THE DAILY STUDY BIBLE SERIES
REVISED EDITION

WILLIAM BARCLAY

INDEX VOLUME

Edited by C. L. Rawlins

D0107886

THE WESTMINSTER PRESS
PHILADELPHIA

Copyright © 1978 The Saint Andrew Press

Published by The Westminster Press®
Philadelphia, Pennsylvania

PRINTED IN THE UNITED STATES OF AMERICA

9 8 7 6 5 4 3 2 1

Library of Congress Cataloging in Publication Data

Rawlins, C   L
    The Daily study Bible, revised edition [by] William
Barclay. : an index volume.

    Index to the Daily study Bible series, rev. ed.
    1. The Daily study Bible series — Indexes.
I. Barclay, William, lecturer in the University of
Glasgow. II. Title.
BS2341.2.R38   220.7′016   78-18316
ISBN 0-664-21370-7
ISBN 0-664-24215-4 pbk.

CONTENTS

		Page
	Introduction	v
	Explanation of Use	x
I	Index of Old Testament References	1
II	Index of New Testament References	31
III	Index of Subjects and Places	89
IV	Index of Personal Names	151
V	Index of Foreign Words, Terms and Phrases	193
VI	Index of Ancient Writings	211

INTRODUCTION

The Daily Study Bible hardly needs an introduction. Since its inception twenty five years ago, 'the little red commentaries'[1] have circulated in their thousands around the world and are to be found from archbishops' palaces to the more humble homes of ordinary people on five continents.

It was in the year of the Coronation that the then relatively unknown lecturer in New Testament studies at the University of Glasgow provided, at short notice, his first commentary; there was no indication then that it would be the precursor of a full series or that it would be selling on a world-wide scale a quarter of a century later. But so it was, and within six years it was complete—an extraordinary event which even pre-planned series with multiple authors and the full backing of fully staffed publishing houses has not equalled. And so the name of William Barclay became an household name with more than sixty books to his credit, countless articles in periodicals both popular and technical, and radio and television appearances which attracted record listening and viewing.[2]

And what is the DSB (as it is familiarly called)? Precisely what its title asserts: a *daily* study of the Bible. It is not just a commentary, if by that term one implies full critical and exegetical treatment of the text, nor if one understands it to mean a fully-worked exposition. To be sure, these matters are not excluded from these studies, and behind them there lies a masterful comprehension of biblical learning, as his other works show.[3] But in this series we have Barclay the pastor rather than Barclay the Professor of Divinity and Biblical Criticism, an important aspect which several critics have overlooked when they have spoken of the unevenness of treatment in this or that part. As the author himself declares, in setting out his aims in the General Introduction, it is 'to make the results of modern scholarship available to the non-technical reader in a form that does not require a theological education

to understand; and then to make the teaching of the New
Testament books relevant to life and work today . . . they are
meant to enable men and women to know Jesus Christ more
clearly, to love him more dearly, and to follow him more
nearly'.[4]

In other words, the books (seventeen in all, extending over
more than four thousand pages) provide us with exposition
which is informative, devotional and relevant, as any *daily*
encounter with the scriptures should be. And how informative!
For those with the inclination and discipline to take them
seriously they are a veritable gold-mine. In these practiced
hands the world of the New Testament comes vibrantly alive,
alive with the authentic ring of first-hand experience and the
touch of the craftsman-writer. Through these pages we are
introduced to the air breathed by the early Christians, made to
sit where they sat, and helped to see things as they saw them.
The message to them thus becomes the message to us, for Dr
Barclay is a most practical writer, a pastor *par excellence*. Ever
ready to enlighten and enliven the most casual reference or
mundane comment, his main task is to home-in on the real
meaning and present-day reality of the passage under con-
sideration. As he says himself, 'Christianity is truth, but it is
truth in action'.[5] Relevance might be his second name. But how
devotional, too! In some commentators' hands the Bible is
handled with clinical precision: introduced, analysed, explained
—and the net result is a descriptive piece which would grace
any museum. . . . Barclay is not such a writer. His work
radiates an infectious love for Christ and mankind, and thus
through his books there develops a powerful encounter between
both. But it is an encounter, and his ethic is one, therefore, of
'reciprocal obligation',[6] towards God and man.

In all this he is clear and frank. Where there are problems he
says so; where there are difficulties he admits them; where there
are discrepancies, weaknesses, contradictions even, he states
them, fully and carefully. If a statement conflicts with present-
day modes of thought or practice he does not baulk the issue or
weaken his stance; the reader is left always in a position to be

responsive to God and his Word. The whole thrust of his exposition is to bring the would-be Christian under the inexorable demands of Christ, demands which are humbling and demanding in a total sense, as Barclay is at pains to declare.

He does not dilute the reality of sin, the danger of compromise or the existence of God's wrath; nor does he obscure the glorious reality of his love and kindness, his willingness to forgive and heal, his power to deliver from enslaving habits, and the hope he inspires. All these, and much more, are found finely stated and illustrated in these commentaries. His exposition is carefully balanced, more so than many—whether 'liberal' or 'conservative'—are prepared to admit. These, with his simplicity and directness of style,[7] are some of the reasons for his great success and usefulness.[8]

This *Index* is simply an aid to the greater and more effective use of the preceding seventeen books. Its format demonstrates the method and strengths of Barclay the commentator. He is primarily a *biblical* theologian. Not only in the sense that his life and energies have been spent in the service of the Bible, by studies linguistic and archaeological, exegetical and practical, classical and modern, but also in the sense that he allows the Bible to create its own theological ethos, dictate its own theological style, provide its own theological language, direct, in a word, its own theological ends. The interpretive rules (or hermeneutic) he uses are themselves biblically oriented. He is not a manipulator of scripture, but one manipulated by it; his authority is of one 'under authority'.[9] In all his writings the axiom of scripture interpreting scripture predominates. In this way he preserves the integrity of scripture and the interrelatedness of its several parts.

Any commentator of whole books of the Bible is placed under the severe discipline of facing unavoidably a wide range of subjects and problems. The second section of this *Index* manifests Barclay's ability to grapple with major and contentious issues fairly and competently. He is not evasive, but brings all matters under the searchlight of the full biblical revelation and record, whether they be matters of the moment or ones of more lasting consequence, personal or public.

Nor does he work in isolation from contemporary scholars or those of past ages. In the third section his indebtedness to their knowledge and experience (never divorced!) is shown. Thanks to great industry, wide reading and a phenomenal memory,[10] his works are replete with quotations and anecdotes of all sorts: practical, philosophical, religious, secular, antiquarian, modern, prose, poetry, and in several languages. From the Hebrides to the Antipodes he draws from a rich fund which never fails to interest or inform. In the final two sections of the *Index* we see much of the sources of Dr Barclay's exposition. Here etymology and ancient practice join hands in a creative act of enlightenment of scripture which could otherwise remain meaningless to the modern reader.

Users of this *Index* should be aware of the 'chain-reference' method whereby they can trace a great deal of information about the subject of their enquiry from small beginnings. In a writer of Barclay's stature this is particularly important, for his use of language is rich and fluent; he moves swiftly through adjectives and synonyms.[11] I have not sought to centralize subjects under single heads, so readers should be alive to a fairly diverse form of reference. For example, those wishing to understand his emphasis on right doctrine should refer to 'Doctrine', 'Belief', 'The Faith', 'Creeds', and 'Orthodoxy'. Further aspects may be explored in other sections, such as under Personal Names (e.g. Jesus or Paul), key scripture references (e.g. Rom. 3:21-25 for 'justification'), or foreign words; by this method the user will be enabled to reach a comprehensive viewpoint of Dr Barclay's thought.

This volume is sent out with the prayer that it may be found to be a worthy servant of the series and the One to whom the whole series looks as both Lord and Master.

A number of people have helped in various ways, to whom I record my deep appreciation and gratitude: Mr Tim Honeyman (Secretary of the Church of Scotland Publications Committee) and Mr Maurice Berrill (its former Publisher) have both supplied much help and encouragement notwithstanding some

delays; Mrs Beryl Barnes produced an admirable typescript
from a difficult manuscript; my wife Veronica willingly
shouldered many extra jobs in addition to her professional and
domestic tasks; but above all to Dr Barclay himself whose
tireless efforts bring to us the ripe fruits of learning year after
year.

C. L. RAWLINS

Postscript

Some months after the above was written, news reached me of
the death of Dr Barclay. He had seen it, and it had met with his
approval, but the Foreword he had promised remains un-
written.

From around the world there has come a flow of apprecia-
tions for this great man, undoubtedly one of the foremost
communicators of the Christian faith of the century. They will
continue, as his work will continue, for it is based on the
unchanging expression of God's will and purposes in Christ
Jesus. Let this small volume stand as part of the living memorial
in William Barclay's honour, who counted not the praise of
men but only of God himself.

C. L. R.

NOTES

1. They were revised and reset in 1974–76.
2. See 'Barclay the Broadcaster' by the late Ronald Falconer, in *Biblical Studies: Essays in Honour of William Barclay*, edited by J. R. McKay and J. F. Miller (William Collins & Sons, 1976, pp. 15–27).
3. See the 'Table of Events and Selected Works' in *Men and Affairs* (A. R. Mowbray & Co., pp. 147–149).
4. Richard of Chichester's prayer is quoted in the General Introduction to both the original and the revised editions of the series.
5. 12.100, a passage which particularly emphasizes the need for Christian action.

6. See, for example, **11**.160f. Dr Barclay twice uses this phrase in the DSB, but the concept pervades the whole of his thought both ethically and theologically.

7. See the Editor's Preface in *Men and Affairs*, pp. viiif.

8. David Edwards, formerly one of Dr Barclay's editors but now Dean of Westminster Abbey, refers to this in the Preface to *Testament of Faith* (A. R. Mowbray & Co., 1975, pp. vii–xii).

9. Matt. 8:9; significantly, Barclay finds the centurion who originally voiced these words 'one of the most attractive characters in the gospels' (**1**.300). Johnston McKay and James Miller, in the Editors' Preface to *Biblical Studies*, refer (somewhat clumsily) to Barclay's 'biblicality' (p.9).

10. See Dr Barclay's modest admission of this in *Testament of Faith* (p. 22f.); David Edwards highlights it in his Preface (p. viii).

11. Note Edwards' reference to this as 'his extraordinary appetite for words' (op. cit., p. ix).

EXPLANATION OF USE

For reasons of space the seventeen volumes of the *Daily Study Bible* have each been given a numerical reference (1–17); these references are printed in *bold type* throughout the book; the key to these will be found at the foot of every page. The main exposition of a passage is printed in italics, thus references to Philippians 3:1 will appear as: **11**.7, 15, *50–53*; **14**.336. It will be found that volume **11** is *Philippians, Colossians and Thessalonians* and volume **14** is *James and Peter*; the primary passage will be found at pages 50–53 of the former volume.

INDEX OF OLD TESTAMENT REFERENCES

Genesis

1–2	13.36
1:1	5.37
1:2	1.22; 5.83; 14.339
1:3	5.7, 28, 45; 17.181
1:6–7	17.47
1:6	5.28; 14.339; 17.181
1:7	16.155
1:9	17.181
1:11	5.28
1:14–18	11.44
1:14	17.181, 209
1:26–27	2.278; 3.287; 11.117f
1:26	1.178; 13.17; 15.75, 97; 17.181
1:27	1.13–14; 3.240; 12.94
1:28	13.23; 14.88
1:31	3.182; 12.94
2:7	6.274; 9.157
2:8–16	17.220
2:8	16.70
2:9	16.69
2:16–17	16.69
2:18	3.343
2:22–23	9.98
2:23–24	2.200, 203
2:24	3.240; 9.56
3	17.82
3:1–19	9.150
3:1	16.70
3:6	17.221
3:8–10	6.17
3:8	3.102; 17.17
3:12–13	14.52
3:17	8.110
3:21	6.90
3:22–24	16.69
3:24	16.158
4:1–15	13.131; 15.189
4:1	6.209; 11.63; 15.54, 185
4:7	6.38
4:10	13.187
5:1	1.12
5:24	13.133; 14.239; 16.122; 17.70
6–8	13.140
6:1–8	1.321; 3.34; 14.240
6:1–5	14.322
6:1–4	15.183; 17.48
6:1–2	3.71; 9.99
6:2	14.239; 15.158
6:5	14.325
6:9	13.142
6:12–13	14.240
8:21	11.86
9:2	14.88
9:3	12.94
9:4	5.224; 17.31
9:18–27	12.79
10:1	1.12
11:10	1.12
11:27	1.12
12:1–3	8.12; 9.252
12:1	9.221; 13.142; 17.151
12:2–3	8.67
12:3	4.34; 10.24
12:7	13.62
14:14	9.15
14:17–20	13.67

14:18–20	13.72
15:5	17.26
15:6	8.66
15:8–21	6.34
15:13	16.9; 17.188
15:18	17.53
16–17	10.41
16:13	4.102
17:5–6	13.62
17:5	5.90; 11.38f; 16.98
17:7–8	10.28
17:7	17.206
17:9–10	11.55
17:9	15.78
17:10–11	8.66; 11.138
17:12	11.57
17:15–22	13.146
17:17	6.34; 8.70; 13.146
17:25	11.57
18–19	14.327
18:1–8	6.26; 13.192
18:1	6.90
18:9–15	13.146
18:10–14	8.128
18:12	13.146
18:18	13.62
18:23	9.15
18:25	16.121
19:1–11	1.371; 14.327; 15.185
19:4–11	17.71
19:12–28	15.185
19:12–26	14.327
19:12–14	9.221; 17.152
19:16	14.328
19:28	17.112
19:29	14.327
19:30–38	12.79
21	10.41
21:1–8	13.146
21:7	13.147
21:12	8.128
22:1–18	13.151
22:1	1.62, 224; 14.42
22:12	8.116
22:16–18	13.62
24:1	6.35
24:50	12.76
25:11	6.90
25:23	8.128
25:25–26	4.17
25:28–34	13.183
25:34	16.133
26:17–25	11.157
26:17–22	9.216
26:24	16.25
27	5.28; 17.181
27:1–39	13.183
27:2	13.153
27:28–29	13.153
27:36	16.133
27:39–40	13.153
28:12	5.94
28:16	17.36
29:35	8.47
32:12	17.26
32:28	5.90; 11.39, 58; 16.98
32:29	17.180
32:30	13.3
32:32	9.80
33:18–19	5.147
35:1–5	6.79
35:17–18	11.58
35:20	1.24
37:34	1.93
37:35	15.36
38	1.17
40:8	1.16
41:42	16.143; 17.23

43:11	17.7	4:10	13.156
45:22	14.115	4:12	1.375
47:29	13.153	4:22	3.71; 6.27; 8.124; 11.119
48:7	1.24		
48:9–22	13.153	6:6–7	2.340; 3.333; 10.109
48:15–16	13.153	6:12	11.55, 139
48:22	5.147	6:20	13.155
49	14.31	7:11	12.194
49:1	15.59	7:14–18	17.71
49:3	14.31	7:17–21	17.127
49:4	16.133	7:20–25	17.125
49:5–7	14.31	7:20–21	17.44
49:8	8.47; 16.133	8:5–14	17.125
49:9	16.169	8:5–11	17.130
49:14–15	14.31	8:7	12.194
49:17	17.25	8:16–18	17.125
49:18	14.31	8:20–24	17.125
49:19	14.31	9–16	8.130
49:20	14.31	9:3–6	17.125
49:22–26	14.31	9:8–11	17.125f
49:27	14.31	9:11	12.194
50:5	1.314	9:22–26	17.125
50:20	14.272	9:24	17.44, 117, 134
50:22–26	13.153	10:12–19	17.125
		10:21–23	17.44, 127
		10:29–30	17.125
		12	3.323, 332; 4.262
		12:5	14.185
Exodus		12:11–13	5.81
		12:11	3.334
1:15–22	13.155	12:12–48	13.158
2:1–10	13.155	12:15ff	9.45
2:11–14	13.156	12:21–23	2.340
2:14–22	13.157	12:22	6.259
3:1–5	4.251	12:34	2.339
3:1	17.143	12:38	12.194
3:2–5	3.37	13:1–10	2.286; 4.140; 17.99
3:6	3.290	13:2	4.24
3:10	8.12	13:7	9.45
3:14	16.29		
4:1–17	6.45		

13:9	2.286; 14.271		20	10.29
13:11–16	2.286; 4.140; 17.99		20:5	6.38; 14.104
13:16	2.286		20:7	1.158
13:19	13.153		20:8–11	4.60
13:21–22	2.161; 9.88		20:9	4.213
14	13.158		20:10	2.208
14:19–31	9.88		20:11	6.77
14:21	17.128		20:13	1.138
15:1–9	17.119		20:14	1.146
15:11	17.94		21:1–6	6.77
15:20	16.105		21:23–25	1.163
15:24	11.43; 15.197		21:33	4.188
16:1–21	1.218		22:1	4.235
16:2	11.43		22:4, 7	4.235; 17.153
16:7	14.259		22:9	6.77; 17.153
16:10	3.210; 5.69; 8.125		22:13	6.61
16:11–21	4.144		22:26–27	1.167
16:11–15	9.88; 16.94		22:28	6.77; 7.164
16:15	5.215; 16.95		23:1	5.254
16:18	9.230		23:7	8.57
16:19	17.42		23:16	5.248
16:29	5.122		24:1–8	4.266; 9.189; 10.109;
16:33–34	16.94			13.81, 91, 108; 14.170;
17:1–7	13.33			15.204
17:3	15.197		24:3–8	3.339; 8.24; 13.4
17:6	5.251		24:3	10.109; 11.142
19–20	16.24		24:7	10.109; 13.81
19:4	17.85		24:10	17.213
19:5–6	14.198		24:15	1.234
19:5	5.59		24:16–18	17.35
19:6	11.10; 16.35		24:16–17	5.69; 8.125
19:9	3.210		24:16	14.259
19:10	17.30		24:18	3.22
19:12–13	13.185		25–31	13.95
19:14	17.30		25:1–7	13.95
19:16	16.43, 155; 17.42		25:8	13.95
19:17	5.30		25:9	17.10
19:18	13.188		25:18–21	16.158
19:22	14.106		25:22	13.97

25:23–30	3.63
25:31–37	16.44
25:40	13.88; 17.10
26:31	16.158
26:33	11.10
27:1	17.211
28:4	16.45
28:16	17.212
28:17	17.214
28:30	13.99
28:41	6.217
29:4	14.234
29:5	16.45
29:7	15.69
29:20–21	14.170
29:38–42	5.81
29:43	8.125; 14.259
30:2	17.211
30:13	2.168
30:19–21	14.107
30:34–38	17.161
31:13	5.30
31:18	2.159
32:6	9.88
32:28	12.194
32:30–32	3.132
32:32–33	16.123
32:32	8.123; 17.196
33:9–11	13.159
33:9	3.210
33:12–32	6.159
33:17	6.5
33:18–22	8.125
33:19	8.130
33:20	5.73; 13.3; 17.222
33:23	17.222
34:5	2.161
34:7	6.38
34:14	14.104

34:15–16	14.102; 16.108
34:15	5.143; 17.106
34:22	5.248
34:29	2.159
34:30	9.190
34:33	9.192
35–40	13.95
36:5–7	13.95
40:13	15.69
40:34–38	17.35
40:34–35	17.122
40:34	2.161; 5.69; 14.259

Leviticus

1:4	1.52
1:9, 13, 17	11.86
2:13	3.234
4:2	13.45
4:7	17.11
4:13	13.45
5:7	14.233
6:5	4.235
6:30	14.233
8	13.78
8:30	14.170
11–15	3.165; 10.32
11	2.111; 3.166, 172; 7.81; 8.182; 10.20; 13.196
11:10	17.30
11:12	1.271
11:13-21	2.112
11:22–23	3.116
11:44	14.188
12	4.24
12:3	5.242; 11.57

12:8	2.245; 3.273; 4.24; 6.10
13–14	4.58
13	3.44
13:45–46	1.296, 365; 4.58, 218
13:47–52	15.205
13:47	3.44
14	1.299; 3.45
14:1–7	14.170
14:22	2.245; 3.273
14:33	3.44
15:14	2.245; 3.273
15:19–33	4.113
15:25–27	1.346; 3.129
15:29	2.245
16	13.97, 101
16:4	14.107; 16.45
16:12	17.40
16:15	13.103
16:19	6.77
16:21–22	13.103
16:27	13.197
16:29	13.98
16:31	1.233
16:32	15.69
16:33	13.98
17:11–14	17.10
17:11	13.107
18:5	8.138
18:8	9.44
18:16	3.150
19:2	14.188; 15.29
19:9	2.16
19:13	14.118
19:15	14.63
19:18	1.165; 2.278; 3.295; 4.140; 14.111; 15.44
19:23–25	3.282
20:5	1.330

20:7	14.188; 15.29
20:10	1.146; 6.2
20:14	17.149
20:21	3.150
20:26	11.11; 14.188; 15.29
21:6	11.10
21:9	17.149
21:16–23	13.78
23:10–11	3.323; 9.150
23:21	7.21
23:27–32	13.101
23:39	5.248
23:40	5.249
24:5–9	2.23; 4.70
24:9	3.63
24:16	3.49; 6.76, 234
24:19–20	1.163
25:23	5.59
25:39–42	6.23
26:5	5.168
26:11–12	9.223; 17.203
26:21–26	17.9
26:26	17.7
26:41	11.55, 139
27:30	2.293; 11.10
27:32	6.56; 11.10

Numbers

4:3	6.36
5:2	4.218
5:6–7	1.57
5:7	4.235
6:1–21	7.138; 12.119
6:22–27	16.135
8:4	17.10
9:12	6.261
9:15	17.121

11:12	5.74
11:16–30	14.262
11:16–17	4.133; 12.70
11:24–25	4.133
12:3	1.98
12:6–7	13.29
12:7–8	13.159
12:8	15.145
13–14	13.36; 15.182
13:23	2.251
13:26–14:29	15.158
13:33	14.322
14:18	6.38
14:24	14.35; 16.25
14:30–32	9.88
14:32–33	15.182
15:22–31	13.45
15:30–31	2.41
15:37–41	1.192, 347; 2.286; 3.295; 4.113
15:38–40	3.130
15:38	3.299
16	9.89
16:1–35	15.191
16:3	16.80
16:5	12.177
16:23–26	17.152
16:26	12.177
16:41	11.43
16:46	8.24; 17.40
17:7	17.121
18:2	17.121
18:14	2.17
18:16	4.24
18:19	3.234
18:20–21	13.76
18:21	4.224
18:28	2.276
19	3.165; 13.103
19:2	2.239; 3.266
19:11	4.139; 7.80
19:16	2.296; 4.156
20:1–13	13.33
20:1–11	9.88
20:4	16.80
21:4–9	5.134
21:4–6	9.89
21:11	4.295
22–24	14.333; 15.190
22:22	3.22; 12.194; 17.81
23:19	12.170
24:14	15.59
24:17	17.228
24:29	15.197
25	14.333; 15.190
25:1–9	9.88
25:1–5	16.66
25:3	8.24
25:11–13	11.60
27:17	6.59
27:18–21	6.105
28:3–8	13.116
28:9	2.24
28:26	7.21
29:7–11	13.101
29:7	13.99
30:2	1.158; 2.116
31:8	14.333; 15.190
31:16	15.190; 16.67, 80
32:10–13	15.182
35:30	6.14

Deuteronomy

1:16	5.254
1:17	5.187

2:24	8.124	12:9	13.33
3:6	8.124	13:1–5	6.48; 14.315, 319;
3:9	1.260		14.89; 17.131
3:24	14.271	13:6	5.74; 7.61
4:2	17.231	13:8–11	8.124
4:11	13.185	13:13	9.104; 11.212
4:12	5.73, 197	14:1	8.124
4:23	13.91	14:2	5.59; 14.166
4:24	13.189	14:21	2.112
4:34	14.42	14:22	2.293; 4.224
5:23–27	13.185	15:4	14.173
5:32–33	6.157	15:7–11	1.169; 9.235
6:4–9	1.192; 2.286; 3.295;	15:9	1.246
	4.140; 17.99	15:11	3.326; 6.113
6:4	3.295; 4.140; 8.60;	15:23	5.224
	9.252	16:13–16	5.248
6:5	2.278	17:2–7	13.124
6:8	2.286; 3.295	17:6	5.195; 6.14; 15.112
6:13	1.70; 4.44	17:7	6.234; 9.48
6:16	1.69; 4.44	17:12	13.46
7:6	5.59; 14.166	18:3–4	2.17
7:13	17.6	18:15	2.9; 4.115; 5.78, 206,
7:19	14.42		252; 6.72
8:3	1.68; 4.43	18:18	5.206, 252; 6.72;
8:8	2.251		17.71
9:3	5.30	18:20	14.315
9:19	13.186	19:10	14.173
9:26	14.271	19:15	2.188; 5.195; 6.13;
9:27	14.35		15.112; 17.70
9:29	14.267	19:18	1.164
10:12	9.207	19:19	9.221
10:16	11.55	19:21	1.163
10:20	4.44	21:1–9	2.362
11:4–9	3.295	21:3	2.239; 3.266
11:13–21	1.192; 2.286; 3.295;	21:17	4.204
	4.140; 17.99	21:19	2.143
11:13	4.140	21:22–23	2.372; 6.260
11:14	14.121; 17.6	21:23	7.27; 9.17; 10.26
11:18	2.286	22:10	9.221

---

1 Matt, v.1	3 Mark	5 John, v.1	7 Acts	9 Cor
2 Matt, v.2	4 Luke	6 John, v.2	8 Rom	10 Gal, Eph

22:12	1.347; 2.286; 4.113	32:6	6.27; 8.124
22:13–24	6.2	32:8	15.183
23:3	1.17	32:9	5.59
23:18	11.54; 17.227	32:11–12	17.85
23:21–22	1.159	32:15	12.18
23:24–25	2.253	32:16	14.104
23:25	2.21; 3.63; 4.69	32:21	8.122, 142; 14.104
24:1	1.151; 2.197, 200;	32:31	2.140
	3.238–40; 4.211	32:32	15.185
24:5	4.194	32:35f	13.125
24:7	9.48	32:39	2.276; 5.186; 14.112
24:14–15	14.118	32:43	8.198; 13.19; 17.165
24:19	2.16	33:1	12.134
25:1–3	9.253	33:17	16.171
25:4	9.79; 12.116	33:27	5.30
25:5–10	2.277; 3.289	34:1–4	14.181
25:5–6	4.41, 249	34:5–6	2.159; 6.90, 177
25:7	2.143; 14.263	34:5	14.293
26:18	5.59		
27:4	5.157		
27:14–26	11.142		
27:26	10.26, 30	*Joshua*	
28:6	6.59		
28:35	17.126	1:2	8.12; 11.10; 12.227
28:51	17.6	1:5	13.194
29:4	8.145	2:1–21	13.161; 14.78
29:17–18	17.44	2:1–7	1.17
29:18	13.182	2:9–11	13.161
29:23	15.185	3:10	16.48; 17.22
29:28	14.37	3:17	17.128
30:6	11.55, 139	5:14–15	13.17
30:12–13	8.138	6:1–20	13.160
30:14	14.57	6:17	8.124
30:15–20	1.278; 5.146	6:25	13.161
30:19	16.109	7	8.79
31:16	2.276; 5.143; 14.102;	7:1–26	8.124
	16.108; 17.106	7:19	6.48
31:29	6.157	7:21	1.239
32:4	2.140	9	1.73
		9:6	13.90

10:11	**17.134**
14:7	**3.281**
19:28–29	**3.178**
24:15	**1.278; 5.146; 16.109**
24:29	**6.178; 8.12; 12.227; 14.35, 293; 16.25**
24:32	**5.147; 13.153**

Judges

2:2	**13.90**
2:8	**11.10; 16.25**
2:17	**17.106**
2:22	**14.42**
3:1, 4	**14.42**
4–5	**13.163**
4:4	**16.105**
5:14	**11.58**
5:19–21	**17.132**
5:31	**16.51**
6–7	**13.163**
6:49	**16.25**
7:21	**14.115**
8:23	**6.236; 10.108**
8:27, 33	**17.106**
9:8–15	**3.89**
9:13	**12.79**
10:4	**6.118**
11–12	**13.163**
13–16	**13.163**
13:18	**17.180**
13:20	**13.18**
13:22	**10.129**
14:12	**14.116**
18:30	**17.25**
20:16	**6.55**
20:26	**1.234**

Ruth

1:4	**1.17**
1:22	**1.24**
2:14	**6.146**

1 Samuel

1	**13.163**
1:16	**17.59**
2:1–10	**4.15**
2:2	**2.140; 17.120**
2:6	**5.187; 14.112**
2:12	**17.59**
2:27	**12.134**
3:1–14	**6.126**
3:14	**2.42**
6:7	**2.239**
7:6	**1.234**
9:1–2	**11.58**
9:6	**12.134**
9:16	**15.69**
10:1	**15.69**
10:2	**1.38**
12:12	**6.236**
15:22	**3.296; 13.114**
16:1–13	**13.163**
16:1	**1.24; 16.133**
16:3, 12	**15.69**
16:13	**16.133**
17:12	**1.24**
17:34–36	**6.61**
18:4	**16.46**
20:6	**1.24**
21:1–6	**2.23; 3.63; 4.70**
22:2	**2.140**
23:14–15	**1.24**
23:18	**13.90**

---

1 Matt, v.1	**3** Mark	**5** John, v.1	**7** Acts	**9** Cor
2 Matt, v.2	**4** Luke	**6** John, v.2	**8** Rom	**10** Gal, Eph

24:5–11	16.46	6:23–30	16.158
24:14	11.54	7:49	16.45
25:17, 25	17, 59	8:2	5.248
26:21	16.65	8:10–11	2.161; 3.210; 14.259; 17.122, 203
28:14	2.276		
29:4	1.225; 3.22; 17.81	8:11	5.69
		8:17–18	15.87
		8:18	1.101
		8:53	14.35
		8:66	16.25
		11:14, 23	17.81

2 Samuel

3:18	3.281; 14.293	11:29–32	2.240; 3.339; 4.239; 7.154; 13.13
7:14	3.71; 9.223; 13.19; 17.206		
		11:30–32	3.264
9:7, 13	6.142	11:36	16.25
10:4	16.143	12:21	11.58
11–12	1.17	12:22	12.134
12:1–14	16.145	12:29	17.25
12:1–13	3.50	13:22	17.72
12:1–7	3.85, 89	14:13	16.121
13:28–29	12.79	16:31	16.105
14:4	3.268	17–18	14.132
16:7	17.59	17:1–7	17.79
17:23	6.118	17:1	14.132; 17.42, 71
18:15	13.164	17:17ff	13.166
19:22	1.225; 3.22	18	6.45
19:26	6.118	18:1	14.132
22:5	11.212	18:13	16.106
22:32	2.140	18:15	17.42
		18:17–40	1.64
		18:19	6.143; 16.106
		18:26	1.196
		18:37	6.100

1 Kings

2:22	16.133	18:42	14.132
3:7	6.59	19:1–8	4.126; 6.126; 13.164; 17.79
4:25	2.251; 5.93		
5:4	1.225; 3.22; 17.81	19:3	1.64
6:20	17.212	19:4	17.143
		19:8	3.22

19:9–12	2.159
19:10–18	8.144
19:11	17.20
19:12	16.50
19:13	1.281
19:15–16	15.69
19:19	1.281
20:8	14.263
20:35–43	12.102
21	16.106
21:10	11.212; 17.59
21:11	14.263
21:13	11.212; 17.59
22	14.314f
22:11	16.171
22:19	13.17; 16.151, 153

2 Kings

1:8	1.44, 282; 3.16
1:9–10	17.71
2:11	2.159; 17.70, 72
2:12	2.287
3:14	17.42
4:8ff	13.166
4:18–37	4.86
4:29	4.134
5	3.127
5:5	14.116
5:6	5.186; 17.42
5:7	14.112
5:22	1.239; 14.116
6:17	3.24
6:26	3.268
6:31ff	13.164
6:32	14.263
7:3–3	1.365

8:13	11.54
9:13	2.239; 3.266
9:22	16.106
9:27	17.132
9:36	16.25
10:10	16.25
15:5	1.365
17:6	5.149
17:23	14.37
17:24	5.149
17:28	5.159
17:29	5.157, 159
18:4	5.134
18:17–37	17.22
19:15	16.158
19:34	16.25
19:35–36	12.150; 13.18
20:1–7	13.164
20:6	16.25
20:20	6.43
21:1–9	9.221
21:10	16.25
22:14	16.105
23:3ff	9.221
23:10	1.141; 3.231
23:29–30	17.132
24:14–16	14.37
25:26	14.39

1 Chronicles

5:26	14.37
9:33	17.34
17:4	16.25
21:1	17.59
24:5, 7–18	16.153
29:10–12	16.179

2 Chronicles

3:7	**16.**158
5:13–14	**2.**161
7:1–13	**17.**35
7:2	**2.**161
11:6	**1.**24
13:5	**3.**234
13:7	**17.**59
13:19	**6.**106
24:6	**16.**25
24:20–2	**2.**298; **4.**159; **13.**166
25:6–31	**16.**153
26:18	**6.**77
28:3	**1.**141; **3.**231
32:3–8, 30	**6.**43
33:6	**3.**231
33:13	**1.**58
34:17	**12.**70

Ezra

2:61–63	**4.**40; **13.**68
2:62	**1.**12
4:1	**11.**58
10:8	**6.**47

Nehemiah

1:7	**16.**25
6:1	**1.**231
6:11	**15.**50
7:63–65	**4.**40; **13.**68
8:1–8	**2.**282
9:1	**1.**234
10:29	**16.**25
13:15–19	**5.**182
13:28	**5.**150

Esther

3:10	**17.**23
6:6–11	**16.**144
8:2	**17.**23

Job

1:6–9	**17.**81
1:6–7	**1.**226; **3.**22, 71
1:6	**14.**322; **16.**153
1:8	**14.**35; **16.**25
1:11–12	**17.**81
2:1–6	**17.**81
2:1	**14.**322; **16.**153
2:2	**3.**22
2:6–7	**12.**54
2:7	**17.**126
3:21	**17.**51
4:4	**9.**143; **10.**158; **13.**122
4:7	**1.**181; **3.**47, 173
4:16	**6.**126
4:18	**11.**124; **14.**322
5:13	**9.**34
5:17	**14.**246; **16.**145
8:6	**1.**181
9:3	**17.**192
9:33	**13.**89
11:4	**1.**181
11:7	**11.**16; **14.**295
13:15	**14.**125
13:26	**6.**3
14:1	**4.**13
14:7–12	**6.**93
15:14	**4.**13
15:15	**11.**124
16:19	**14.**125
19:25–27	**9.**139

---

11 Phil, Col, Thes
12 Tim, Tit, Phlm
13 Heb
14 Jas, Pet
15 John, Jude
16 Rev, v.1
17 Rev, v.2

19:25	14.125	8:2	2.249
21:20	17.111	8:4–6	13.23
22:29	14.109	8:4	2.26
23:3	3.25	8:5	13.24
25:4	4.13	8:6–8	14.89
26:6	17.51	9:10	1.205; 4.143; 5.62;
26:13	15.62		6.210; 15.53
27:9	6.48	9:13	16.52
28:17	16.156	9:18	1.91
28:19	17.214	10:7	8.55
28:22	17.51	14:1–3	8.55
28:28	9.207	14:1	1.140; 3.314f
29:3	6.13	15	3.293
31:12	17.51	15:3	1.274
33:4	1.22	16:5	14.174
37:4	16.155	16:8–11	14.181
37:9–10	17.20	16:9–11	6.92; 9.139
38–41	8.27	16:10	5.117
38:7	14.322	16:11	6.158
38:31	16.48	18	16.25
40:15–24	17.77	18:2	2.140
42:7	16.25	18:10	16.158
42:12	14.125	18:15	17.20
		18:31	2.140
		18:49	14.127
		18:50	8.198
Psalms		19:1–2	16.159
		19:4	8.141
1:1	1.88	19:9	9.208
2	14.181	19:10	17.57
2:2	17.73, 132	20:7	1.206; 5.60f; 6.210;
2:5	10.18		15.54
2:7	1.60; 4.38; 13.19, 47	21:3	14.49
2:8–9	16.110	22	2.368; 12.220; 14.181
2:8	1.70	22:7–8	2.368
2:9	17.75, 78, 182	22:16	11.54
5:9	8.55	22:18	2.368; 6.255
6:5	6.91; 9.138; 14.237;	22:20	11.54
	16.181	22:22	6.210; 13.27
8	13.23		

22:25–31	2.368	40:3	16.176
23	12.201	40:6–9	13.113f
23:1–2	1.211; 6.53	40:11	12.25
23:1	14.215; 17.38	41:9	3.335; 6.142
23:2	17.39	42:1	5.154; 14.192
23:5	3.255; 6.110	42:2	16.48; 17.22
24:1	1.250	42:3	14.338
24:4	14.107f	42:6	1.260
24:5	12.18	42:7	3.255; 17.86
25:11	15.54	42:11	11.83
26:3	6.158	43:5	11.83; 12.19
26:6	14.107	45:7–8	13.19
27:1	6.13	46:1	1.211
27:2	17.148	46:4	17.220
27:3	6.152	46:7	1.211
27:10	9.199	46:9	17.4
27:11	6.157	46:10	2.163
29	17.55	47:8	16.151
29:10	10.142	50:3	14.341
30:9	6.92; 9.138; 14.237; 16.181	50:10	1.250; 17.191
		50:12	1.250
30:11	10.50	50:14	13.115
31:3	15.54	50:20	14.111
31:5	4.288	51:1–7	17.30
32:2	5.93; 17.108	51:16	5.113; 8.58; 13.115
32:5	1.57	51:17	1.95
32:6	17.86	53:1	15.200
33:2	16.174	55:12–14	6.143
33:3	16.176	55:22	14.272
33:6	1.22; 5.29	57:3	12.25
34:6	1.91	66:18	6.48
34:8	14.192	68:5	14.61
34:15	6.48	68:6	15.103
35:10	1.91	68:8	13.188
35:19	6.187	68:10	1.91
36	16.25	68:17	17.53
36:1	8.55	68:18	10.143
36:9	5.154; 17.39, 216	68:20	14.112
37:25	1.181; 3.246	69:4	6.187

69:9	5.114; 8.197; 11.60		89:3	11.10; 15.25
69:21	6.259		89:4	6.128
69:22–23	8.145		89:6	14.322
69:28	16.123; 17.196		89:10	15.62; 17.58
72:4	1.91		89:12	3.210
73:9	14.85		89:17	16.171
73:13	14.108		89:20ff	3.298; 6.178
73:23–26	14.174		89:20	11.10
73:23–24	3.292; 6.92; 9.139		89:27	11.119; 16.33; 17.206
73:27	5.143		90	12.134
74:12–14	17.77		90:4	3.108; 14.250, 342;
74:13	17.47			17.188
75:4	16.171		90:15	16.9; 17.188
75:8	3.255; 17.111		91:6	12.214
77:18	13.188; 16.155		91:7–10	1.181
77:20	6.53		91:11–12	1.69
78:1–3	2.69		92:5	17.119
78:24–25	16.95		94:11	9.34
78:24	5.215		94:12	14.246; 16.145
78:45	17.130		95:7–11	13.33, 37
78:70	11.10; 14.293		95:7	6.53
79:3	17.72		96:1	16.176
79:5–10	17.12		97:1	17.172
79:10	14.338		97:7	13.19
79:13	6.53		98:1	16.176; 17.119
80:1	6.53; 16.158; 17.38		98:2	17.120
80:8	6.172		98:5	16.174
82:6	6.77		99:1	16.158
83:13–14	14.85		99:3	17.120
83:13	17.20		100:3	6.53; 14.216
85:2	1.56		101:5	14.111
86:9	17.120		101:7	17.228
86:11	6.158		102:25–27	17.195
86:14–16	12.25		102:25–26	17.15
87:4	17.58		102:26–27	13.19
88:5	6.92		103:2	4.219; 17.28
88:10–12	6.92; 9.138; 14.237;		103:15	14.48
	16.181		103:22	16.159
88:11	17.51		104:2	16.122, 151; 17.75

1 Matt, v.1	3 Mark	5 John, v.1	7 Acts	9 Cor
2 Matt, v.2	4 Luke	6 John, v.2	8 Rom	10 Gal, Eph

104:3	16.155; 17.54		118:6	13.194
104:4	13.19		118:22–23	3.283; 4.247; 8.135
104:30	1.22		118:22	2.264; 14.194
105:6	6.~5; 14.166		118:25	2.239; 5.249
105:26	14.293; 16.25		118:26	2.2, 239; 3.266
105:30	17.130		118:29	5.249
105:33	2.151		119:30	6.158
105:41	5.251		119:103	17.57
105:43	14.166		119:174	14.192
106:1	17.169		120–134	3.324
106:2	1.196		121:3	15.207
107:18	16.52		121:6	3.119
107:20	5.29		121:8	6.59
107:30	5.210		122	3.324
107:41	1.91		124:4	3.255; 17.86
109:6	17.81		124:8	15.87
109:14	6.38		130:8	1.19
110	14.181		132:10	16.25
110:1	2.279; 3.298; 4.252; 13.19		132:15	1.91
			133:1	11.14; 14.209
110:4	13.67, 71, 72, 80		135:1	17.169, 171
111:1	17.169		135:4	5.59
111:2	17.119		135:20	17.171
111:9	17.120		136	1.390; 2.342; 3.338
112:1	17.169		136:5–6	5.168
112:3	9.235		137	14.37
112:9	9.235; 16.171		137:8	17.153
113–118	2.342; 3.338; 5.249; 6.116; 17.169		139:1–4	5.163
			139:12	17.219
113–114	3.338		139:14	17.119
113:1	17.169		140:3	8.55
114:7	13.188		141:2	16.174
115–118	3.338		141:8	6.152
115:17	6.92; 9.138; 14.237		144:9	16.176
116:8	9.173		144:10	16.25
117:1	8.198; 17.169		145:1	10.108
118	3.267		145:15	1.176
118:1	5.249		145:17	17.120
118:5–6	6.116		145:19	6.48f

146:1	**17**.169	
147:1	**17**.169	
147:7	**16**.174	
147:15	**5**.29	
148	**16**.159, 182	
148:1	**17**.169	
148:4	**16**.155	
148:14	**16**.171	
149:1	**16**.176; **17**.169	
150:1	**17**.169	

Proverbs

1:7	**9**.207; **14**.209	
1:9	**14**.49	
2	**11**.117	
3:6	**6**.208	
3:11–12	**13**.177	
3:12	**16**.144	
3:13–26	**5**.31	
3:18–20	**5**.31	
3:18	**6**.208; **16**.69	
3:24	**12**.186	
3:27–28	**14**.118	
3:34	**8**.37; **14**.105, 270	
4:5–13	**5**.31	
4:9	**14**.49	
6:23	**6**.158	
8	**11**.117	
8:1–9:2	**5**.31f	
8:22–30	**5**.31f	
9:10	**9**.207	
10:11	**17**.220	
10:12	**14**.253	
10:17	**6**.158	
10:19	**14**.55	
10:25	**1**.290	
11:9	**6**.208	

11:28	**14**.117	
11:30	**16**.69	
11:31	**14**.261	
13:3	**14**.55	
13:12	**16**.69	
13:14	**17**.220	
13:24	**16**.145	
14:27	**17**.220	
15:1–4	**14**.82	
15:4	**16**.69	
15:11	**17**.51	
15:17	**9**.220	
15:29	**6**.49	
16:6	**9**.207	
16:22	**17**.221	
16:27	**14**.85	
16:32	**1**.98; **12**.252
17:15	**8**.57	
17:28	**14**.55	
19:14	**12**.76	
20:1	**12**.79	
20:27	**5**.251	
22:2	**14**.63	
23:6	**1**.246	
23:13–14	**16**.145	
23:29–35	**12**.79	
24:29	**1**.165	
25:21	**1**.165	
26:11	**14**.335	
27:1	**14**.113	
27:6	**16**.145	
27:20	**17**.51	
28:13	**1**.57	
28:22	**1**.246	
29:15, 17	**16**.145	
29:20	**14**.55	
29:33	**14**.110	
30:5–6	**17**.231	
31:6	**12**.79	

35:12	**14**.63	1:18	**16**.49; **17**.30
36:9	**17**.221	1:21	**17**.142
		1:30	**16**.70
		2:2–4	**17**.216
		2:2	**15**.59
Ecclesiastes		2:4	**16**.10
		2:12	**7**.25
2:5	**16**.70	3:9	**15**.185
2:15–16	**16**.84	3:16–17	**17**.154
2:24	**9**.154	3:18–24	**14**.221
3:12	**9**.154	4:3	**17**.196
5:2	**1**.196	5:1–7	**3**.281; **4**.245; **6**.172
5:18	**9**.154	5:7	**2**.261
7:20	**14**.82	5:8	**14**.117
8:15	**9**.154	6	**13**.17
9:2	**16**.84	6:1	**16**.151
9:4–5	**9**.138; **16**.84	6:3	**5**.69; **16**.127, 162
9:7	**3**.38; **9**.154	6:4	**17**.122
9:8	**16**.122	6:5–6	**14**.107
9:10	**6**.92; **9**.138; **14**.237	6:5	**10**.102; **17**.36
		6:6	**17**.41
		6:8	**1**.360; **8**.12
Song of Solomon		6:9–13	**8**.145
		6:9–10	**2**.68; **3**.92; **4**.99;
3:11	**14**.49		**6**.132; **8**.145
5:2–6	**16**.147	7:3	**8**.145
6:3	**17**.203	8:12	**8**.145
6:10	**17**.75	8:7–8	**17**.137
8:7	**9**.125	8:13–15	**2**.265
		8:13–14	**14**.195
		8:13	**14**.229
Isaiah		8:14	**8**.135
		8:17	**13**.27
1:9–10	**17**.71	8:18	**8**.145
1:9	**15**.185	9:1–2	**1**.75
1:11–20	**13**.115	9:2–7	**3**.298
1:11–17	**5**.112	9:7	**3**.193; **6**.128
1:15	**6**.48; **12**.65	9:12	**8**.145
1:16–17	**12**.256	9:18	**14**.85
1:16	**1**.54; **14**.107		

---

11 Phil, Col, Thes	**13** Heb	**15** John, Jude	**16** Rev, v.1
12 Tim, Tit, Phlm	**14** Jas, Pet		**17** Rev, v.2

9:19	8.25	22:15–25	16.133
10:22–23	8.120, 133	22:22	2.145; 16.128
11:1–9	3.298	23	2.12
11:1	1.40; 3.193; 16.2, 170; 17.228	23:1, 14	14.115
		23:16–17	17.142
11:2	16.31, 116	24:21–22	14.237
11:4	16.51; 17.178, 182	24:21	17.47
11:6–9	3.24; 16.10	24:23	16.153; 17.47
11:10	8.198; 16.2, 170	25:6	17.174
11:12	17.19, 216	25:8	16.11; 17.203
11:13	16.10	26:1	17.210
11:16	17.128	26:3	1.261
12:3	5.154, 249	26:19	2.276
13:6–16	3.304; 7.25	27:1	15.62; 17.58, 77
13:6	14.115; 17.16	27:12	16.8
13:8	17.16	27:13	3.319; 17.42
13:9	4.257; 6.197; 8.25; 11.204; 14.344	28:1–2	14.49
		28:2	17.134
13:10–13	4.257; 14.344	28:7	14.315
13:10	2.303; 3.319; 16.7; 17.14	28:9–12	9.131
		28:16	2.265; 8.121, 135, 139; 14.194
13:13	2.303; 17.15		
13:19–22	16.8, 149	29:6	14.341
13:19	15.185	29:10	8.145
14:12	15.183; 16.111; 17.59, 80	29:13	3.167
		29:14	9.17
14:13	17.133	30:21	6.157
14:31	14.115	30:30	14.341
15:2–3	14.115	31:4	6.61
16:7	14.115	32:15	16.10
19:2	17.5	33:15	3.294
20:3–4	7.154; 14.36	33:18	9.17
20:3	16.25	33:24	16.11
20:4	16.143	34:4	3.319; 17.14, 15
20:7	14.293	34:8–10	17.112
21:9	17.111	34:9–10	17.170
22:5	11.204	34:11–15	17.150
22:9–11	6.43	35:1	16.10
22:14	2.42	35:5–6	6.72

35:6	5.186		45:22	17.217
35:7	5.154		45:23	1.369; 8.187
35:8–10	3.319		48:12	16.48, 52, 81
35:8	6.157		48:13	5.30
35:10	17.203		48:20	17.152
37:16	16.158		49:2	16.51
37:32	8.133		49:6	5.55; 6.63; 16.8;
38:10	16.52			17.217
38:18	6.92; 9.138; 14.237;		49:10	1.67; 5.154; 17.37
	16.181		49:23	16.130
39:13	9.138		49:24–26	2.36
40:3–5	4.6, 32		50:3	17.14
40:3	1.44; 5.78f		50:9	14.229
40:6–8	14.189		51:2	14.222
40:6–7	14.48		51:3	16.10
40:7	17.20		51:5	16.8; 17.217
40:11	6.54; 14.215; 17.38		51:6	17.195
40:24	17.20		51:9	15.62; 17.47, 58, 77
40:25	16.127		51:17	3.255; 17.111
40:31	7.11; 17.85		52:6	6.210
41:5	17.14		52:7	8.141
41:8	6.25, 178		52:11	9.223
42:1–4	2.33		52:13–	14.181
42:1	1.60; 4.38		53:12	
42:6	5.55; 6.63		52:15	5.79; 8.203
42:9–10	16.176		53	1.60; 5.81; 7.69, 129;
43:2	17.86			9.18; 14.185, 214
43:15	16.127		53:1–2	6.131; 8.141
43:18–19	17.204		53:4	1.310f
43:21	14.198		53:7	5.81; 14.120; 16.171
44:1–2	16.25		53:9	5.93; 17.108
44:3	1.48; 5.154		54:5	5.143; 9.246; 14.101;
44:6	16.48, 52, 81; 17.204			16.108; 17.76, 172
44:9–17	17.21		54:11–12	17.200
45:1	2.33		54:12–13	16.9
45:3	6.5; 13.60		55:1	5.154; 17.230
45:4	14.166; 16.25		55:2	5.212
45:14	10.122; 16.8, 130		55:5	17.217
45:20–22	16.8		55:6	5.246

11 Phil, Col, Thes
12 Tim, Tit, Phlm

13 Heb
14 Jas, Pet

15 John, Jude

16 Rev, v.1
17 Rev, v.2

55:11	1.369; 5.29
56:1	3.294
56:6–8	17.217
56:7	2.247; 3.274f
56:8	6.63
56:11	3.178
56:12	9.154
57:15	14.110
57:19	10.111
58:11	5.250
59:7–8	8.55
59:20–21	8.152
59:21	5.83
60:10–20	17.201
60:12	1.304; 10.122
60:14	16.130
60:19–20	17.216
60:19	6.13
61	4.48
61:1	5.84; 15.69
61:2	15.36
61:6	16.35
62:2	16.99
62:5	9.246
63:1–3	17.181
63:3	17.116
63:6	16.8
63:16	6.27
64:4	3.292
64:6	17.30
64:8	6.27
65:1	8.142
65:6–7	6.38
65:14	14.115
65:17	8.109; 17.197
65:19	17.203
65:20–22	16.10
65:25	16.10
66:15–16	14.341; 16.7

66:15	17.20
66:19	17.217
66:22	17.197
66:24	3.232

Jeremiah

1:4–5	8.12
1:5	6.77, 216
2:2	16.63
2:7	5.59; 14.173
2:13	5.154; 17.220
2:21	6.172
2:23	14.173
2:35	1.57
3:2	14.173
3:6–11	2.49
3:6–10	17.76
3:14	17.172
3:17	17.217
3:18	16.10
3:20	14.101; 16.108
4:13	17.20
4:24	17.15
5:24	14.121
6:10	11.55, 139
6:14	1.281; 14.314
7:11	2.247; 3.274
7:22	5.112
7:25	3.281; 8.12; 11.10; 12.227; 14.36
7:34	17.167
8:3	17.51
8:11	1.281
8:13	2.251

---

1 Matt, v.1	**3** Mark	**5** John, v.1	**7** Acts	**9** Cor
2 Matt, v.2	**4** Luke	**6** John, v.2	**8** Rom	**10** Gal, Eph

8:16	17.25	27:22	7.154
9:14–15	17.44	28	14.315
9:23–24	9.22	28:10–11	2.240; 3.339
11:17	8.149	29:5	16.70
11:19	5.81; 16.171	30:7	11.204
11:20	16.109	30:9	3.193; 16.2
13:1–11	4.239; 7.154; 13.13	30:23	17.20
13:8	14.49	30:24	15.59
15:2	17.97	31:3	5.220
15:19	14.134	31:8–9	5.186
16:9	17.167	31:12	16.10
16:18	5.59	31:18	1.53
16:19–21	17.217	31:31–34	13.92
17:13	5.154	31:33	17.203
17:15	14.338	31:34	13.118
17:19–27	5.182	33:14–18	3.298
17:21–24	4.60; 5.122	35:5–7	12.119
17:24	3.39	37:17	15.22
18:1–6	8.132	47:2	17.137
21:8	1.278	47:4	2.12
22:4	3.193	48:47	15.59
22:13	14.119	49:18	15.185
23:1–4	6.54	49:36	17.20
23:3	8.145	50:8	17.152
23:5ff	3.298	50:13	8.24
23:5	3.193; 16.2	50:29	17.153
23:14	14.315; 15.185	50:39	17.150
23:15	17.44	50:40	15.185
23:16	14.312	51:6	17.152
23:19	17.20	51:7–8	17.111
23:20	15.59	51:7	17.137
23:29	5.29; 17.181	51:13	17.134
23:32	14.315	51:34	17.77
25:10	17.167	51:36	17.128
25:15	17.111	51:37	17.150
25:22	2.12	51:45	17.152
27	3.339	51:48	17.165
27:1–11	4.239; 13.13	51:56	17.4
27:1–6	2.240	51:63–64	17.166

11 Phil, Col, Thes   **13** Heb   **15** John, Jude   **16** Rev, v.1
12 Tim, Tit, Phlm   **14** Jas, Pet   **17** Rev, v.2

B

Lamentations

1:12	6.254
1:15	17.116
1:30	1.30
3:24	14.174
3:30	1.165
4:6	15.185
5:16	14.49
5:21	12.44

Ezekiel

1:6	16.157
1:7	16.50
1:10	16.157
1:13	16.155
1:18	16.157
1:22, 26	16.157
1:28	5.69; 16.51; 17.54
2:1	8.220
2:9-10	16.165
3:1, 3	17.57
3:12	16.43
3:14	17.143
3:15	16.39
3:18	6.17
3:23	16.51
3:27	17.225
4	7.154
4:1-8	3.339
4:1-3	4.239; 13.13
4:16	17.7
5:1-4	3.339; 4.239; 7.154; 13.13
7:2	17.19
7:19	8.25
8:3-18	9.221

8:3	17.143
8:18	6.48
9:1-7	17.23
9:6	2.242; 14.261
10:2	17.41
10:8	14.263
10:20, 22	16.158
11:24	17.143
13:3	14.312
13:16	14.314
14:14, 20	8.145
14:21	17.9
14:22	8.145
15	6.172
16	17.172
16:15	17.142
16:37-39	16.143
16:46, 49, 53, 55	15.185
17:22ff	3.110
17:23	4.179
18:4	8.26; 10.82
18:18	6.17
18:23	14.343
18:31	5.131
19:10	6.172
20:34	9.223
20:37	6.56
20:43	14.173
21:2	13.23
22:27	1.281
23:26-29	16.143
24:6	17.167
26-27	17.158
26:3-7	2.12
26:13	17.166
26:16	16.46
27:3	17.154
27:28-30	17.164

28:12–22	2.12
28:17	16.151
30:2	13.23
31:1ff	3.110
31:6	2.76; 4.179
32:7–8	3.319
32:7	17.14
33:12	1.56
34	6.54
34:9–10	15.194
34:23ff	3.298
34:23	14.215; 16.2; 17.38
34:24	16.25
36:25	5.79
36:26–27	1.48; 5.84, 131
37:9	6.274
37:14	1.48
37:24	3.298; 14.215; 16.2; 17.38
37:25	6.128; 16.25
37:27	9.223; 17.203
38–39	17.194
38	17.60
38:8	17.133
38:14–39	16.8
38:19	17.13
38:21	17.133
38:22	17.134
39:2, 4	17.133
39:15	1.314
39:17–19	17.184
39:17	17.133
39:29	1.48
40:2	17.209
40:3	17.67, 211
40:6	17.67
41:21	17.212
43:1–2	17.151
43:2	16.48, 50
43:3	16.51
43:16	17.212
44:7, 9	11.139
44:13	14.106
45:2	17.212
47:1–12	5.154, 251
47:1–7	17.220
47:12	17.221
48:20	17.212
48:30–35	17.210
48:31–35	17.201
48:35	16.135

Daniel

2:34f, 44f	2.265; 8.135
2:44	17.187
3	9.119; 13.129
3:19–28	13.164
3:19–25	1.117
3:24–25	8.166
4:10, 21	3.110
5:29	16.144
6:17	17.23
6:18, 23	13.164
7:1–14	5.185f; 16.36
7:1–8	6.121
7:3–7	17.88
7:8	17.94
7:9	16.48f
7:10	17.196
7:13–14	17.115
7:13	2.355; 5.185; 6.121; 16.45
7:14	6.128; 17.187, 217
7:20	17.94
7:27	16.9; 17.187
8:9–12	17.60, 62

8:10	17.77		6:6	1.335; 2.24; 3.296;
8:26	17.225			13.115
9:11	14.35; 16.25		8:13	5.112
9:27	3.309		9:1	14.102; 16.108; 17.106
10:5	16.46		9:3	5.59
10:6	16.49f; 103		10:1	6.172
10:13, 20f	16.54		10:8	17.16
11	17.194		11:1	1.35f; 3.71; 8.124
11:31	3.309; 15.62		11:8	15.185
12:1	16.54, 123		11:10	17.54
12:2–3	16.9		12:5	16.39
12:3	14.134; 16.111		13:5	8.114
12:7	17.69		13:15	17.20
12:10	17.225		14:6	8.149
12:11	2.306; 3.309; 15.62			

Hosea

Joel

1:7–18	17.49
2–3	3.304
2:1–11	17.49
2:1–2	4.257; 6.197; 7.25; 14.344; 16.7

1:5	17.4
1:6, 9	14.197
1:10	8.121, 133; 14.197; 16.48; 17.22

2:1	17.16, 42
2:10	3.319; 17.13, 44
2:11	17.16
2:23	14.121
2:28	1.48
2:30–31	2.303; 4.257; 11.204; 14.344; 16.7
2:30	14.341
2:31	17.14
2:32	8.121, 140
3:2, 12	17.116
3:13	17.115
3:15	3.319; 16.7
3:16	17.54
3:18	5.251; 17.220

1:11	16.10
2:1	14.197
2:3	16.143
2:4	6.28
2:8	17.6
2:9	16.143
2:12	2.251
2:18	3.24; 16.10
2:19–20	16.76; 17.172
2:22	17.6
2:23	8.133; 14.197
4:6	6.208
4:17	8.29; 16.145
5:6	5.112
5:8	11.58

Amos

1:14	17.20
3:2	8.114; 11.11
3:7	2.5; 3.281; 6.51; 8.12; 11.10; 12.49, 227; 13.12; 14.36; 14.293; 15.170; 16.25, 168
3:8	17.54
3:10	14.116
3:12	6.60
4:11	15.185
5:4	6.208
5:11	14.117
5:16-20	3.304
5:18-20	4.257; 7.25
5:18	11.204
5:27	7.60
7:7-9	17.67
7:14-15	3.28
8:3	14.115
8:4-7	14.117
8:8	17.13
8:9	3.319; 17.14
9:3	17.47
9:5	16.39
9:8-10	8.145
9:11	16.2
9:13	5.168
9:14	12.79

Jonah

3:10	1.54

Micah

1:1-4	17.16
1:8-11	16.143
2:12	8.145
3:3	17.148
3:8	5.83
3:11	14.315
4:1	15.59
4:4	2.251; 5.93
4:6	13.182
5:2-4	16.2
5:2	1.24, 30
5:3	8.145
6:6-8	8.58; 13.115; 14.61
6:8	3.294
7:6	3.313
7:8	6.13
7:12	3.319
7:18	1.56

Nahum

1:3	17.19
1:4	17.20
1:5-6	14.341
1:5	17.15
3:4	17.142
3:5	16.143
3:14	17.167

Habakkuk

2:3	13.127
2:4	3.294; 10.26
2:14	6.208
2:20	17.36

11 Phil, Col, Thes	**13** Heb	**15** John, Jude	**16** Rev, v.1
12 Tim, Tit, Phlm	**14** Jas, Pet		**17** Rev, v.2

Zephaniah

1:3	17.44
1:7	7.25
1:12	9.45
1:14–18	2.303; 4.257; 14.344
1:14–16	11.204
1:14	16.7; 17.16
1:16	17.42
2:9	15.185
2:11	5.158
2:13–15	17.150
3:3	1.281
3:8	8.25
3:9	17.217
3:12–13	8.145
3:13	17.108

Haggai

2:6	13.188; 17.13
2:7–9	16.9
2:9	17.201

Zechariah

1:5	6.33
1:6	3.281; 14.36
1:18	16.171
2:1	17.67
2:5	17.210
2:12	5.59
2:13	17.217
3:1–5	17.30
3:1–2	17.81
3:2	3.22
3:10	2.251

4:2	16.45
4:10	16.172
5:3	1.370
6:1–8	16.2
6:1–5	17.19
7:6–10	14.61
8:2	14.104
8:20–23	17.217
8:22–23	16.130
9:9	2.240; 3.264; 4.240; 6.117f
9:14	17.20, 42
10:6–11	3.319
10:11	17.128
11:10	2.337
11:16	6.62
12:6	14.85
12:10	6.261; 16.36f
12:11	17.132
13:1	5.79, 154
13:4	1.282
13:7	2.343
14	17.60
14:1–11	16.8; 17.194
14:1–4	17.116
14:8	5.154; 17.220
14:9	17.217
14:13	16.7; 17.5
14:16–18	5.248

Malachi

1:2–3	8.128
1:8–9	14.63
1:11	5.158
2:7	16.54
2:9	14.63

1 Matt, v.1	3 Mark	5 John, v.1	7 Acts	9 Cor
2 Matt, v.2	4 Luke	6 John, v.2	8 Rom	10 Gal, Eph

2:10	6.27	3:5	14.119
2:16	1.151; 11.196	4:1	11.204; 14.341
2:17	14.338	4:4	14.35, 293
3:1–4	5.108	4:5–6	1.44; 2.6, 136, 164;
3:1–3	16.7; 17.16		3.213; 4.19, 90;
3:1	1.69; 2.242; 3.12;		5.78; 16.6
	17.70	4:5	17.70

INDEX OF NEW TESTAMENT REFERENCES

(Page numbers in italics indicate the main treatment of the N.T. passages)

Matthew

1:1–17	**1**.9, *11–18*; **3**.298; **4**.12, 40f
1:2	**4**.3
1:5	**13**.161
1:16	**4**.41
1:18–25	**1**.*18–23*; **4**.12
1:21–23	**1**.6
1:21	**8**.20; **14**.176
1:24–25	**14**.20
2:1–2	**1**.*23–27*
2:2	**1**.9; **17**.21
2:3–9	**1**.*28–30*
2:9–12	**1**.*31–33*
2:13–15	**1**.*33–36*
2:13	**17**.79
2:14–15	**1**.6
2:15	**4**.137
2:16–18	**1**.6, *36–38*; **3**.149
2:17	**4**.137
2:19–23	**1**.*38–40*
2:22	**7**.93
2:23	**1**.6; **4**.137
3:1–6	**1**.*43–46*
3:2	**1**.51
3:3	**4**.6; **5**.79
3:7–12	**1**.7, *46–58*; **2**.3; **3**.20; **7**.141
3:8	**14**.72
3:9	**6**.26
3:11	**5**.84; **7**.141; **15**.108
3:12	**17**.117
3:13–17	**1**.*58–60*
3:16–17	**15**.108
3:17	**3**.20
4:1–11	**1**.*61–70*
4:1	**3**.6; **17**.82, 143
4:2	**1**.234
4:3–4	**5**.204
4:3	**17**.82
4:5	**17**.82
4:8–9	**16**.33
4:8	**17**.82
4:10	**2**.150; **17**.82
4:11	**17**.82
4:12–17	**1**.*70–76*, 364
4:12	**5**.2
4:18–22	**1**.*76–79*
4:21	**14**.9
4:23–25	**1**.*80–83*
5–7	**1**.8; **4**.76
5:1	**1**.*86–87*, 198
5:3	**1**.*88–92*; **4**.5; **14**.66
5:4	**1**.*93–95*; **14**.108; **15**.36; **17**.204
5:5	**1**.*96–98*; **10**.51
5:6	**1**.*99–102*; **17**.36
5:7	**1**.*102–105*; **2**.194; **14**.70
5:8	**1**.*105–108*; **2**.119; **14**.108; **15**.75; **16**.122; **17**.34, 222
5:9	**1**.*108–110*
5:10–12	**1**.*110–118*
5:10	**12**.198

5:12	1.179; 17.172	6:5–8	1.*191–198*
5:13–16	2.54	6:5	1.186
5:13	1.85, *118–122*	6:9–15	1.*198–200*
5:14–15	1.*122–125*	6:9	1.*200–210*
5:14	16.53	6:10–11	1.364
5:15	1.85; 3.98	6:10	1.*210–214*, 258, 267;
5:16	1.*125f*; 14.72, 204		2.86, 289; 3.42;
5:17–20	1.6, *126–133*; 2.282,		4.54f; 14.347
	285	6:11	1.*215–219*
5:18	1.85	6:12	1.103, *219–224*; 3.276;
5:21–48	1.*133–137*		14.228
5:21–22	1.*137–141*; 15.83	6:13	1.*224–232*; 9.196;
5:21	1.9, 134		17.82
5:22	1.140; 3.231	6:14–15	1.103, *219–224*; 2.195;
5:23–24	1.*142f*; 12.65		3.276; 14.22, 71, 228
5:25–26	1.*144–146*	6:14	14.134
5:26	4.171	6:15	12.65
5:27–28	1.*146*	6:16–18	1.*232–238*, 335
5:27	1.9, 134	6:16	1.186
5:28	14.331	6:19–21	1.*238–243*
5:29–30	1.*147–150*; 11.150	6:19	14.116
5:29	1.140; 3.231	6:21	2.218
5:30	1.140; 2.183; 3.231	6:22–23	1.*243–247*
5:31–32	1.85, *150–157*; 4.212	6:24	1.*248–254*; 14.103;
5:31	3.237		15.57; 16.109
5:33–37	1.*158–162*; 2.292;	6:25–34	1.*254–261*; 14.272
	14.126	6:26–30	2.54
5:33	1.134	7:1–5	1.85, *261–265*
5:34–37	14.22	7:1–2	2.89; 6.6; 14.66, 71,
5:34	1.9		121
5:38–42	1.*162–172*	7:2	3.98; 17.153
5:38	1.9, 134	7:3–5	6.6
5:43–48	1.*172–178*	7:6	1.*265–269*; 3.178;
5:43	1.9, 134		11.54
5:47	9.163	7:7–12	1.85
6:1–18	1.*179–185*	7:7–11	1.85, *270–272*
6:1	1.*185f*	7:7	4.8; 5.246
6:2–4	1.*187–191*	7:11	3.27
6:2	1.186	7:12	1.*272–277*

7:13–14	1.*277–280*	9:20–22	1.*345–348*
7:15–21	14.72	9:21	8.20; 14.176
7:15–20	1.*281–288*; 16.63	9:23–26	1.*342–345*
7:15	16.63	9:24	6.86
7:16–20	14.22	9:27–31	1.*349–351*
7:16	3.271	9:27	3.298
7:21–23	1.*288–290*	9:30	1.298; 6.97
7:21	3.271	9:31–34	1.325
7:22	12.177	9:32–34	1.*351–352*
7:24–27	1.*290–294*; 2.54; 4.82	9:35	1.*352–354*
7:28–29	1.133	9:36	1.*354–356*; 3.7; 6.54; 14.269
8	1.358		
8:1–4	1.*295–300*	9:37	1.*356–357*
8:5–13	1.*300–307*; 5.174	10	1.8
8:9	8.54f	10:1–4	1.*357–362*
8:10	6.64	10:1	2.166
8:11	1.6, 210; 6.64; 17.174	10:2	14.8
8:14–15	1.*307–309*	10:3	5.94; 14.8
8:14	2.175	10:4	4.3
8:16–17	1.*309–310*	10:5–8a	1.*362–366*
8:16	1.2	10:5–6	1.6; 4.6; 6.63
8:17	1.311	10:6	14.269
8:18–22	1.*311–315*	10:8b–10	1.*366–368*
8:23–27	1.*316–319*	10:11–15	1.*368–371*
8:25	8.20; 14.176	10:15	15.185
8:28–34	1.*319–323*	10:16–22	1.*372–378*; 6.155
8:28	1.319; 12.182	10:16	1.281; 6.61
9	1.358	10:17–22	6.182
9:1–8	1.324, *325–328*; 3.2	10:18–19	7.174
9:9–13	4.64	10:22	14.176
9:9	1.5, *328–332*; 14.8	10:23–29	6.182
9:10–13	1.324, *332–335*; 2.183	10:23	1.*378–382*
9:11	1.7	10:24–25	1.*382–384*
9:13	1.18	10:26–31	1.*384–390*
9:14–17	1.325	10:26	3.98
9:14–15	1.*335–337*	10:28	1.140, 312; 3.231; 14.112
9:16–17	1.*337–340*; 2.54		
9:18–31	1.*340–342*; 6.100	10:29	4.161, 171
9:18–19	1.*342–345*	10:32–33	1.*390–392*; 2.42;

	12.170; **15**.68; **16**.123	12:30	**2**.*39–41*
10:33	**15**.119	12:31–33	**2**.*41–45*
10:34–39	**1**.*393–397*	12:31–32	**4**.161
10:34	**6**.185	12:34–37	**2**.*45–47*
10:36	**1**.228; **3**.75; **4**.103	12:36–37	**14**.82
10:37–39	**2**.151	12:38–42	**2**.*48–50*
10:39	**6**.124; **17**.84	12:38–40	**2**.129
10:40–42	**1**.*397–400*	12:39	**16**.108
10:42	**1**.179	12:43–45	**2**.20, *50–52*
11	**11**.1	12:45	**14**.335
11:1–6	**2**.*1–4*; **5**.245; **6**.163	12:46–50	**2**.20, *52f*; **14**.9
11:4	**5**.196	13	**1**.8; **2**.*53–56*
11:5	**14**.66	13:1–9	**2**.*56–63*; **14**.57, 189
11:7–11	**2**.*4–7*	13:8	**6**.154
11:12–15	**2**.*7–9*	13:10–17	**2**.*63–71*
11:16–19	**2**.*9–10*	13:12	**3**.98
11:16–17	**2**.54	13:13	**4**.99
11:20–24	**2**.*11–13*	13:14–15	**6**.132
11:23–24	**1**.371	13:18–23	**2**.*56–63*
11:24	**15**.185	13:19	**15**.24
11:25–27	**2**.*13–15*	13:24–30	**2**.*71–75*; **12**.179;
11:27	**15**.67		**17**.115
11:28–30	**2**.*15–18*	13:31–32	**2**.*75–78*; **4**.179
11:29	**10**.51	13:33	**2**.*78–83*
11:30	**10**.51; **11**.157; **15**.104	13:34–35	**1**.6; **2**.63–71
12	**2**.*18–20*	13:36–43	**2**.*71–75*; **12**.179
12:1–8	**2**.19, *21–27*, 42	13:37–43	**17**.115
12:7	**1**.335	13:39	**17**.82
12:9–14	**2**.19, *27–32*	13:43	**16**.122
12:10–13	**4**.72	13:44	**2**.*83–86*
12:14	**1**.7; **2**.19	13:45–46	**2**.*86–88*
12:15–21	**2**.*32–34*	13:46	**17**.215
12:15	**1**.2	13:47–50	**2**.*88–90*; **12**.179
12:16	**1**.298	13:51–52	**2**.*90f*
12:22–29	**2**.19, *34–39*	13:53–58	**2**.*91f*
12:23	**1**.15; **3**.298	13:55	**3**.6; **4**.13; **14**.9, 14,
12:24	**1**.7		19; **15**.170
12:25–29	**15**.78	13:57	**5**.172
12:28	**12**.90	13:58	**1**.3

14:1–12	2.*92–98*
14:3–12	1.71
14:3	7.93
14:5–12	4.36
14:12–21	1.1; 3.2
14:13–21	2.*98–103*
14:13	4.117
14:14	1.354
14:15–21	2.125
14:15	4.87
14:19	2.125
14:22–27	2.*104–106*
14:27	16.52
14:28–33	2.*106f*
14:30	8.20
14:33	16.146
14:34–36	2.*108*
14:36	1.347
15:1–9	2.*109–117*
15:1–6	2.215
15:10–20	2.*118–120*; 11.145
15:13	1.7
15:17	11.145
15:21–28	2.*120–124*; 5.175
15:21	2.125
15:22	1.9, 15, 349; 3.298
15:24	1.6; 6.64
15:28	1.363
15:29–39	2.*124–128*
15:32	1.354f; 4.87
16:1–4	2.*128–130*
16:1	14.102
16:3	1.7
16:4	16.108
16:5–12	2.*130–132*
16:6	2.79
16:12	1.7
16:13–23	1.7
16:13–16	2.*133–138*
16:13	5.230; 15.32
16:16	15.68
16:17–19	2.*139–146*
16:18	14.195
16:20–23	2.*147–150*
16:21	2.227; 14.263
16:23	1.65; 2.150
16:24–26	2.*151–155*
16:24–25	2.107
16:24	6.155
16:25	6.124; 17.84, 118
16:27–28	2.*155f*
16:28	1.381
17:1–8	2.*156–163*; 14.310
17:1	14.9
17:2	16.51; 17.54
17:7	16.52
17:9–13	2.*164f*
17:9	1.298
17:14–20	2.*165–168*
17:20	2.75; 3.275
17:22–23	2.*164f*, 227
17:24–27	2.*168–172*
17:27	4.172
18	1.8; 2.*172–174*
18:1–4	2.*174–176*
18:2	3.7
18:3	5.127; 12.44
18:5–7	2.*176–181*
18:8–9	2.*181–184*
18:8	3.43
18:9	1.140; 3.231
18:10	1.321; 2.*176–181*; 3.35; 13.18; 16.54
18:12–14	2.*184–186*; 14.269
18:12	6.54, 283
18:15–18	2.*186–190*
18:16	5.195
18:17	1.7

11 Phil, Col, Thes	**13** Heb
12 Tim, Tit, Phlm	**14** Jas, Pet

15 John, Jude	**16** Rev, v.1
	17 Rev, v.2

18:19–20	**2.***190–192*	21:15–17	**2.***248–250*
18:19	**6.**180	21:15	**1.**9, 15; **3.**298
18:21–35	**2.***192–195*; **14.**71	21:18–22	**2.***250–257*
18:24	**4.**172	21:23–27	**2.***257–259*
18:35	**1.**102; **12.**65	21:23	**14.**263
19:1–9	**2.***195–205*	21:28–32	**2.***259f*, 271
19:3–9	**1.**157; **3.**240	21:31–32	**2.**187
19:4–6	**17.**106	21:33–46	**2.***260–265*, 271
19:10–12	**2.***205–210*	21:33	**1.**250
19:13–15	**2.***211–212*; **3.**7	21:41	**1.**7; **14.**166
19:16–22	**2.***213–216*	21:42	**8.**135; **14.**194
19:19	**2.**201	22:1–14	**2.**271
19:20	**2.**213	22:1–10	**1.**333; **2.***265–268*
19:21	**1.**313	22:2, 10–11	**17.**172
19:23–26	**2.***216–219*		
19:24	**17.**2	22:11–14	**2.***268–271*
19:27–30	**2.***220f*	22:15–22	**2.***271–274*
19:27–29	**16.**154	22:16	**14.**62
19:28	**14.**269; **17.**193	22:21	**14.**205
20:1–16	**2.***221–226*	22:23–33	**2.***274–277*
20:2	**4.**171	22:30	**14.**324
20:17–19	**2.***227f*	22:34–40	**2.***277–279*
20:17	**3.**7	22:41–46	**2.***279f*
20:20–28	**2.***228–235*	23	**1.**7, 8
20:20–23	**3.**253	23:1–4	**2.***284f*
20:20	**1.**3; **5.**16; **6.**256	23:2	**1.**7
20:21	**17.**148	23:4–7	**14.**81
20:29–34	**2.***235–237*	23:4	**15.**104
20:30–31	**1.**15, 349	23:5–12	**2.***285–287*
20:30	**2.**280	23:5	**1.**347; **3.**295, 299
20:34	**1.**354; **4.**87	23:12	**11.**38; **14.**110
21:1–11	**2.**9, *237–243*	23:13–26	**2.**288
21:35	**1.**6	23:13	**2.***288f*
21:5	**10.**51	23:15	**1.**140; **2.***289–291*; **3.**231
21:9	**1.**9, 15; **2.**280; **3.**298; **4.**252		
		23:16–22	**2.***291–293*
21:12–14	**2.***243–248*	23:23–24	**2.***293f*
21:12–13	**5.**4, 107	23:25–26	**2.***295f*
21:13	**5.**111	23:27–28	**2.***296f*

23:29–36   2.297–299
23:33   1.140; 3.231
23:37–39   2.299f
23:37   3.263; 5.3, 106
24–25   1.8
24   1.7; 2.300–302
24:1–31   2.301–304
24:1–2   2.302, 304f
24:3   2.312f; 14.122
24:4–5   2.304, 311
24:5   5.199; 15.64
24:6–8   2.304, 308f
24:8   16.7
24:9–10   2.309f
24:9   17.10
24:11–13   2.304, 311
24:11   12.92; 15.4
24:12   15.3
24:13   14.125, 176; 16.40
24:14   1.6; 2.312f; 14.347;
              17.109
24:15–22   2.302, 305–308
24:15   15.62
24:21   17.17, 29
24:23–26   2.304, 311
24:23   17.61
24:24   5.199
24:27–28   2.312f
24:27   2.312; 14.122, 123
24:29–31   2.308
24:29   17.14
24:30   16.36
24:31   16.43; 17.42
24:32–41   2.313–316
24:32–35   2.314f
24:33   14.121
24:36–51   14.123
24:36–41   2.315f
24:36   11.205; 14.123

24·37, 39   2.312; 14.122, 123
24:42–51   2.316–318
24:42–43   16.119
24:44   17.61
24:48–51   16.132
25:1–13   1.7; 2.318–321
25:1   17.172
25:14–30   1.7, 179, 184; 2.321–
              324; 4.172
25:15   1.250
25:21, 23   4.39
25:25   2.84
25:29   3.98
25:31–46   1.7–8, 180; 2.324–326;
              17.195
25:35   14.255
25:40   3.225; 13.199
25:41   3.23
25:43   14.255
26:1–5   2.327f
26:3   14.263
26:6–13   2.328–331
26:14–16   2.331f
26:15   3.328
26:17–19   2.338–340
26:18   5.102
26:20–25   2.333f
26:26–30   2.341–343
26:29   17.174
26:31–35   2.343f
26:31   6.54
26:33–35   2.106
26:33   6.285
26:35   8.100; 14.90
26:36–46   2.347–350
26:38–46   14.272
26:39   15.115
26:40   11.166
26:41   16.119

26:42	15.115	27:62–66	2.374
26:45	5.102	27:66	6.266; 16.166; 17.23, 191
26:47–50	2.334–336		
26:50–56	2.350–352	28:1–10	2.375f
26:52	17.97	28:2	4.291
26:53	6.67; 17.182	28:3	17.121
26:56	14.154, 268	28:9	6.270
26:57–58	2.344–347	28:10	6.271
26:57	2.352–356; 14.263	28:11–15	2.377
26:59–68	2.352–356	28:16–20	2.377f
26:61	5.115	28:18	1.9
26:63	1.161; 6.245	28:19–20	1.6, 363; 6.64
26:64	16.36	28:20	6.192; 7.10; 17.232
26:65–66	2.357; 6.235		
26:69–75	2.344–347; 14.90		
27:1–2	2.353, 356–362		
27:1	14.263		
27:3–10	2.336–338	*Mark*	
27:3–5	3.330; 7.16	1:1–4	3.11–15
27:3	14.263	1:3	4.6; 5.78f
27:9	1.6	1:5–8	3.15–18
27:11–26	2.353, 356–362	1:8	15.108
27:11	1.9	1:9–11	3.18–21; 15.108
27:14	6.245	1:11	6.127
27:15–26	6.248	1:12–13	3.21–24
27:17, 22	2.361	1:12	1.64; 3.6
27:27–31	2.362–364	1:13	17.82
27:32–44	2.365–367	1:14–15	3.24–26
27:34	4.284	1:14	1.210; 5.2, 141; 7.11
27:35	1.6; 14.267	1:15	1.51; 4.54
27:37	1.9	1:16–20	3.26–29
27:45–50	2.367–370	1:19–20	5.16; 10.149; 14.9
27:50	2.369; 3.364; 4.288; 6.258	1:19	14.273
		1:20	3.254; 4.16; 6.229
27:51–56	2.370f	1:21–28	1.308
27:54	1.301; 6.193, 205	1:21–22	3.29–32
27:56	5.16; 6.256; 14.8, 16	1:21	4.187
27:57–61	2.371–374	1:22	1.133; 3.6
27:57	2.219	1:23–28	3.33–36

1:25	3.115	3:21	1.3, 228; 2.52; 4.102;
1:27	3.6		7.15, 96; 9.144, 208;
1:29–31	3.*36–38*		11.188; 14.9, 19
1:29	14.9	3:22–27	3.*77–79*
1:32–34	3.*39f*	3:27	17.190
1:34	1.2, 298	3:28–30	3.*79–81*; 4.161
1:35–39	3.*40–42*	3:31–35	3.*81–83*; 14.9, 19
1:38	1.210	3:34	16.49
1:40–45	3.*42–46*	3:35	15.102
1:41	1.354f; 4.87; 5.9;	4:1–2	3.*84–87*
	6.39	4:1	1.317
1:43	6.97	4:3–9	3.*88–90*
2:1–12	1.1; 3.2	4:10–12	3.*90–94*
2:1–6	3.*46–48*	4:11–12	2.68
2:1	1.326	4:12	6.132
2:5	14.131	4:13–20	3.*94–97*
2:7–12	3.*49–52*	4:15	17.82
2:14	14.8; 17.107	4:21–25	3.98
2:13–14	3.*52–55*	4:21	3.*97–100*
2:14–17	1.332	4:22–23	3.*101f*
2:15–17	3.*55–58*	4:24	3.*103f*
2:17	3.8	4:25	3.*104–106*
2:18–20	3.*58–60*	4:26–29	3.*106–109*
2:19	17.172	4:29	17.115
2:21–22	3.*60–62*	4:30–32	3.*109–112*
2:23–28	3.*62–66*	4:33–34	3.*112–114*
2:23	5.4	4:35–41	3.*114–117*
2:27	2.26	4:35	1.317
3:1–6	3.*66–70*; 4.72	4:38	3.7
3:5	1.3; 3.7; 10.156;	4:41	3.6
	16.49	5:1–20	3.184
3:7–12	3.*70–72*	5:1–19	1.322
3:10	1.2	5:1–13	3.*117–120*
3:13–19	3.*73–75*, 360	5:1	1.319
3:14–15	3.219	5:7	1.322
3:14	1.360f; 4.74	5:14–17	3.*121–124*
3:17	5.16; 14.8	5:18–20	3.*124–126*
3:18	5.94; 14.8	5:21–43	6.100
3:20–21	3.*75–77*	5:21–24	1.342; 3.*126–128*

11 Phil, Col, Thes   **13** Heb   **15** John, Jude   **16** Rev, v.1
12 Tim, Tit, Phlm   **14** Jas, Pet   **17** Rev, v.2

5:22	5.9	7:9–13	2.215; 3.*169–171*
5:25–29	3.*128–131*	7:11	3.8
5:26	1.346; 4.113	7:14–23	3.*171–175*; 11.145
5:30–34	3.*131–133*	7:15	12.244
5:35–39	3.*133–136*	7:19	11.145
5:37	5.16; 14.9	7:22	10.47
5:40–43	3.*136f*	7:24–30	3.*176–179*
5:41	3.8	7:24	2.125
5:43	1.298	7:31–37	3.*179–182*
6:1–6	3.*137–141*	7:31	2.125f
6:3	3.6; 14.9, 14, 15, 19; 15.170	7:33	6.41
		7:34	3.6, 8
6:4	5.172	7:36	1.298
6:5–6	1.3	8:1–10	3.*182–185*
6:6	3.7	8:2	4.87
6:7–11	3.*141–144*	8:11–13	3.*185f*
6:12–13	3.*144–146*	8:12	3.6
6:14–15	3.*146–148*	8:14–21	3.*187–189*
6:16–29	3.*148–154*	8:22–26	3.*189–191*
6:17–29	4.36	8:26	1.298
6:17	7.93	8:27–33	1.7
6:30–44	1.1; 3.1f, 27	8:27–30	3.180, *191–193*
6:30–34	3.*154–156*	8:27	5.230
6:30	4.117	8:29	2.137
6:31–44	2.125	8:31–33	3.*199–201*
6:31	3.7	8:31	3.220, 252
6:34	3.6f; 6.39, 54; 14.215, 270	8:33	3.7
		8:34–37	2.151
6:35–44	3.*157–159*	8:34–35	3.*201–203*
6:39	2.125; 5.4	8:35	6.124; 17.84
6:40	3.7	8:36	3.*203–205*
6:44	3.184	8:37	3.*206f*
6:45–52	3.*159–161*	8:38–9:1	3.*207–209*
6:45	5.208	8:38	14.102; 15.119; 16.108
6:51	3.6		
6:53–56	3.*161–163*	9:1	1.381f; 2.155, 314; 14.310
7:1–4	3.*163–167*		
7:3	14.107	9:2–8	3.*209–211*; 14.310
7:5–8	3.*167–169*	9:2	5.16; 14.19

9:4	**17.71**
9:5	**5.4**
9:7	**6.127**
9:9–13	3.*212–214*
9:14–18	3.*214–216*
9:14	**5.9**
9:19–24	3.*216–218*
9:22	**1.354**
9:25–29	3.*218–220*
9:30–31	3.*220f*
9:31	**3.252**
9:32–35	3.*221–224*
9:36–37	3.*224f*
9:38–40	3.*225–228*
9:38	**5.16**
9:40	**2.40**
9:41–42	3.*228–230*
9:43–48	3.*230–233*
9:43	**1.141**
9:44–48	**1.141**
9:45	**1.141**
9:47	**1.141**
9:49–50	3.*233–236*
10:1–12	3.*236–240*
10:9	**9.62**
10:11–12	**2.201**
10:13–16	**3.7**, *241f*
10:14	**1.3; 3.7**
10:17–22	**2.213**; 3.*243–245*
10:18	**2.213**
10:21	**3.7; 5.19; 6.145; 16.49; 17.107**
10:23–27	3.*246–248*
10:23	**16.49**
10:24	**3.6**
10:25	**7.2**
10:26	**3.6**
10:28–31	3.*248–250*
10:32–34	**2.227**; 3.*251–253*

10:32	**3.7**
10:35–45	**2.228**
10:35–40	3.*253–256*
10:35	**1.3; 5.16; 14.9**
10:37	**17.148**
10:41–45	3.*256–259*
10:41	**14.9, 190**
10:42–44	**14.267**
10:45	**14.317; 16.177**
10:46–52	3.*259–262*
10:47ff	**1.349; 3.298**
11:1–6	3.*262–265*
11:1–2	**3.8**
11:1	**2.238**
11:7–10	3.*266–268*
11:9	**11.2**
11:11	3.*268f*; **16.49**
11:12–14	**2.251**; 3.*269–272*
11:12	**3.7**
11:13	**2.252**
11:15–19	3.*272–275*
11:15–17	**5.4, 107**
11:17	**5.111, 113**
11:20–21	**2.251**; 3.*269–272*
11:22–26	3.*275–278*
11:27–33	3.*278–280*
12:1–12	3.*280–284*
12:9	**14.166**
12:10	**14.194**
12:13–17	3.*284–288*
12:14	**14.62**
12:18–27	3.*288–292*
12:28–34	**2.278**; 3.*292–297*
12:28–31	**15.102**
12:35–37a	**1.349**; 3.*297–299*
12:37b–40	3.*299–301*
12:41–44	3.*301–303*
12:42	**4.171**
13	3.*303*

13:1–2   3.*306–309*
13:2   3.350
13:3–6   3.306, *314–317*
13:3   14.9
13:6   5.199; 15.64; 17.61
13:7–8   3.306, *317–320*
13:8   16.7
13:9–13   3.306, *312–314*; 6.182;
            17.10
13:14–20   3.306, *309–311*
13:14   15.62; 17.79
13:19   17.17, 29
13:21–23   3.306, *314–317*
13:22   5.199; 12.92, 131
13:24–27   3.306, *317–320*
13:24   17.14
13:26   16.36
13:28–37   3.307, *320f*
13:29   14.121; 16.146
13:31   17.195
13:32   7.14; 11.205; 14.123
13:37   16.119
14:1–2   3.*322–325*
14:3–9   3.*325–327*
14:3   6.109
14:5   2.329; 6.97
14:10–11   3.*328–330*
14:12–16   3.*330–334*; 6.292
14:17–21   3.*334–336*
14:22–26   3.*336–340*
14:27–31   3.*340–342*
14:27   6.54
14:32–42   3.*342–345*
14:33   4.16; 14.9
14:36   2.349; 3.8
14:41   5.102
14:43–50   3.*345f*
14:43   3.8
14:44   14.279

14:51–52   3.*347f*
14:53   3.*348–351*
14:54   3.*351–353*
14:55–65   3.*348–351*
14:58   5.116
14:61   6.245
14:62   16.36
14:66–72   2.345; 3.*351–353*
15:1–5   3.*354f*
15:5   6.245
15:6–15   3.*356–358*; 6.248
15:6   4.280
15:16–20   3.*358f*
15:21–28   3.*359–362*
15:21   2.366; 4.283; 8.215
15:25   2.368
15:29–32   3.*362f*
15:33–41   3.*363–365*
15:34   2.368; 3.8
15:37   2.369; 4.288; 6.258
15:40   2.229; 6.256; 14.8, 16
15:42–47   3.*365–367*
15:46   2.368
15:47   2.374
16:1–8   3.*367–369*
16:1   5.16
16:5   4.291; 17.121
16:7   9.143
16:8   3.5, 370; 6.271
16:9–20   3.5, *369–371*
16:9   6.256
16:15   6.64

Luke

1:1–4   4.*7f*
1:3   7.2

1 Matt, v.1   3 Mark   5 John, v.1   7 Acts   9 Cor
2 Matt, v.2   4 Luke   6 John, v.2   8 Rom   10 Gal, Eph

1:5–25	4.*8–11*	3:23	1.41; 3.139; 4.37, 41;
1:5	5.76		14.19
1:26–38	4.*11–13*	3:38	4.3
1:36	2.96; 5.82	4:1–13	4.*41–44*
1:39–45	4.*13f*	4:1	3.6
1:46–56	4.4, *14–16*	4:2–3, 5	17.82
1:46–47	12.18	4:6–7	16.33
1:47	15.207	4:13	2.148; 17.82
1:55	15.78	4:14–15	4.*44–46*
1:57–66	4.*16–18*	4:16–30	4.*46–49*
1:67–80	4.4, *18f*	4:16	16.26
1:80	17.143	4:18	14.66
2:1–7	4.*20f*	4:24	5.172
2:7	14.20	4:25–27	4.5
2:8–20	4.*22f*	4:25	14.132
2:21–24	4.*23–25*	4:31–37	4.*49–51*
2:24	4.5	4:35	7.2
2:25–35	4.*25–27*	4:38–39	4.*51–53*
2:29–32	4.4	4:38	4.187
2:36–40	4.*27f*	4:40–44	4.*53–55*
2:36	16.105	4:40	1.2
2:41–52	4.*28f*	4:43	1.210; 4.120
2:48	4.12	5:1–11	4.*55–57*
2:49	2.169; 4.120	5:7–10	5.16
3:1–6	4.*30–32*	5:8	3.80; 5.163; 10.102
3:1–2	4.3; 7.93	5:10	14.9
3:3–11	7.141	5:11	16.51
3:4, 6	4.6; 5.79	5:12–15	4.*57–59*
3:7–18	4.*32–35*	5:16–17	4.*59–61*
3:7–13	3.20	5:16	4.4
3:8	3.271; 6.26; 14.72	5:17–26	1.1; 3.2
3:16	5.85; 7.141; 15.109	5:18–26	4.*61–63*
3:18	5.2	5:27–32	1.333; 4.*63–65*, 234
3:19–20	4.*35f*	5:33–35	4.*65–67*
3:19	7.93	5:36–39	4.*67–69*
3:20	5.2	6:1–5	4.*69–71*
3:21–22	4.*37f*; 15.108	6:6–11	4.*71–73*
3:21	4.4	6:6	4.187
3:23–38	3.298; 4.12, *38–41*	6:7	2.19

---

11 Phil, Col, Thes   **13** Heb   **15** John, Jude   **16** Rev, v.1
12 Tim, Tit, Phlm   **14** Jas, Pet   **17** Rev, v.2

6:12–19	4.*73–75*	8:14	14.99
6:12	4.4	8:16–18	4.*100–102*
6:13–19	1.84, 360	8:16	1.85
6:13	1.361	8:19–21	4.*102–104*
6:14	14.9	8:22–25	4.*104–106*
6:15	4.3; 14.8	8:26–39	4.*106–109*
6:16	1.359; 14.8; 15.169	8:26	1.319
6:19	1.2	8:28	1.322
6:20–49	1.85	8:31	17.191
6:20–26	4.*75–77*; 14.108	8:36	8.20
6:20	4.5; 14.66; 16.78	8:38–39	4.228
6:22	6.47	8:40–56	6.100
6:24	14.117	8:40–42	1.342; 4.*109–112*
6:26	16.118	8:43–48	4.*112–114*
6:27–38	4.*77–80*	8:49–56	1.342; 4.*109–112*
6:37–42	1.85	8:51	14.9
6:39–46	4.*80–82*	8:52	16.169
6:47–49	5.*82f*	9:1–9	4.*114–116*
7:1–10	4.*83–86*; 5.174	9:10–17	1.1; 3.2; 4.*116–118*
7:3	14.263	9:18–22	4.7, *119f*
7:9	4.5	9:18	4.4; 5.230
7:11–17	4.*86–88*; 6.100	9:20	2.137
7:13	1.354f; 16.169	9:22	4.120
7:15	5.9	9:23–27	2.151; 4.*120–122*
7:18–29	4.*88–91*	9:24	6.124; 17.84
7:18–22	9.261	9:26	15.119
7:22	4.5; 5.196	9:27	1.381f; 14.310
7:24	15.23	9:28–36	4.*123–125*; 14.310
7:30–35	4.*91–93*	9:28	14.9
7:36–50	2.329; 4.5, *93–95*;	9:29	2.157; 4.4
	11.157	9:31	2.160
7:45	14.279	9:32	2.157; 11.166; 14.269
7:47	14.134	9:37–45	4.*125–127*
8:1–3	4.*96f*	9:37	2.157
8:1	1.210	9:38	7.2
8:2	6.256	9:46–48	4.*127f*
8:4–15	4.*98–100*	9:49–56	4.*129–131*
8:10	6.132	9:49	5.16
8:12	17.82	9:50	2.40

9:51–56	4.5; 14.90		12:2–9	6.182
9:51	4.119; 8.206		12:5	1.141; 3.231
9:54	5.16; 14.9		12:6	1.389; 4.171
9:57–62	4.131f		12:8–9	16.123
9:57–58	2.107; 6.80, 155		12:13–34	4.163–166
9:59	17.108		12:16–21	14.113
10:1–19	3.23		12:19	9.154
10:1–16	4.132–135		12:24	13.29
10:7	12.116; 14.118		12:32	6.54
10:12–13	1.371		12:35–48	4.166–168
10:12	15.185		12:36	16.146
10:17–20	4.135f		12:49–53	4.169f
10:18	15.78, 183		12:51–53	6.182
10:21–24	4.136–138		12:54–59	4.170–172
10:22	15.67		12:58–59	1.145
10:23–24	14.178		13:1–5	4.172–174
10:25–37	4.138–141		13:1–4	4.281
10:25	4.171		13:6–9	2.253, 271; 4.174–176
10:30–37	4.5		13:10–17	4.176–178
10:30	1.363		13:13	4.187
10:37	6.64		13:16	17.82
10:38–42	4.141f, 104; 6.91		13:18–19	4.178–180
11:1–4	4.143f		13:20–21	4.180–182
11:1	1.198		13:22–30	4.182–184
11:5–13	4.4, 144–146		13:27	12.177
11:9–13	1.85		13:28	1.210; 4.54
11:11	3.27		13:29	4.5; 6.64
11:12	1.271		13:31–35	4.184–186
11:14–23	4.147f		13:31	4.94
11:22	16.180; 17.190		13:33	4.120
11:24–28	4.149f		13:34	5.3
11:26	14.335		13:35	2.2
11:29–32	2.49; 4.150–152		14:1–6	4.186–189
11:30	2.49		14:7–11	4.189f
11:33–36	4.152–154		14:11	11.38; 14.111
11:37–44	4.154–157		14:12–14	4.190f
11:41	14.134		14:14–24	1.333; 4.192–195
11:45–54	4.157–159		14:15	1.216
12:1–12	4.159–162		14:25–33	4.195–197

11 Phil, Col, Thes
12 Tim, Tit, Phlm
13 Heb
14 Jas, Pet
15 John, Jude
16 Rev, v.1
17 Rev, v.2

14:25–27	2.151	18:18	2.213
14:26	1.313	18:19	2.213
14:34–35	4.85, *197f*	18:24	14.117
15	3.316	18:25	7.2
15:1–7	4.*199–201*	18:31–34	2.227; 4.*230f*
15:4–7	14.269	18:31	3.7
15:4	6.54	18:35–43	4.*231–233*
15:8–10	4.*201–203*	18:38–39	4.252
15:8	4.172	19:1–10	4.5, *233–236*
15:11–32	4.5, *203–206*	19:9	2.219
15:13	12.235	19:11–27	4.172, *236–238*
15:17–18	3.14	19:28–40	4.*238–240*
15:17	16.64	19:38	2.2
15:18	16.65	19:39–40	2.249
15:22	16.144	19:41–48	4.*240–242*
15:24	16.116	19:45–46	5.4, 107
16:1–13	4.*207–210*	19:46	5.111
16:14–18	4.*210–212*	20:1–8	4.*243f*
16:16	2.8	20:9–18	4.*244–247*
16:17	1.85	20:16	2.69; 14.166
16:18	2.201; 9.62	20:17	14.194
16:19–31	4.5, *212–214*; 6.102	20:19–26	4.*247–249*
16:21	11.54	20:21	14.62
16:22–31	6.34	20:27–40	4.*249–251*
17:1–10	4.*215–217*	20:41–44	4.*252f*
17:6	3.275	20:45–47	4.*253f*
17:11–19	4.5, *217–219*	21:1–4	4.*254–256*
17:18–19	4.228; 6.64	21:5–24	4.*256–260*
17:20–37	4.*219–221*	21:8	17.61
17:20–21	4.*220f*	21:12, 18	17.10
17:21	1.211; 4.54	21:21–24	4.173
17:25	4.120	21:25–37	4.*260f*
17:29	1.371; 15.185	21:38	6.291
17:33	2.151; 6.124; 17.84	22:1–6	4.*262–264*
18:1–8	4.4, *221–223*	22:3	3.23, 330
18:9–14	2.187; 4.*223–225*	22:7–23	4.*264–267*
18:14	11.38	22:24–30	4.*267f*
18:15–17	3.7; 4.*225–227*	22:24	6.138; 14.190
18:18–30	2.213; 4.*227–230*	22:28	1.65

22:31–38	*4.268–271*		24:34	9.143f
22:31–32	**12.11**		24:36–49	*4.297f*
22:31	17.82		24:39	6.270; **15.23**
22:32	4.4		24:42	3.27
22:39–46	*4.271–273*		24:47	15.53
22:42–44	1.65		24:50–53	*4.299f*; **7.13**
22:47–53	*4.273–275*		24:52	7.14
22:54–62	*4.268–271*			
22:61–62	14.269; **16.49**			
22:61	14.155			
22:63–71	*4.275–277*		*John*	
23:1–12	*4.277–279*		1	5.26; **13.1**
23:1–2	3.354		1:1–18	*5.25–37*
23:2	2.357		1:1–2	*5.37–40*
23:3	12.136		1:3	5.13, *40–42*; **16.141**
23:6–12	4.173		1:4	*5.42–46*
23:7ff	7.93		1:5	5.45, *47–49*; **15.27**
23:9	6.245		1:6–8	*5.49–53*
23:13–25	*4.279–281*		1:7–8	5.52
23:17–25	6.248		1:8	5.12, 50
23:24	7.62		1:9	5.9, *54–56*; 6.18; **13.56**
23:26–31	*4.282–284*		1:10–11	*5.56–60*
23:26	7.99		1:10	6.18
23:30	17.16		1:11	7.161
23:32–38	*4.284–286*		1:12–13	*5.60–63*
23:39–43	*4.286f*		1:12	5.128
23:43	4.5; **16.71**		1:13	14.171, 189
23:44–49	*4.287–289*		1:14	4.137; 5.13, *63–70*;
23:45	17.14			15.7, 23, 93; **16.180**
23:46	2.369; 3.364; 4.4;		1:15–17	*5.70–73*
	6.258; 14.262		1:15	15.112
23:47	4.84		1:18	*5.73–75*; **15.114**
23:50–56	*4.289f*		1:19–2:11	5.76
23:50f	2.373		1:19–34	*5.75f*
24:1–12	*4.290–293*		1:19–28	*5.75–80*
24:5	6.271		1:19–20	5.195
24:7	4.120		1:20	5.50
24:13–35	*4.293–296*		1:20ff	5.12
24:28	16.148		1:23	4.6

1:26	5.195	3:7–13	5.*130–133*
1:28	5.6	3:11	16.32, 140
1:29–31	5.*80–82*	3:14–15	5.*134–137*
1:29	5.195; 15.77; 16.170	3:16	5.13, 43, *137–138*;
1:32, 34	5.*82–85*; 15.108, 112		6.18; 12.19, 55;
1:35–39	5.75, *85–88*		15.40; 17.205
1:35–36	1.78; 5.195	3:17–21	5.*138–140*
1:36	16.170	3:17	6.18
1:40–42	5.75, *88–91*; 8.221	3:19–20	5.46, 47
1:40–41	5.5	3:19	15.27
1:41–51	5.76	3:21	5.68; 14.133; 15.29
1:41–42	14.292	3:22–30	5.2, *141–144*
1:43–51	5.76, *91–95*	3:25–30	5.50
1:43	17.107	3:28	5.12
1:44	5.6, 202	3:29	17.173
1:45	5.52	3:31–36	5.*144–146*
1:48	2.252; 6.82	3:36	5.44
1:51	16.140, 150	4	5.5
2:1–13	5.2	4:1–9	5.*146–151*
2:1–12	5.106, 232	4:1–4	5.172, 228
2:1–11	5.5, 76, *95–105*	4:1	5.50
2:1	5.6; 14.19	4:1–2	5.2, 12, 228
2:4	5.15, 231	4:4–42	1.363
2:6	5.5	4:5	5.6
2:11	5.9, 68, 75	4:6	5.14
2:12–16	5.*105–114*	4:9	4.5, 129; 5.6; 7.65
2:13–22	5.4	4:10–15a	5.*151–156*; 6.86
2:13–17	10.156	4:14	5.250; 17.37
2:13	3.263; 5.2, 4, 80	4:15b–21	5.*156–158*
2:15	5.14	4:16–17	5.15
2:16	5.111	4:21	5.116
2:17–22	5.*114–117*	4:22–26	5.*158–162*
2:20	5.6	4:26	6.72
2:23–25	5.*117–120*	4:27–30	5.*162–164*
2:23	5.228	4:29	9.132
3:1–15	5.5; 14.171	4:31–34	5.*164–166*
3:1–6	5.*120–130*	4:31	5.14
3:3–8	6.86	4:35–5:1	5.2
3:3, 5	16.140	4:35–38	5.*166–169*

4:39–42	5.*170f*
4:39	5.53, 228
4:40	6.64
4:43–5:1	5.106
4:43–45	5.*172–173*
4:46–54	5.*174–176*
4:46	5.6, 232
4:54	5.176
5–7	5.176
5:1–9	5.*177–181*, 232
5:1	3.263; 5.2, 106
5:2	5.6
5:6	5.15
5:9	4.187
5:10–18	5.*181–184*
5:10	5.6, 176
5:19–29	5.*184–187*
5:19, 20	5.*187–189*
5:21–23	5.*189–190*
5:22	3.51; 17.194
5:24	5.43f; *190–191*
5:25–29	5.*191–193*
5:29	5.43
5:30–32	15.112
5:30	5.*193–194*
5:31–36	5.*194–196*
5:33	15.112
5:36	5.12, 51, 166; 15.112
5:37–43	5.*196–199*
5:37	5.51; 15.112
5:39	5.52; 15.112
5:40	5.43
5:41	5.69
5:43	17.61
5:44–47	5.*199–200*
5:46	5.52
5:47	5.238f
6:1–7:14	5.2, 106
6	5.10
6:1–13	5.*200–205*, 232
6:1	4.117; 5.176
6:2	5.228
6:4	5.4, 106, 177, 208
6:5–7	5.5
6:5	5.14
6:6	5.15
6:8–9	5.5, 89
6:8	15.175
6:9	3.159; 5.5
6:14, 15	5.*206–207*
6:15	2.104
6:16–21	5.*207–210*
6:17	5.48
6:19	5.5
6:20	5.14
6:22–27	5.*210–213*
6:27	5.43
6:28, 29	5.*213–214*
6:30–34	5.*215–216*
6:31–35	16.95
6:32	5.9
6:33–38	5.14
6:33–35	1.215
6:35–40	5.*216–218*
6:35	17.36, 230
6:38	5.166
6:39–40	14.175
6:40	5.43
6:41–51	5.*218–220*
6:42	4.13
6:44	14.175
6:47	5.44
6:51–59	5.*221–226*
6:54	14.175
6:59–65	5.*226–228*
6:61–64	5.15
6:66–71	5.*228–230*
6:70–71	6.111

7:1–9	*5.230–233*; 6.83
7:1–5	14.19
7:1	5.176
7:2	5.2, 106; 6.10
7:3–9	14.9
7:5	2.52; 6.257; 7.96; 9.144; 14.9
7:6, 8	5.102
7:10–13	*5.233–238*
7:10	3.263; 5.2, 15, 106
7:14	*5.242–245*
7:15–24	5.239
7:15–18	*5.238–240*
7:16	16.23
7:17	12.171
7:18	5.69
7:19–24	*5.241–242*
7:21–23	5.6
7:25–30	*5.242–245*
7:30	5.231
7:31–36	*5.245–247*
7:33	6.156
7:37–44	*5.247–252*
7:37	6.10; 17.37
7:38–39	17.221
7:39	6.81
7:45–52	*5.253–254*
7:53–8:11	*6.1–9*
8:2–11	6.292f
8:12–20	*6.9–15*
8:12	5.45, 48; 6.64; 15.27; 17.229
8:14	5.51
8:15	6.292
8:16	5.9
8:18	5.51; 15.112
8:20	5.231
8:21–30	*6.15–20*
8:23	6.18
8:25	6.19
8:28	5.135; 16.23
8:29	5.166
8:31–32	5.67; *6.20–22*
8:33–36	*6.22–24*
8:33	15.78
8:37–41	*6.24–26*
8:37	15.78
8:39	6.64
8:40	5.67; 9:146
8:41–45	*6.27–29*
8:44	9.147
8:45	5.68
8:46–50	*6.29–32*
8:48	4.140
8:50	5.69
8:51–55	*6.32–33*
8:54	5.69
8:56–59	*6.34–36*
8:58	5.14
9	5.10; 6.50–52
9:1–5	*6.37–41*
9:3	5.9
9:4	4.168
9:5	1.122; 5.45; 13.56
9:6–12	*6.41–44*
9:6	5.6
9:13–16	*6.44–45*
9:14	4.187; 5.6
9:17–35	*6.46–49*
9:25	5.53
9:35–41	*6.49–50*
9:35–38	15.68
9:37	6.72
9:38	5.53
9:39	5.139
9:41	7.35
10:1–18	14.215, 270
10:1–6	*6.52–57*

10:7–10	6.*58–60*	11:36	6.145
10:7, 9	16.129	11:38	5.14
10:10	5.43; 14.298	11:47–53	6.101, *103–106*
10:11–15	6.*60–63*	11:54–57	6.*106–108*
10:11	10.148; 17.38	11:55	5.106
10:12	1.281	11:57	3.328; 4.239; 6.108
10:14	10.148; 17.38	12:1–8	6.*108–113*
10:16	6.*63–66*, 289	12:1, 3	5.6
10:17, 18	6.*66–67*	12:4–5	5.5
10:18	5.15, 166	12:5	2.329
10:19–21	6.*68–69*	12:6	2.331; 3.173, 328
10:22–28	6.*69–73*	12:9–11	6.*113–114*
10:22	5.2, 106	12:12–19	6.*115–119*
10:23	5.6	12:16	6.81
10:25	5.52	12:17	5.53
10:28	5.43; 16.61	12:20–22	6.*119–120*
10:29, 30	6.*74–76*	12:21	5.6
10:30	4.137	12:22	5.5, 89
10:31–39	6.*76–78*	12:23–26	6.*121–125*
10:40, 41	6.*78–79*	12:23	5.102; 6.81, 203
10:41	5.12, 50	12:25	2.151; 17.84
11	5.5, 10	12:27–34	6.*125–130*
11:1–44	6.*100–103*	12:27	5.231
11:1–5	6.*80–82*	12:31	9.44, 196; 15.78; 17.82
11:3	5.19		
11:4	5.9, 69	12:32	2.371; 3.29, 367; 5.135; 6.234, 264; 7.28; 12.55; 15.40
11:5	5.19		
11:6–10	6.*82–85*		
11:10	5.45		
11:11–16	6.*86–88*	12:35–36	6.*130–131*
11:14	5.15	12:35	5.48; 15.27
11:16	5.5; 6.275	12:36	5.45, 46
11:17–19	6.*88–90*	12:37–41	6.*131–133*
11:20–27	6.*90–96*	12:42, 43	6.*133–134*
11:24	14.175	12:42	6.47
11:28–33	6.*96–98*	12:44–50	6.*134–136*
11:33	5.14	12:44–45	15.67
11:34–44	6.*98–100*	12:46	5.45, 46, 48; 15.27
11:35	5.14	12:48	14.175
		12:49	5.239; 16.23

13:1–17	5.5; 6.*136–142*	14:25–31	6.*170–171*
13:1	6.292	14:30	9.196; 17.82
13:2	17.82	15:1–10	6.172–176
13:4–5	14.270	15:1	5.9
13:18–20	6.*142–144*	15:7	15.115
13:21–30	6.*144–147*	15:10	6.75
13:23–25	5.19	15:11–17	6.*176–181*
13:27	3.330; 17.82	15:14	2.53
13:29	6.293	15:16	8.12; 11.103
13:30	3.348; 5.48; 6.85	15:18–21	6.*181–186*
13:31, 32	6.*147–149*	15:18–19	6.18; 14.87
13:33–35	6.*149–150*	15:19	15.4
13:34–35	14.227; 15.88, 141	15:22–25	6.*186–187*
13:34	6.75; 15.44	15:22	7.35
13:36–38	6.*151–152*	15:24	5.52
14–17	5.5	15:26, 27	6.*187–188*
14:1–3	6.*152–156*	15:26	5.53, 67; 15.112
14:4–6	6.*156–159*	15:27	5.53
14:5	5.5	16:1–4	6.*189–191*
14:6–9	15.67	16:2	6.47; 17.10
14:6	5.43, 66f	16:5–11	6.*191–194*
14:7–11	6.*159–163*	16:11	9.44, 196; 17.82
14:8–9	5.5	16:12–15	6.*194–196*
14:9	1.21; 2.15; 4.137, 288; 6.210; 9.197; 13.103; 14.197; 16.22	16:12–13	5.24
		16:13–14	14.133
		16:13	5.67
		16:16–24	6.*196–200*
14:10	5.239	16:22	1.89; 11.51; 16.97
14:11	5.52	16:25–28	6.*200–201*
14:12–14	6.*163–165*	16:29–33	6.*201–203*
14:14	15.115	16:33	6.18; 16.178
14:15–17	6.*166–168*	17:1–5	6.*204–209*
14:15	6.75; 15.141	17:1	5.102
14:17	5.67; 6.18; 14.87	17:2	5.43
14:18–24	6.*168–169*	17:4	4.167; 5.166
14:19	4.88; 16.53	17:5	5.14, 69
14:21	5.128; 6.75	17:6–8	6.*209–213*
14:22	14.87; 15.169	17:9–19	6.*213–217*
14:23–24	5.166; 6.75	17:11	6.75

17:14	**15**.4
17:15	**1**.287
17:20, 21	**6**.75, *217–218*
17:21–23	**14**.224
17:22–26	**6**.*219–220*
17:22	**5**.69
17:25	**6**.18
18:1–11	**6**.*220–224*
18:1	**5**.6
18:10	**2**.351; **3**.346; **5**.220
18:13	**4**.32, 242
18:12–14	**6**.*225–227*
18:15–18	**6**.*227–231*
18:15	**4**.270
18:19–24	**6**.*225–227*
18:25–27	**6**.*227–231*
18:28–	**6**.*231–249*
19:16	
18:28	**6**.293
18:33–34	**2**.138
18:36	**14**.87
18:37	**5**.67; **12**.200; **14**.133; **16**.32
18:40	**3**.173
19:6–7	**4**.280
19:10–11	**6**.67
19:11	**5**.15
19:12	**4**.281
19:13	**5**.6
19:14	**6**.293
19:17–22	**6**.*249–252*
19:17	**4**.282; **5**.6
19:23, 24	**2**.367; **4**.285; **6**.*253–255*
19:23	**3**.142; **5**.5
19:25–27	**5**.19; **6**.*255–257*
19:25	**14**.8, 16, 17
19:26–27	**14**.154; **15**.138
19:26	**5**.98; **14**.18
19:28–30	**6**.*257–259*
19:28	**5**.14
19:30	**2**.369; **3**.364; **4**.288
19:31–37	**6**.*260–262*
19:34	**5**.251
19:35	**5**.19, 53
19:38–42	**6**.*262–264*
19:39	**2**.219; **5**.5, 121
20:1–10	**6**.*264–268*
20:1	**5**.48
20:2	**5**.19
20:11–18	**6**.*268–272*
20:12	**4**.291
20:19–23	**6**.*272–274*
20:20	**6**.282
20:24–29	**5**.5; **6**.*275–279*
20:27	**6**.270
20:28	**14**.294
20:29	**14**.161, 179
20:30, 31	**6**.*279*
20:31	**5**.43
21	**6**.280
21:1–14	**6**.*280–284*
21:1	**2**.105; **5**.208
21:2	**5**.6, 94
21:6	**5**.220
21:11	**5**.220; **6**.284
21:15–19	**6**.54, *284–287*; **14**.269
21:16	**10**.148; **14**.215
21:18–19	**14**.287, 308
21:19–22	**17**.108
21:20–24	**6**.*287–288*
21:20	**5**.19
21:24	**5**.19, 53
21:25	**2**.11; **4**.134; **6**.*288–289*

Acts

1:1–6:7	**7**.5

NEW TESTAMENT REFERENCES

54

Ref	
1–5	7.6
1:1–5	7.9–11
1:1	7.2
1:5	15.109
1:6–8	7.11–13
1:7	11.205
1:8	7.4, 19, 193; 17.170
1:9–11	7.13–14
1:9	17.78
1:12–20	7.14–17
1:13	5.16; 14.8, 9; 15.169
1:14	14.10, 14; 15.171
1:15	12.91
1:16	7.18
1:21–26	7.17–18
1:21–22	10.3, 146
1:22	9.78, 115; 14.155
1:25–26	16.133
1:26	14.267
2:1–13	7.20–22
2:4	15.109
2:13	7.22
2:14–39	9.17
2:14–21	7.22, 24–25; 14.250
2:14–16	14.140
2:17	14.175
2:18	14.293
2:19–20	14.148
2:20–31	14.141
2:22–36	7.26–28
2:22–26	14.141
2:24	2.143
2:27	2.143; 13.83
2:31	5.117
2:32	9.178
2:33	5.135; 7.27; 15.109
2:37–41	7.28–29
2:37	6.192
2:38–39	14.141
2:40	8.20
2:41	2.145
2:42–47	7.29–31
3:1–10	5.16; 7.31–33
3:1	1.195
3:2	6.37
3:11–16	7.33–34
3:12–26	9.17; 14.140
3:13–14	14.141
3:13	7.27; 14.141
3:14	6.248; 14.120
3:15	9.78; 13.25
3:17–26	7.34–36
3:17	4.285
3:18	7.26
3:19–23	14.141
4:1–13	5.16
4:1–4	7.36–37
4:5–12	7.38–39
4:5	14.263
4:8–12	9.17; 14.140
4:10	7.27
4:11	3.283; 4.247; 8.135; 14.141
4:12	16.94
4:13–22	7.39–41
4:13	5.239
4:16	7.32
4:19	14.206
4:23–31	7.41–42
4:28	7.26
4:31	7.19; 15.24
4:32–37	7.43
4:32	14.224
4:33	9.78
4:36–37	7.90, 99; 13.8
5:1–11	7.44–45
5:3	17.82
5:5, 10	12.54

1 Matt, v.1　3 Mark　5 John, v.1　7 Acts　9 Cor
2 Matt, v.2　4 Luke　6 John, v.2　8 Rom　10 Gal, Eph

5:12–16	*7.45–46*		8:25	**7.77; 15.24**
5:17–32	*7.46–48*		8:26–40	**7.6,** *67–69*
5:17	**14.316**		8:29	**7.19**
5:29	**14.206**		9:1–9	**6.**193; *7.69–71*
5:30–31	**14.141**		9:2	**7.**139; **9.**186
5:30	**7.27**		9:4	**17.85**
5:31	**5.**135; **13.**25; **14.**141		9:9	**9.258**
5:32	**7.20**		9:10–18	*7.71–72;* **12.44**
5:33–42	*7.48–50*		9:11	**15.169**
6:1–7	*7.50–52*		9:13	**11.11**
6:1	**12.106**		9:19–22	*7.72–73*
6:2	**15.24**		9:23–25	*7.74–75;* **9.255**
6:3	**7.19**		9:25	**3.184**
6:5	**16.67**		9:26–31	*7.75–76*
6:7	**15.24**		9:26–28	**12.44**
6:8–9:31	**7.5**		9:27, 30	**7.90**
6:8–15	*7.52–53*		9:31–	**7.6**
6:12	**14.263**		10:48	
6:14	**5.115**		9:32–	**7.5**
6:15	**14.259**		12:24	
7:1–7	*7.53–55*		9:32–43	*7.76–78*
7:6	**14.201**		9:32	**11.11**
7:8–16	*7.55–57*		9:43	**7.80**
7:17–36	*7.57–59*		10	**2.**145; **11.**145; **14.**292
7:37–53	*7.59–61*		10:1–8	*7.78–80*
7:51	**7.19**		10:6	**14.254**
7:52	**14.120**		10:9–16	*7.80–81*
7:53	**10.**29; **13.**17; **16.**24		10:17–33	*7.81–83*
7:54–8:1	*7.61–63*		10:17	**1.301**
7:55	**7.19**		10:19	**7.19**
7:60	**4.**285; **6.**86; **8.**168		10:22–23	**1.**300; **4.**84
8:1–4	*7.63–64*		10:26	**1.301**
8:5–13	*7.64–65*		10:28	**4.85**
8:9, 11	**1.26**		10:34–43	*7.83–84;* **14.**140
8:14–25	*7.65–67*		10:34	**14.**62, 141
8:14–17	**10.23**		10:36–43	**9.17**
8:14	**5.16**		10:38	**15.**70, 108; **17.**82
8:17–18	**15.89**		10:39–42	**14.141**
8:17	**13.**55; **15.**70, 109		10:39	**14.178**

11 Phil, Col, Thes **13** Heb **15** John, Jude **16** Rev, v.1
12 Tim, Tit, Phlm **14** Jas, Pet **17** Rev, v.2

c

10:42, 43	14.141		13:5	11.170; 12.217; 15.24
10:44–48	7.84–85		13:6–12	9.21
10:44–46	7.66		13:6	1.26
10:44–45	15.90		13:7	15.24
10:44	10.23; 15.109		13:8	1.26
10:46	7.21		13:9	7.19
11:1–10	7.85–86		13:11	12.54
11:1	15.24		13:12	7.3
11:11–18	7.86–87		13:13	3.3; 7.100–102;
11:12	7.19			10.39; 11.170;
11:19–30	7.6			12.217; 14.275
11:19–21	7.87–89		13:14–15	7.102–103
11:20	8.215f		13:15	16.26
11:22–26	7.89–90		13:16–41	7.103–105
11:24	7.19		13:26	15.24
11:27–30	7.91–92, 97		13:27	4.285
11:28	7.19		13:29	7.26
11:30	14.264		13:35	5.117; 13.83; 15.24
12:1–11	7.92–94		13:38	15.53
12:2	2.230; 3.256; 7.1, 101;		13:42–52	7.105–107
	14.15		13:44, 49	15.24
12:12–19	7.94–96		13:50	12.197; 14.149; 16.79
12:12	3.3, 347; 12.217		14:1–7	7.107–108
12:15	16.54		14:2	16.79
12:17	14.10		14:3	15.24
12:20–25	7.96–97		14:4	10.145
12:24	15.24		14:5–6	12.197
12:25– 16:5	7.5		14:5	16.79
			14:8–21	12.21
12:25– 14:8	7.6		14:8–18	7.108–109
			14:8	6.37
12:25	3.3		14:14	10.145; 14.17
13–14	7.97		14:15	17.10
13:1–3	7.98–99; 12.49		14:17	8.27
13:1	3.361; 7.91; 8.219;		14:19, 20	7.109–110
	14.79; 17.127		14:19	12.197; 16.79
13:2	7.19, 101; 8.13		14:21–28	7.110–112
13:4–12	7.99–100		14:21–23	15.137
13:4	7.19, 101		14:22	12.198; 16.40

14:23	12.71, 234; **16**.264; **15**.133	16:6–10	7.*121–122*; **11**.179
14:27	**16**.129	16:6	**7**.19
15:16	**7**.6	16:10–17	**7**.6
15	2.145; 7.4; **14**.10, 292	16:11–15	7.*122–123*
15:1–5	7.*112–113*	16:13–14	**11**.73
15:2	**14**.264	16:14	**16**.102
15:5	**14**.316	16:16–40	**11**.188
15:6–12	7.*114–115*	16:16–24	7.*124–125*
15:7	**15**.24	16:19	5.220; **11**.30; **14**.143
15:13–21	7.*115–116*	16:20–21	**11**.4
15:13	**14**.36	16:25–40	7.*125–127*
15:14	2.145; **14**.145, 292	16:25–34	**11**.73
15:17	**14**.23	16:25, 29	**14**.143, 275
15:22–35	7.*116–118*	16:31	**14**.73
15:22	**14**.17, 143, 275; **15**.169	16:32	**15**.24
15:23	**14**.23, 36	16:35ff	**7**.3
15:24	**14**.80	16:36–40	**16**.15
15:27	**14**.143, 275; **15**.169	16:37	**14**.143, 275
15:28–29	**16**.67	17:1–14	**11**.47
15:28	**7**.19	17:1–9	7.*127–128*; **11**.181
15:29	**16**.107	17:4	2.290; **9**.21, 73
15:32	7.91; **14**.143, 275; **15**.169	17:5–9	**8**.220
		17:5	**16**.79
15:39	**15**.24	17:6	1.376; 2.83, 182
15:36–18:23	**7**.119	17:10–15	7.*128–129*
		17:10–12	**11**.181
15:36–41	7.*118–119*; **11**.170; **12**.218	17:12	**9**.21, 73
		17:14–15	**12**.22
15:37–40	3.3; **14**.143, 275	17:16–21	7.*129–131*
15:38	**7**.101	17:22–31	7.*131–132*; **9**.23
16-28	**7**.6	17:31	**17**.195
16	11.5, 47; **17**.93	17:32–34	7.*132–133*; **9**.23
16:1–5	7.*119–120*	17:32	**2**.236
16:1–3	**12**.20	17:34	**9**.21
16:1	11.47, 22; **12**.119, 199	18	**17**.93
16:4	**14**.264	18:1–17	9.5, 6; **16**.15
16:6–19:20	**7**.5	18:1–11	7.*133–136*
		18:2	8.7, 208f; **9**.167; **12**.222

11 Phil, Col, Thes
12 Tim, Tit, Phlm
13 Heb
14 Jas, Pet
15 John, Jude
16 Rev, v.1
17 Rev, v.2

18:5	11.47; 12.22; 14.143, 275
18:8	9.16
18:9–10	11.27, 215
18:11	9.31
18:12–17	7.136–137; 14.146
18:12	7.3
18:14	7.4
18:18–23	7.137–138
18:18	8.8, 209
18:19	16.60
18:24–28	7.138–141
18:24–26	8.209; 13.9
18:24	9.14; 12.266; 16.60
18:26	11.68; 13.9; 16.60
19	9.253; 16.59; 17.93
19:1–7	5.11; 7.141–142
19:3–4	5.50
19:6	7.21; 13.55
19:8–12	7.142–143
19:9	7.139
19:10	8.20; 11.94
19:13–41	16.15
19:13–20	7.143–144
19:13	1.289
19:19	17.206
19:21–28:31	7.5
19:21–41	14.203
19:21ff	15.153
19:21, 22	7.144; 8.2; 11.47; 12.22
19:22	12.222
19:23–41	7.145–147
19:23	7.139
19:24–27	1.378
19:25	12.214
19:28	12.89
19:29	11.169; 15.147
19:31	7.3, 140
19:33	8.216
19:34	1.196
19:37	7.4
20:1–6	7.147–148
20:4	8.220; 9.169; 12.22, 222; 15.148
20:5–16	7.6
20:5	16.28
20:7–12	7.148–150
20:13–16	7.150–151
20:17–38	7.151–152; 16.60
20:17	16.28
20:28–29	14.264; 15.194
20:28	10.148
20:17–35	10.63
20:17	12.71
20:23	7.19
20:28	6.54; 7.19; 12.71; 14.161
20:29–31	16.119
20:29–30	15.4, 64; 16.63
20:29	1.281; 6.61
20:31	9.31; 10.63; 16.60
20:32	15.24
20:33	14.116, 266
21–22	17.93
21:1–18	7.6
21:1–16	7.153–154
21:9–10	7.91; 12.68
21:9	16.105
21:15–17	14.161
21:16	14.254
21:17–26	7.154–156
21:18–25	14.11, 14, 264
21:27–36	7.156–157
21:28–29	10.112
21:29	12.222
21:30–40	16.15

21:37–40	7.*158–159*	25:25	7.4
21:38	1.69	26:1–11	7.*175–177*
21:40	11.59	26:4–23	11.60
22:1–10	7.*159–160*	26:9–11	6.190
22:2–21	11.60	26:10	9.61; 10.173
22:3	11.59	26:11	9.106
22:4	7.139	26:12–18	7.*177–178*
22:11–21	7.*160–162*	26:18	9.44; 10.122; 11.111;
22:14	14.120		12.45
22:22–30	7.*162–163*	26:19–23	7.*178–179*
22:26	4.84	26:24–31	7.*179–180*
23:1–10	7.*163–165*	26:24	9.208; 11.188
23:2	9.251	27:1–	7.6
23:6–10	2.128	28:16	
23:6	11.59	27	12.215
23:8	9.137	27:1–8	7.*180–182*
23:11–24	7.*165–166*	27:2	11.169
23:11	8.2	27:9–20	7.*182–183*
23:12–31	16.15	27:21–26	7.*183–184*
23:17	4.84	27:27–38	7.*185–186*
23:23–24	1.301; 4.84	27:39–44	7.*186–187*
23:25–35	7.*166–168*	27:43	1.301; 4.84
23:26–30	14.23	28:1–6	7.*187–188*
23:26	14.36	28:2	9.229
23:29	7.4	28:7–10	7.*188–189*
24:1–9	7.*168–169*	28:11–15	7.*189–190*
24:1	14.263	28:16–29	7.*190–192*
24:5	14.316	28:16	7.193; 11.20
24:10–21	7.*169–170*	28:17–29	11.170
24:14	7.139	28:17, 20	11.21
24:17	9.162, 164	28:25	7.19
24:22–27	7.*170–171*	28:27	6.132
24:22	7.139	28:30–31	7.*192–193*; 12.10
24:23	1.301; 4.84	28:30	11.20; 12.283
24:26	12.283		
25:1–12	7.*171–173*	*Romans*	
25:10–11	16.15		
25:13–21	7.*173–174*	1–8	8.5f
25:22–27	7.*174–175*	1:1–7	8.*11–14*

1:1	8.xi; **14**.17, 35, 293; **15**.171, 176; **16**.25	4:4	**12**.23
		4:9–12	8.*65–67*
1:3	**1**.15; **3**.298; 8.101	4:13–17	8.*67–69*
1:7	8.xi, 10; **11**.12; **12**.23; **14**.36; **15**.176	4:15	8.26; **14**.7
		4:18–25	8.*70–71*
1:8–15	8.*14–18*	5:1–5	8.*71–75*
1:8	8.xi	5:1	**13**.72
1:11	8.2	5:2	**14**.235
1:15	8.2, 10	5:6–11	8.*75–77*
1:16–17	8.*18–23*	5:9	8.26; **17**.31
1:18–23	8.*23–28*	5:12–21	8.*77–82*
1:19–20	**5**.56	5:12	**14**.248
1:20	**3**.89	5:13	**6**.29
1:24–25	8.*28–30*	6	**3**.315; **10**.163; **12**.169, 174; **14**.247, 349; **15**.160
1:26–27	8.*30–32*		
1:28–32	8.*33–40*		
1:30	**14**.111	6:1–18	**5**.184
2:1–11	8.*40–44*	6:1–11	**5**.126; 8.*82–86*
2:4	**10**.51, 139; **14**.348	6:1–4	**7**.69
2:5	**16**.22	6:3ff	**10**.32
2:6	**14**.72	6:4	**12**.6, 169
2:8	**15**.29	6:8	**12**.169
2:11	**14**.62	6:10	**14**.233
2:12–16	8.*44–46*	6:12–14	8.*86–88*
2:14–15	**11**.142; **14**.57	6:13	**16**.116
2:17–29	8.*46–50*; **14**.80	6:15–23	8.*88–92*
2:24	**14**.319	6:17–20	**6**.23
2:28–29	**17**.24	6:23	**9**.12
2:28	8.101	7:1–6	8.*92–94*
3:1–8	8.*50–54*	7:5	8.101
3:5	8.26	7:7–13	8.*94–97*
3:9–18	8.*54–56*	7:10–11	**14**.7
3:10	**14**.82	7:14–25	8.*97–100*
3:19–26	8.*56–59*	7:15–24	**14**.51
3:23	**14**.82	7:22–23	**14**.50
3:25	**14**.348; **17**.31	8:1–4	8.*100–103*
3:27–31	8.*60–61*	8:4–5	8.101
3:28	**14**.72	8:5–11	8.*103–105*
4:1–8	8.*61–65*	8:6–8	8.101

1 Matt, v.1	**3** Mark	**5** John, v.1	**7** Acts	**9** Cor
2 Matt, v.2	**4** Luke	**6** John, v.2	**8** Rom	**10** Gal, Eph

8:7–8	14.103	10:4	1.126; 10.115; 14.59
8:9	8.102	10:9	11.39; 12.136
8:11	11.64	10:11, 13	8.121
8:12–17	8.*105–107*	10:14–21	8.*140–143*
8:12	8.102	10:14	5.170
8:13	11.150	10:19	8.122
8:14–17	15.74	11:1–12	8.*143–147*
8:15–16	15.101	11:2	14.343
8:15	4.143	11:6	12.23
8:17	14.258	11:8	6.132
8:18–25	8.*108–111*	11:11	16.133
8:23	10.79	11:13–24	8.*147–151*
8:26–30	8.*111–115*	11:25–32	8.*151–155*
8:28	14.272; 15.177	11:26	8.122
8:31–39	8.*115–119*	11:29	15.177
8:32	1.214; 6.153; 11.122; 14.272	11:33–36	8.*154f*
		11:36	17.205
8:34	15.38	12–15	8.5f
8:35–39	11.51	12	8.6; 14.22
8:38–39	4.299; 16.85	12:1–2	8.*155–158*
9–11	8.5, *119–123*, 136	12:1	11.16; 14.191, 197
9:1–6	8.*123–126*	12:2	14.87, 326; 16.109; 17.152
9:3	8.101		
9:6–9	16.130	12:3–8	8.*158–163*; 14.255
9:6–7	17.24	12:4	14.225
9:6	15.65	12:8	1.245
9:7–13	8.*127–129*	12:9–13	8.*163–167*
9:7–8	14.41	12:11	16.142
9:11	2.71	12:13	7.123; 12.81; 14.255; 15.149
9:14–18	8.*129–131*		
9:17	8.120	12:14–21	8.*167–170*
9:19–29	8.*131–133*	12:15	14.227
9:22	10.51; 14.348	12:16	14.225
9:25	8.121	12:19	8.26
9:27	8.120	13:1–7	8.*170–174*; 14.159, 205; 16.15; 17.63
9:29	1.371; 15.185		
9:30–33	8.*133–135*	13:1–6	17.93
9:32–33	3.283	13:5	3.26
10:1–13	8.*136–140*	13:6–7	14.206

13:8–10	8.*175–176*		16:3–5	9.167
13:11–14	8.*176–179*; **14**.123		16:3–4	8.*208–211*
13:11	8.21; **16**.118		16:3	**12**.222
13:12	**14**.73, 249; **15**.27		16:5–11	8.*211–213*
13:13	**10**.47		16:5	**11**.172; **13**.9; **14**.254
14:1	8.*179–181*		16:7	**10**.145; **14**.17
14:2–4	8.*182–183*		16:12–16	8.*214–217*
14:5, 6	8.*183–185*		16:12	**16**.62
14:7–9	8.*185–197*		16:13	3.249, 361; **4**.283
14:10–12	8.*187–189*		16:16	**14**.279
14:10	**17**.195		16:17–20	8.*217–219*
14:12	**14**.72		16:17	8.8
14:13–16	8.*189–190*		16:19	**11**.172
14:15–23	8.9		16:20	**11**.82
14:17–20	8.*190–193*		16:21–23	8.*219–220*
14:17	**10**.50; **13**.72		16:21	**11**.47; **12**.22
14:20	**12**.244		16:22	8.xii, 45; **11**.74
14:21–23	8.*193–194*		16:23	9.16, 21; **11**.103;
15:1–6	8.*195–197*			**12**.222; **15**.148
15:5	**11**.83		16:25–27	8.9, *220–222*
15:6	9.163		16:25	**15**.206; **16**.22; **17**.109
15:7–13	8.*197–200*		16:27	**15**.163
15:9	**12**.25; **14**.27			
15:13	**10**.50; **11**.82			
15:14–21	8.*200–203*			
15:14–15	**15**.66		*1 Corinthians*	
15:14	**10**.51		1–4	9.8
15:15	**10**.124; **12**.24		1:1–3	8.xi; 9.*9–11*
15:19	7.148		1:1	**11**.9, 103; **14**.17;
15:22–29	8.*204–205*			**15**.176
15:24	8.3; **12**.10, 12, 283		1:2	**15**.176
15:25–26	7.145; 8.3; 9.162		1:3	**14**.36
15:28	8.3; **12**.10, 283		1:4–9	9.*11–13*
15:30–33	8.*206*; **11**.25		1:4	8.xi; **12**.24
15:30–31	8.3; **11**.216		1:3	8.xi; **11**.12; **12**.23
15:33	1.109		1:9	**15**.74
16	8.xi, 5, 7, 9; 9.186;		1:10–17	9.*13–16*
	12.68		1:10	**14**.225
16:1–2	8.*207–208*		1:11	9.6

1:12	13.9; **14.**145	5:5	**8.**21; **12.**54; **15.**118
1:14	**8.**220; **15.**148	5:6–8	2.79
1:18–25	9.*16–20*	5:7	5.81
1:18	**15.**25	5:9–13	**9.**42, *46–48*
1:20	**14.**87	5:9	9.5f, 221f
1:22	1.48	6:1–8	**9.**42, *48–51*
1:24	**16.**179	6:2	17.193
1:26–31	9.*20–23*	6:9–20	**9.**42
1:26–27	**14.**27, 66	6:9–11	7.134; **9.***51–54*, 261
1:26	**15.**177	6:9–10	2.79; **9.**4
2:1–5	9.*23–25*	6:11	**12.**262; **17.**30
2:6–9	9.*25–27*	6:12–20	9.*54–58*
2:6	13.50	6:13ff	11.64
2:7–8	**12.**91	6:20	**11.**9; **16.**177
2:9	3.292	7:1–	9.57
2:10–16	9.*27–28*	15:58	
2:10	**16.**108	7	**10.**172; **12.**76
2:14–15	**14.**313	7:1–2	9.57, *58–59*
2:14	**15.**188	7:1	9.6
3:1–9	9.*29–31*	7:2	**10.**172
3:1–2	5.126	7:3–7	9.57, *59–61*
3:2	13.50; **14.**192	7:8–16	9.*61–64*
3:3	**14.**225	7:8–9	9.57
3:4	13.9	7:9	**10.**52, 172
3:8	**14.**73	7:10–11	9.57
3:10–15	9.*31–33*	7:12–17	9.57f
3:11	2.141	7:13–16	**14.**219
3:16–22	9.*33–35*	7:17–24	9.*64–66*
3:16	**17.**68	7:18	9.58
3:22	**14.**145	7:20	**15.**177
4:1–5	9.*35–38*	7:22	**14.**293
4:6–13	9.*38–40*	7:23	**14.**317; **16.**177
4:7	**11.**48	7:24	9.58
4:14–21	9.*40–42*	7:25	9.58, *66–68*
4:17	7.120; **9.**6; **11.**47; **12.**22	7:26–35	9.58, *68–70*
		7:32–33	**10.**172
4:19	**14.**114	7:36–38	9.58, *66–68*
4:21	**10.**52	7:38–40	9.58
5:1–8	**9.**42, *43–46*	7:39–40	9.*70–74*, 172

8–10	9.71; **16**.106	11:32	**16**.145
8	9.73, *74–76*	12	9.95; **14**.255
8:6	5.41; **11**.100	12:1–3	9.*106–107*
9	9.73	12:3	15.90
9:1–14	9.*77–81*	12:4–11	9.12, *108–112*
9:1	10.146	12:9	6.164
9:5	2.175; **14**.145, 277; 15.171	12:10	15.90
		12:12–31	9.*112–116*; **14**.225
9:6–7	12.161; **14**.17	12:12–27	8.159
9:12	14.266	12:12	6.273
9:15–23	9.*81–84*	12:13	12.272
9:16	14.265	12:26	14.226
9:22	16.93	12:28	6.164; **14**.79; **17**.127
9:24–27	9.*84–86*; **12**.161	12:30	6.164
9:24	11.45	13	9.95, *116–119*; **12**.201
9:25	10.52; **16**.83	13:4–7	9.*119–125*
9:26–27	11.45	13:8–13	9.*125–126*
10:1–13	9.73, *87–90*	13:11	10.34
10:4	5.251	13:12	6.220; **14**.179
10:5–11	15.182	14	7.21; **15**.90
10:11	14.250	14:1–23	9.96
10:14–22	9.73, *91–93*	14:1–19	9.*126–130*
10:17	14.225	14:2	15.90
10:23–11:1	9.*93–96*	14:6	**16**.22
		14:15	14.127
10:23–26, 27–28	9.73	14:20–25	9.*131–133*
		14:20	13.50
10:29–11:1	9.74	14:22	14.124
		14:23–33	9.96
10:31	14.214	14:23	7.22; **15**.90
11–14	9.95	14:24–36	9.96
11:2–16	9.95, *96–100*	14:26–33	9.*133–135*
11:10	14.322	14:26–27	15.90
11:17–22	9.95, *100–102*; **15**.192	14:26	14.127
11:18–19	14.316	14:29	16.63
11:21	15.194	14:33	11.82; **15**.90
11:23–34	9.*102–105*	14:34–40	9.*135–137*
11:24–34	9.95	14:34	16.105
11:30	15.118	15	9.*137–141*; **12**.30

1 Matt, v.1	**3** Mark	**5** John, v.1	**7** Acts	**9** Cor
2 Matt, v.2	**4** Luke	**6** John, v.2	**8** Rom	**10** Gal, Eph

15:1–11	9.*141–146*
15:3	14.233
15:5	14.145
15:6	6.86
15:7	7.96, 115; 10.145; 14.11
15:8–10	11.60
15:10	12.24; 16.62
15:12–19	9.*146–149*
15:14ff	11.64
15:17	8.21
15:18	17.114
15:20–28	9.*149–152*
15:21	8.78
15:23	14.122
15:24	8.118
15:28	11.40
15:29–34	9.*152–156*
15:35–49	9.*156–159*
15:50–58	9.*159–161*
15:51–52	11.27
15:52–53	17.42
15:52	16.43
16:1–12	9.*161–165*
16:1–2	7.145; 8.2
16:3	9.163
16:7	14.114
16:9	16.129
16:10–11	11.48; 12.22
16:12	11.103
16:13–21	9.*165–169*
16:13	16.118
16:14	14.124
16:15	9.16
16:17	9.6
16:19	8.xi, 8, 209; 12.222; 14.254
16:20	14.279
16:21	8.xii

2 Corinthians

1–9	9.7, 8
1:1–7	9.*169–171*
1:1	8.xi; 11.9; 12.22; 14.17
1:2	8.xi; 11.12; 12.23; 14.36
1:3	8.xi; 11.83
1:5	11.64
1:8–11	9.154, *171–173*
1:11	11.25
1:12–14	9.*173–175*
1:12	12.24
1:15–22	9.*175–177*
1:19	12.22; 14.143, 275
1:20	14.297
1:22	9.205
1:23–2:4	9.*178–180*
1:23	1.161
2:4	9.7, 237
2:5–11	9.*180–182*
2:11	17.82
2:12–17	9.*182–185*
2:12–13	9.224
2:12	16.28, 129
2:13	9.7; 12.219, 233
3:1–3	9.*185–197*
3:4–11	9.*187–191*
3:5	11.83
3:12–18	9.*191–194*
3:14	6.132
4:1–6	9.*194–197*
4:2	14.133
4:5	16.25
4:6	15.27
4:7–15	9.*197–201*
4:10–11	11.64
4:16–18	9.*201–203*

4:17	4.77
5:1–10	9.*203–206*
5:4	14.308
5:7	8.21
5:10	14.73; 17.195
5:11–19	9.*206–209*
5:14	4.193; 14.265
5:17	4.90; 5.126; 17.204
5:18–19	12.55
5:19	15.25
5:20–6:2	9.*209–212*
5:21	2.369
6:3–10	9.*212–218*
6:6	10.51
6:7	15.25
6:10	16.78
6:11–13	9.*218–220*
6:14–7:1	9.6, 8, 218, *220–223*
6:14–15	17.153
6:15	11.212; 17.59
6:16	17.68
6:17	16.93
6:18	16.38; 17.173
7:2–4	9.*218–220*
7:5–16	9.*223–227*
7:5	9.7
7:6	12.219
7:8	9.7, 237
7:13	9.7; 12.219
8–9	9.162
8:1–15	9.*227–230*
8:1–5	9.232
8:1	12.24
8:4	9.163
8:6	12.232
8:9	1.191; 11.34; 16.179
8:10	12.232
8:16–24	9.*230–231*
8:16	12.232

8:18	12.216, 233
8:20	9.164
8:23	12.233
9:1–5	7.145; 8.2; 9.*231–233*
9:1	9.163
9:5	9.164
9:6–15	9.*233–237*
9:11	1.245
9:12–13	9.163f
10–13	9.7, 8, 237
10:1–6	9.*237–241*
10:1	10.52
10:7–18	9.*241–245*
10:10	9.145, 257f; 10.38
11:1–6	9.*245–247*
11:1–2	14.102; 16.108
11:2	5.143; 17.76, 173
11:7–15	9.*247–250*
11:7–12	11.86
11:9	7.136; 11.6
11:16–33	9.*250–255*
11:22	7.159
12:1–10	2.256; 9.*255–260*
12:2	17.78
12:7–8	7.102; 10.38
12:7	17.82
12:11–18	9.*260–262*
12:14	9.6; 14.266
12:18	12.219, 233
12:19–21	9.*262–266*
12:20	14.111
12:21	10.47
13	9.*266–268*
13:1–2	9.6
13:1	5.195
13:5	8.21
13:11	1.109; 11.83; 14.225
13:12	14.279
13:13	8.xi

Galatians

1:1–5	10.*1–9*
1:1	8.xi; 11.9; 14.17
1:3	8.xi; 11.12; 12.23; 14.36
1:4	14.233
1:6–10	10.*9–11*
1:6	12.24
1:7	7.73
1:8–9	17.230
1:11–17	10.*11–13*; 12.13
1:12	16.22
1:13	11.60
1:15–24	7.73
1:15	8.12; 12.24
1:17–18	7.74
1:18–25	10.*11–15*
1:18	14.145
1:19	7.115; 10.145; 14.10, 15
1:20	1.161
1:21	7.73
2:1–10	10.*15–17*
2:1	12.232
2:2	16.21
2:5	3.25
2:6–10	10.4
2:7	10.124
2:9	5.16; 10.124; 14.10, 22, 145; 16.134
2:10	8.205; 9.162; 14.75
2:11–13	10.*18–19*
2:11	14.145
2:14–17	10.*19–21*
2:14	14.145; 15.29
2:16	14.72
2:18–21	10.*21–23*
2:19–20	1.137
2:20	11.149
3:1–9	10.*23–25*
3:7	15.29
3:10–14	10.*25–27*
3:13	9.106; 14.317; 16.34, 177
3:15–18	10.*27–28*
3:16	15.78
3:19–22	10.*29–30*
3:19	13.17, 89; 16.24
3:23–29	10.*31–33*
3:23–24	14.7
3:24	9.41
3:26–27	15.74
3:28	12.68, 272
3:29	15.78; 17.24
4:1–7	10.*33–35*
4:4	4.13
4:5	10.79; 16.34
4:6–7	15.74
4:6	4.143
4:8–11	10.*36–37*
4:10	8.184
4:11	16.62
4:12–20	10.*37–40*
4:13	7.102
4:14–15	9.258
4:21–5:1a	10.*40–42*
4:26	17.199
5:1b–12	10.*42–44*
5:7	14.133
5:9	2.79
5:13–15	10.*44–46*
5:13	5.183; 14.207, 335, 349; 16.68
5:16–21	10.*46–49*
5:19–21	8.102; 10.101; 14.200
5:19	10.47
5:22–26	10.*49–52*

5:22–23	14.301; **17**.222	2:1–3	**10**.*95–101*
6:1–5	**10**.*52–53*	2:1	**16**.116
6:1	**10**.149	2:2	**9**.192; **17**.80
6:6–10	**10**.*53–55*	2:4–10	**10**.*101–105*
6:11–18	**10**.*55–57*	2:5	**16**.116
6:11	**9**.258	2:11–12	**10**.*106–110*
6:15	**5**.126	2:11–13	**14**.291
6:16	**14**.41, 166; **16**.130;	2:11	**10**.62
	17.24	2:12	**14**.172
6:17	**11**.64, 175	2:13–18	**10**.*110–117*
		2:13–14	**14**.225
		2:18	**6**.58; **10**.129; **14**.235
		2:19–22	**10**.*117–119*
Ephesians		2:20–21	**17**.68
		2:20	**2**.141; **3**.283; **8**.135
1:1–14	**10**.*73–74*	3:1–13	**10**.*119–120*
1:1–2	**10**.*74–76*	3:1–7	**10**.64, 120–125
1:1	**8**.xi; **10**.63; **11**.9	3:1	**10**.61; **11**.21, 174
1:2–3	**10**.129	3:2–13	**10**.119f
1:2	**8**.xi; **11**.12; **12**.23;	3:2	**10**.63
	14.36	3:3	**16**.22
1:3–14	**10**.64, 76	3:6	**3**.25
1:3–4	**10**.*76–79*	3:8–13	**10**.*125–127*
1:3	**8**.xi; **14**.153	3:8	**16**.179
1:4	**14**.153; **17**.96, 108	3:10	**8**.118
1:5–6	**10**.*79–80*	3:12	**10**.129; **14**.235
1:7–8	**10**.*81–83*	3:14–21	**10**.*127–128*
1:7	**17**.31	3:14–17	**10**.*128–132*
1:9–10	**10**.66, *83–85*	3:18–21	**10**.*132–133*
1:11–14	**10**.*85–88*	3:20	**15**.206
1:13	**3**.25; **15**.25	4	**10**.*133–134*
1:15–23	**10**.64, *88–94*	4:1–10	**10**.*134–145*
1:15	**10**.63	4:1–3	**10**.*134–140*
1:17	**10**.129, 130; **16**.22	4:1	**10**.61; **11**.174; **15**.177
1:18	**15**.177	4:2	**10**.52
1:20, 21	**14**.153	4:3–6	**14**.225
1:21	**8**.118	4:4–6	**10**.*140–143*
1:23	**6**.273	4:4	**15**.177
2:1–10	**10**.*94–95*	4:6	**10**.130; **17**.205
2:1–9	**10**.64		

4:7–10	10.*143–145*
4:9–10	14.242
4:11–13	10.*145–150*
4:11	6.54; 14.79; **17.**127
4:13ff	13.50
4:14–16	10.*150–151*
4:15	14.133
4:17–24	10.*151–154*
4:17	10.63
4:19	8.29; 10.47
4:22–24	5.126
4:25–32	10.*154–160*
4:26	4.168
4:32	4.285; 14.228
5:1–8	10.*160–163*
5:6	8.26
5:8	15.27
5:9–14	10.*164–166*
5:9	10.51
5:11	15.28
5:15–21	10.*166–167*
5:18	4.149
5:19	14.128
5:20	10.130
5:21–23	16.173
5:22–32	5.143; 17.106
5:22–26	9.69
5:22–23	10.*167–175*
5:24–28	14.102; 16.108
5:26	12.262
5:27	17.108
6:1–9	14.222
6:1–4	10.*175–178*
6:4	9.41
6:5–9	10.*178–180*; 12.272
6:5	9.24
6:6	14.293; 16.25
6:9	14.62
6:10–20	10.*181–184*

6:11	17.82
6:12	8.118; 15.28
6:14	14.153
6:15	3.25
6:17	16.94
6:20	10.61; 11.21, 174; 12.280
6:21–24	10.*184–185*
6:21	7.192; 10.62; 11.169; 12.219, 265
6:23	10.129

Philippians

1:1–3:1	11.7
1:1, 2	11.*9–12*
1:1	8.xi; 11.47; 12.22, 71; 14.35, 293; 15.171; 16.25
1:2	7.120, 192; 11.9–12; 12.23; 14.36
1:3–11	11.*13–19*
1:3	8.xi
1:4	10.50
1:7	11.5, 21
1:12–14	11.*19–22*
1:12–13	7.193
1:13–14	11.21
1:14	15.24
1:15–18	11.*22–24*
1:18	11.14
1:19–20	11.*24–26*
1:21–26	11.*26–29*
1:21	11.149
1:25	10.50; 11.14
1:27–30	11.5, 7, *29–31*
1:27	14.225
2:1–11	11.6

11 Phil, Col, Thes	**13** Heb	**15** John, Jude	**16** Rev, v.1
12 Tim, Tit, Phlm	**14** Jas, Pet		**17** Rev, v.2

2:1–4	11.*31–34*	3:17–21	11.*67–70*
2:2	14.225	3:20	11.4
2:5–11	11.*34–40*	4:1	11.7, 15, 45, *70–72*
2:5	15.83	4:2–3	11.*72–74*; 12.68
2:9–11	17.179	4:2	11.7; 14.225
2:9	5.135	4:3	16.123; 17.196
2:10	14.242	4:4–23	11.7
2:11	9.107; 10.141; 12.136, 153; 14.350; 15.68; 16.180	4:4–5	11.*74–76*
		4:5	14.124, 249
		4:6–7	11.*77–78*
2:12–18	11.*40–46*	4:8–9	11.*78–83*
2:12–13	14.300	4:10–18	9.248; 11.6
2:15	16.53; 17.209	4:10–13	11.*84–85*
2:16	15.25	4:10–11	11.6, 15
2:17	11.14; 17.11	4:14–20	11.*85–87*
2:19–24	11.*46–48*	4:16	11.6
2:19–22	3.72	4:18	7.192
2:19–20	7.120; 8.219; 12.22	4:19	4.118
2:20, 22	12.22	4:21–23	11.87
2:24	12.10	4:21–22	8.xi
2:25–30	9.230; 11.*48–50*	4:22	8.212
2:25	12.159		
2:28	11.15		
2:29–30	11.6, 15		

Colossians

3:1	11.7, 15, *50–53*; 14.336	1:1	7.120, 192; 8.xi; 11.9, 47, *103–105*; 12.22
3:2–4:3	11.7	1:2–8	11.*105–107*
3:2–3	11.*53–56*	1:2	8.xi; 11.12; 12.23; 14.36; 16.28
3:2	3.178; 11.7		
3:3	17.24	1:4	11.94
3:4–7	11.*57–61*	1:5	3.25; 15.24, 25
3:4–5	7.159	1:6	11.94
3:5–6	9.252	1:7	11.94, 171
3:5	8.13	1:8	11.94
3:8–9	11.*61–63*	1:9–11	11.*107–110*
3:10–11	11.*63–65*	1:12–14	11.*111–112*, 136
3:10	14.258; 17.204	1:12	14.267
3:12–16	11.*65–67*	1:13	9.44; 15.27
3:14	11.45; 15.177		

1:14	10.65	3:6	8.26
1:15–23	11.*112–125*	3:8	1.139
1:15	11.95, 119; 16.32, 141	3:9b–13	11.*154–157*
1:16	5.41; 11.95, 96, 114	3:9	14.73
1:17	11.95	3:11	11.179; 12.272
1:18	16.141	3:14–17	11.*158–160*
1:19	5.71; 10.65; 11.95	3:17	14.214
1:20	17.31	3:18–4:1	11.*160–165*
1:21	11.94	3:19	14.128
1:22	11.95, 115; 17.108	3:20–4:1	14.222
1:23	3.25	3:22–4:1	12.272
1:24–29	11.*125–127*	3:25	14.62
1:24	11.64	4:2–4	11.*166–167*
1:27	11.94; 12.19	4:3	11.21; 16.129
1:28	11.97, 116	4:5–6	11.*167–168*
2:1	11.93, *127–128*	4:7–11	11.*168–170*
2:2–7	11.*129–132*	4:7	10.61; 12.219, 265
2:2	11.95	4:9	12.274
2:3	10.65	4:10	3.4; 7.192; 12.217
2:5	11.94	4:11–12	7.2
2:8–23	11.*133–135*	4:12–15	8.xi; 11.*171–172*
2:8–10	11.*135–138*	4:12–13	11.94
2:8	11.95, 96	4:12	14.293; 16.25
2:9	5.71; 10.65; 11.95, 115	4:13	12.273; 16.28
2:10	8.118; 11.96	4:14	4.1; 7.3; 12.213, 216; 15.153
2:11–12	11.*138–140*	4:15–16	12.273
2:12	10.32	4:16	10.68, 70; 11.*172–174*; 12.273
2:13–15	11.*140–143*		
2:14	12.283	4:17–18	11.*174–175*
2:15	8.118; 11.96; 15.78	4:17	12.273; 16.140
2:16–23	11.*143–146*	4:18	8.xii; 11.21
2:16–17	8.184; 11.96		
2:18	11.97		
2:20	11.95	*1 Thessalonians*	
2:21	11.96		
3:1–4	11.*147–149*	1	11.*185–187*
3:5–9a	11.*149–154*	1:1	8.xi; 11.12; 12.22, 23; 14.36, 143
3:5–8	11.94, 97		

11 Phil, Col, Thes
12 Tim, Tit, Phlm
13 Heb
14 Jas, Pet
15 John, Jude
16 Rev, v.1
17 Rev, v.2

1:3	8.xi
1:5	11.190
1:8	15.24
1:10	8.26
2:1–12	11.*187–190*
2:3–12	11.183
2:5	11.182
2:6–7	10.145; 11.182
2:7	14.192
2:9	7.136; 11.182; 14.266
2:11	11.182
2:13–16	11.*190–192*
2:13	15.24
2:14	11.182
2:17–20	11.*192–194*
2:17	11.181
2:19	14.124; 16.83
2:20	11.182
3:1–10	11.*194–196*
3:1–2	11.181
3:2–6	7.120
3:2	12.22
3:4–6	11.182
3:4	12.198
3:5	11.181
3:6	11.48; 12.22
3:11–13	11.*196–197*
3:13	14.122, 123
4:1–8	11.*198–200*
4:3–8	11.182
4:9–12	11.*200–202*
4:9–10	11.182
4:9	15.66
4:11	11.182
4:13–18	11.182, *202–203*
4:13	6.86
4:14, 16	11.27
4:15	14.122
4:16	16.43; 17.42, 114

4:17	17.78
5:1–11	11.*204–206*
5:2	2.303; 4.257; 7.25; 11.182; 14.123
5:4–5	15.27
5:6	11.182; 16.119
5:12–22	11.*206–208*
5:12–14	11.182
5:21	16.63
5:23–28	11.*208*
5:23	1.109; 11.82; 14.122f
5:25	11.25, 216; 15.116
5:26	8.xi; 11.189; 14.279

2 Thessalonians

1	11.*208–211*
1:1	8.xi; 11.12; 14.143, 275
1:2	8.xi; 12.23; 14.36
1:3	8.xi
1:4	8.21
1:7–9	16.132
1:11	10.51; 15.177
2:1–12	11.*211–213*
2:1	14.122
2:3–4	15.63
2:3	3.310; 12.92; 17.56
2:5	17.61
2:6–7	17.93
2:7	16.15; 17.61
2:8	16.51
2:9	14.122
2:10	14.133
2:13–17	11.*214–215*
2:16	12.24
3:1–5	11.*215–216*
3:1–2	11.25

3:1	**15**.24	3:7	**12**.74
3:6–18	**11**.*217–219*	3:8–13	**12**.3
3:8	7.136	3:8–10	**12**.*84–86*
3:17	**8**.xii	3:8	**14**.266
		3:10	**12**.72
		3:12–13	**12**.*84–86*
1 Timothy		3:11	**12**.*86–87*
		3:14–15	**12**.*88–89*
1:1–2	**12**.*17–25*	3:15	**13**.32
1:1	**15**.207	3:16	**12**.4, *89–91*
1:2	3.71	4:1–5	**12**.*91–95*
1:3–7	**12**.*25–34*	4:1–3	**15**.199
1:3	16.60	4:1	**12**.3
1:4	**12**.5, 6, 28, 29	4:3	**12**.30
1:6–7	**14**.80	4:4–5	**12**.5, 30
1:7	**12**.6	4:4	9.12
1:8–11	**12**.*34–41*	4:6–10	**12**.*95–97*
1:12–17	**12**.*41–48*	4:6	**12**.3; **14**.134
1:15	4.95; **12**.13	4:7–8	**11**.46; **12**.29
1:16	10.51, 139	4:10	**12**.29; **15**.207
1:17	**12**.29; **15**.163	4:11–16	**12**.*97–102*
1:18–20	**12**.*48–54*	5:1–2	**12**.*102–105*
1:18	3.71; **12**.159	5:3–16	**12**.3
2:1–7	**12**.*54–64*	5:3–8	**12**.*105–108*
2:1–2	**8**.171	5:6	**16**.116
2:1	**15**.117; **17**.93	5:9–10	**12**.*109–113*
2:2	**14**.205	5:9	**15**.149
2:3	**15**.207	5:10	**14**.255
2:4	**12**.5, 29; **14**.343; **15**.40	5:11–16	**12**.*113–115*
2:5	**12**.29	5:17–22	**12**.*115–118*
2:6	**16**.177	5:17–19	**12**.3
2:8–15	**12**.*64–69*	5:17	**12**.73; **14**.264
2:8	**13**.83; **14**.107	5:18	**12**.73; **14**.118
2:13–17	**17**.93	5:19–22	**12**.73
3:1–7	**12**.3, *69–84*, 234	5:19	5.195
3:2	**8**.167; **14**.255; **15**.150	5:22	**17**.152
3:3	**14**.266	5:23	**12**.13, *118–120*
3:5	**12**.74	5:24–25	**12**.*120–121*
3:6	**17**.80	6:1–2	**12**.*121–123*

6:3-5	12.*123–128*
6:4	12.5, 29
6:5	12.6; 14.315
6:6-8	12.*128–131*
6:6	15.198
6:9-10	12.*131–133*; 14.117
6:10	1.252
6:11-16	12.*133–136*
6:11	14.301
6:15	15.163
6:16	16.151
6:17-19	12.*137–138*
6:20-21	12.*138–141*
6:20	12.6, 28

2 Timothy

1:1-7	12.*142–145*
1:2	12.23
1:5	7.120; 11.147; 12.21, 68
1:8-11	12.*145–150*
1:10	3.25; 16.53
1:12-14	12.*150–154*
1:12	4.120; 9.78; 14.296
1:13	15.25
1:14	12.4
1:15-18	12.*154–157*
1:16	12.222
2:1-2	12.*157–158*
2:3-4	12.*159–160*
2:5	11.46; 12.*160–162*
2:6-7	12.*162–163*
2:8-10	12.*163–168*
2:8	1.15; 3.298; 12.4; 15.25
2:11-13	12.*168–170*

2:11-12	6.220
2:12	14.258; 16.40
2:14	12.*170–172*
2:15-18	12.*172–176*
2:15	15.25
2:16	12.29
2:17	12.53
2:18	12.6, 30
2:19	12.*176–178*
2:20-21	12.*178–179*
2:22-26	12.*179–181*
2:23	12.5, 29
2:24	14.293
3:1	12.*182–183*; 14.175
3:2-5	12.*184–191*
3:5	16.118
3:6-7	12.*191–193*
3:6	12.5, 30
3:8-9	12.*193–195*
3:8	12.3; 15.30
3:10-13	12.*195–198*
3:14-17	12.*198–202*
3:15	12.1
4:1-5	12.*202–208*
4:1	14.122; 17.195
4:3	14.80
4:4	12.29
4:5	10.147
4:6-8	12.*308–312*
4:6	17.11
4:8	11.45; 14.49; 16.83
4:9-15	12.*212–220*
4:10	11.171; 14.103; 15.153
4:11	3.4; 7.1f, 101, 192; 11.171
4:14	12.53
4:16-22	12.*220–223*
4:18	8.21

4:19	8.8, 209	2:10	15.207
4:20	12.11	2:11–14	12.*256–257*
		2:11	12.5
		2:13	14.122
		2:15	12.*257–258*
Titus		3:1–2	12.*258–260*
1:1–4	12.*227–234*	3:1	8.171
1:1	6.178; 14.293; 15.171;	3:3–7	12.*260–263*
	16.25	3:3	14.99
1:3	15.207	3:4	15.207
1:4	12.23, 218, 233	3:5	5.125
1:5–7a	12.*234–235*	3:8–11	12.*263–265*
1:5–6	12.3	3:9	12.5, 6
1:5	12.9, 71, 72; 14.264	3:10	14.316
1:6–9	12.71	3:12–15	12.*265–266*
1:7–16	12.3	3:12	12.9
1:7	14.266		
1:7b	12.*235–238*		
1:8–9	12.*238–240*	*Philemon*	
1:8	8.167; 13.83; 14.255;		
	15.150	1–7	12.*277–279*
1:10–11	12.*240–242*	1	7.120, 192; 12.22
1:10	12.6	2	11.172; 12.159, 273;
1:11	12.6; 14.266, 315		14.254
1:12	12.*242–243*	3	11.12, 21; 12.23;
1:13–16	12.*244–246*		14.36
1:13	12.3	8–17	12.*279–282*
1:14	12.6, 29	9	11.174
1:15	12.5, 30	10	3.249; 12.269
1:16	12.5, 30	11	12.271
2:1–2	12.*246–248*	12	12.281
2:3–5	12.*248–251*	13–14	12.274
2:3	12.68	13	11.21; 12.270
2:4	12.5	15	12.271
2:5	14.319	16	12.271; 14.213
2:6	12.*251–252*	18–25	12.*282–283*
2:7–8	12.*252–254*	18–19	12.269
2:7	12.233	19–21	12.274f
2:9–10	12.*254–256*	22	11.25, 217; 12.10

24	3.4; **7.**1; **11.**170, 171; **12.**213, 216; **15.**153	6:4–6	**15.**119
		6:9–12	**13.***59–61*
		6:10	**13.**6
		6:13–20	**13.***61–63*
		6:18	**13.**59
Hebrews		6:20	**6.**155
1:1–3	**13.***12–16*	7	**13.***63–71*
1:2	**5.**41; **14.**175	7:1–3	**13.**69, *71–75*
1:4–14	**13.***16–20*	7:3	**13.**68
2:1–4	**13.***20–22*	7:4–10	**13.***75–77*
2:2	**10.**29	7:8	**13.**70
2:3	**13.**5, 6	7:11–20	**13.***77–79*
2:4	**16.**32	7:11	**13.**70
2:5–9	**13.***23–25*	7:15–19	**13.**70
2:10–18	**13.***25–28*	7:19	**14.**106
2:18	**4.**271; **9.**171; **16.**132	7:21–25	**13.***79–83*
3:1–6	**13.***28–32*	7:25	**10.**133; **15.**38
3:1	**15.**177	7:26–28	**13.***83–85*
3:7–19	**13.***32–34*	7:27	**13.**71; **14.**233
3:12	**13.**35	8:1–6	**13.***86–89*
3:18–4:2	**15.**182	8:5	**17.**10
4:1–10	**13.***35–38*	8:7–13	**13.***90–94*
4:2	**15.**24	9:1–5	**13.***94–97*
4:11–13	**13.***38–41*	9:4	**16.**94
4:12	**16.**51, 94; **17.**182	9:6–10	**13.***97–101*
4:14–16	**13.***41–44*	9:11–14	**13.***102–105*
4:14–15	**15.**93	9:14	**17.**31
4:14	**6.**154	9:15–22	**13.***105–108*
4:16	**14.**106; **16.**35	9:23–28	**13.***109–111*
5:1–10	**13.***44–48*, 64	9:23	**17.**10
5:1, 3	**14.**233	9:24	**15.**38
5:11–14	**13.***49–51*	9:28	**14.**233
5:12–14	**5.**126	10:1–10	**13.***112–115*
5:12	**13.**5–7; **14.**192	10:4	**13.**59; **16.**79
5:13	**15.**25	10:10	**14.**233
6	**13.**64	10:11–18	**13.***116–118*
6:1–3	**13.***51–55*	10:19–25	**13.***118–123*
6:2	**14.**192	10:19–23	**13.**2; **15.**114
6:4–8	**13.***55–59*	10:19–22	**16.**35

10:20	6.58	13:1–6	13.*189–194*
10:24–25	14.124	13:2	8.167; 14.255; 15.149
10:26–31	13.*123–126*	13:4	17.106
10:26	13.45	13:7–8	13.*194f*
10:32–39	13.*126–128*	13:7	13.5f; 15.24
10:32–34	13.6	13:8	16.30
10:32	13.5	13:9–16	13.*195–199*
10:37	2.2; 16.133; 17.55	13:14	14.168
11:1–3	13.*128–131*	13:17–20	13.*199–200*
11:4	13.*131–133*	13:18	15.116
11:5–6	13.*133–139*	13:20–24	13.*200–202*
11:6	13.59; 16.145	13:20	1.109; 6.54; 10.148; 17.38
11:7	13.*139–142*		
11:8–10	13.*142–146*	13:22	13.9
11:8	3.62; 7.55; 8.63; 16.145	13:23	11.48
		13:24	13.6
11:9	13.148; 14.201		
11:11–12	13.*146–147*		
11:13–16	13.*147–150*		
11:13	14.201	*James*	
11:17–19	13.*150–153*		
11:20–22	13.*153–154*	1:1	6.178; 14.8, 21, 23, 31f, *35–41*, 137, 293; 15.171; 16.25
11:21	3.62		
11:23–29	13.*154–159*		
11:27	9.203	1:2–4	14.*42–44*
11:30–31	13.*160–162*	1:2	14.29
11:32–34	13.*162–165*	1:5–8	14.*44–46*
11:35–40	13.*165–171*	1:5	1.245
12:1–2	13.*171–173*; 16.132	1:7	14.21
12:2	13.25; 14.303	1:9–11	14.31, *47–48*
12:3–4	13.*174–175*	1:10	14.29
12:4	13.6	1:11	14.29
12:5–11	13.*175–179*	1:12	14.31, *48–49*; 16.83
12:6	14.247	1:13–15	14.*50–53*
12:12–17	13.*179–185*	1:15	14.28
12:18–24	13.*185–187*	1:16–18	14.*53–54*
12:22	17.199	1:17	14.25, 29
12:25–29	13.*187–189*	1:18	5.125; 14.21, 31, 171, 172; 15.79
12:29	17.117		
		1:19–20	14.31, *54–56*

11 Phil, Col, Thes
12 Tim, Tit, Phlm
13 Heb
14 Jas, Pet
15 John, Jude
16 Rev, v.1
17 Rev, v.2

1:20	**1.**139	3:9–12	**14.***89–90*
1:21	10.51; **14.***56–58*	3:11–13	**14.**22
1:22–24	**14.***58–59*	3:11–12	**14.**28
1:25	**14.**7, 21, *59–60*	3:13–14	**14.***91–93*
1:26–27	**14.***61–62*	3:15–16	**14.***93–94*
1:27	**1.**119; **16.**121	3:17–18	**14.***94–98*
2:1–3	**14.**27	4:1–3	**14.***98–101*
2:1	**14.**24, 31, *62–63*	4:1–2	**14.**31
2:2–4	**14.***63–66*	4:1	**14.**28
2:2	**14.**21, 26	4:4–7	**14.***101–106*
2:4	**14.**28	4:4	**14.**28, 29
2-5–7	**14.***66–68*	4:6	**3.**175; **8.**37; **12.**186;
2:5	**14.**28; **16.**78		**14.**29
2:7	**14.**23	4:7	**3.**23
2:8–11	**14.***68–70*	4:8–10	**14.***106–110*
2:8	**14.**21, 111	4:10	**14.**21
2:12–14	**14.***71–74*	4:11–12	**14.***110–112*
2:12–13	**14.**22, *70–71*	4:12	**14.**29
2:12	**13.**7	4:13–17	**14.***112–114*
2:13	**1.**102; **2.**194; **14.**28,	4:13	**14.**28
	29	4:15	**14.**21
2:14–26	**14.**22, 349	4:17	**7.**35
2:14–19	**14.**29	5:1–6	**14.**27, 29
2:14–17	**14.**28, *75–76*	5:1–3	**14.***115–118*
2:14	**14.**28	5:3	**14.**28, 175
2:18–19	**14.**28, *76–78*	5:4–6	**14.***118–121*
2:20–26	**14.***78–79*	5:6	**14.**28
2:20	**14.**29	5:7–9	**14.**22, 26, *121–124*
2:21–23	**14.**29	5:7–8	**14.**21, 29, 31
2:24	**14.**22	5:8	**14.**249; **16.**133
2:25	**13.**161; **14.**29	5:9	**16.**146
2:26	**14.**29	5:10–11	**14.**21, *124–125*
3:1	**14.**26, *79–81*	5:11	**14.**29
3:2	**9.**175; **14.***81–83*	5:12	**14.**22, *126–127*
3:3–6	**14.**29	5:13–18	**14.**31
3:3–5a	**14.***83–84*	5:13–15	**14.***127–130*
3:5b–6	**14.***85–88*	5:13–14	**14.**28
3:6	**1.**141; **3.**231; **14.**25	5:14	**6.**164; **9.**110; **14.**21,
3:7–8	**14.***88–89*		264; **15.**116

5:15   6.180; **14.**21
5:16–18   **14.***130–132*
5:17   **14.**29
5:19–20   12.45; **14.***133–134*
5:19   **15.**30
5:20   **14.**29, 31

1 Peter

1:1–2   **14.**159, *165–170*
1:1   **14.**137
1:2   **15.**140
1:3–4:11   **14.**160
1:3–5   **14.***171–176*
1:3   5.125; **12.**25; **14.**140,
            152, 172
1:5   8.21; **14.**139, 141
1:6–7   **14.***176–178*
1:6   **14.**146, 158
1:7   **14.**122, 139, 141, 156;
            16.22, 143
1:8–9   **14.***178–179*
1:8   **14.**141, 160
1:10–12   **14.**140, *180–182*
1:13–25   **14.**141
1:13   **14.**122, 139, 141, 142,
            153, *182–183*; **16.**22
1:14–25   **14.***184–189*
1:14   **14.**145
1:17   4.143
1:18   **14.**165
1:19–20   **17.**96
1:19   **14.**141; **16.**171, 177;
            17.31, 108
1:20–21   **14.**141
1:21   **14.**141, 142
1:22–23   5.125
1:23–25   **14.**191

1:23   **14.**172; **15.**79
2:1–3   **14.**141, *189–193*
2:1   **14.**111
2:2   **13.**50
2:4–10   **14.***193–199*
2:4–8   2.141
2:4–6   8.135
2:4   3.283
2:5   8.32; **17.**68
2:7   3.283; 4.247; **14.**141
2:9–10   **14.**145; **15.**27
2:10   **14.**165, 291
2:11–12   **14.***200–204*
2:12–17   **16.**15
2:12   **14.**139, 142, 158
2:13–17   8.171; **14.**159; **17.**63
2:13–15   **14.***204–206*
2:15   **14.**158, 159
2:16   **14.**141, *207–208*, 335
2:17   2.274; **12.**59; **14.***208–
            209*
2:18–3:7   **14.**160
2:18–25   **14.***209–217*
2:21   **15.**83; **17.**108
2:22   **14.**142; **17.**108
2:23   **14.**120
2:24   **14.**141, 142
2:25   6.54; **10.**148; **17.**38
3:1–2   **14.***217–219*
3:3–6   **14.***220–222*
3:7   **14.***222–224*
3:8–12   **14.***224–228*
3:13–15a   **14.***228–230*
3:14   **14.**146, 159
3:15b–16   **14.***230–231*
3:15   5.160
3:16   **14.**146, 158
3:17–4:6   **14.***231–232*
3:17–18a   **14.***232–236*

3:17	14.159
3:18–22	6.35; **14.**243–245
3:18b–20	14.236–243
3:18–20	16.52
3:18	14.120
3:19	14.235
3:20	10.51, 139
3:21	14.160
3:22	14.141, 153, 235; 15.78
4:1–5	14.141, 245–248
4:3–4	14.145
4:3	10.47; 14.165
4:4	14.158
4:5	14.141; 16.132
4:6	6.35; 14.235, 236–243, 248–249
4:7a	14.123, 139, 140, 249–251
4:7b–8	14.251–253
4:8–9	14.124
4:9–10	14.254–256
4:9	7.123; 8.167; 12.81; 15.149
4:10	14.177
4:11	14.159, 256–257
4:12–5:11	14.160
4:12–13	14.257–258
4:12	14.146, 158
4:13	14.139, 141, 159; 16.22
4:14–16	14.258–260
4:14, 16	9.12; 14.155, 158
4:17–19	14.260–262
4:17	13.32; 14.139, 141
4:18	14.141
4:19	14.146
5:1–4	14.262–270
5:1–3	14.160

5:1	12.71; **14.**139, 140, 141, 154, 161
5:2–3	6.54; 10.148; 12.71
5:2	14.161, 215
5:4	10.48; 14.139, 141, 160; 16.83
5:5	8.37; 12.186; **14.**105, 270–271
5:6–11	14.271–274
5:8–9	3.23; 14.106; 16.118
5:9	14.146, 158
5:12–14	14.159
5:12	14.143, 274–276
5:13	3.4, 72; 11.170; **14.**160, 276–279; 15.18, 131, 138
5:14	14.148, 279–281

2 Peter

1:1	14.145, 291–294
1:2	14.294–296
1:3–7	14.296–305
1:4, 5–8	14.283
1:8–11	14.305–307
1:9	14.283
1:10	15.177
1:12–15	14.307–309
1:16–18	14.309–311
1:16	14.122
1:19–21	14.311–314
1:20	14.283
2	15.168f
2:1	14.314–318; 16.177
2:2–3	14.318–319
2:2, 3	14.283
2:4–11	14.320–330
2:4–5	3.34; **14.**237, 240, 283

2:6	1.371; **14**.283; **15**.185	1:8–10	**15**.10, 14, *32–34*, 80
2:9	**15**.28	1:8	**14**.82
2:10	**14**.283	2:1–2	**15**.*34–40*
2:12–14	**14**.288, *330–332*	2:1	**15**.13, 14, 52, 81
2:12	**14**.283	2:2	**14**.233; **15**.14
2:13	**14**.283; **15**.193	2:3–6	**15**.*40–43*
2:14–15	**14**.283	2:3–5	**15**.17
2:15–16	**14**.*332–333*	2:4–6	**15**.10
2:15	**14**.283	2:4	**15**.31
2:17–22	**14**.*334–335*	2:7–8	**15**.*43–46*
2:18	10.47; **14**.283	2:8	**15**.16, 27
2:19	**14**.207, 283	2:9–11	**15**.12, 16, 28, *46–49*
2:20–22	**14**.284	2:12–14	**15**.*49–55*
3:1–2	**14**.*336–337*	2:14	**15**.13
3:2	**14**.287	2:15–17	**15**.*55–59*
3:3–4	**14**.284, *337–339*	2:17	**15**.16
3:4	**14**.123, 287	2:18	11.213; **14**.175, 249;
3:5–7	**14**.284		**15**.*59–65*; **17**.62
3:5–6	**14**.*339–340*	2:19–21	**15**.*65–67*
3:7	**14**.*340–342*	2:19	**15**.5
3:8–9	**14**.284, *342–343*	2:22–23	**15**.*67–68*
3:8	**17**.188	2:22	11.213; **15**.6, 13, 32,
3:10	4.257; 6.184, 198;		61, 68; **17**.62
	7.25; **14**.123, 284,	2:24–29	**15**.*68–72*
	343–345; **17**.195	2:26	**15**.6
3:11–14	**14**.284, *345–347*	2:28	**14**.122, 124; **15**.52
3:15–16	**14**.284f, 288, *347–349*	2:29	**14**.172; **15**.17
3:15	10.139	3:1–2	**15**.*72–76*
3:16	**14**.283	3:1	**15**.16
3:17–18	**14**.*350–351*	3:2–3	12.19
		3:2	**14**.179; **15**.43; **16**.84
		3:3–10	**15**.17
1 John		3:3–8	**15**.*76–78*
		3:5	**15**.14
1:1–4	**15**.*21–25*	3:7	**15**.52
1:1, 4	**15**.13	3:9	**14**.172; **15**.*78–81*
1:5	**15**.10, 13, *25–28*	3:10–18	**15**.*81–85*
1:6–7	**15**.*28–32*	3:10–11,	**15**.17
1:6	**15**.10	11–17	
1:7	**15**.12, 15, 16; **17**.31		

---

11 Phil, Col, Thes   **13** Heb   **15** John, Jude   **16** Rev, v.1
12 Tim, Tit, Phlm   **14** Jas, Pet   **17** Rev, v.2

3:13	**15**.16
3:14–17	**15**.12
3:14–15	**14**.227
3:16	**15**.14
3:19–24a	**15**.*85–88*
3:19	**14**.133
3:21	**15**.44
3:22	**15**.17, 115
3:23	**15**.12, 17
3:24	**15**.15
3:24b–4:1	**15**.*88–92*
4:1–7	**15**.91f
4:1–3	**16**.63
4:1	**15**.5, 44
4:2–3	**5**.13, 65, 223; **15**.7, 14, *92–94*
4:2	**15**.142
4:3	**11**.213; **15**.61, 119, 129; **17**.62
4:4–6	**15**.*94–96*
4:4–5	**15**.16, 52
4:7–21	**15**.*96–101*
4:7–12	**15**.17
4:7–10	**15**.13
4:7–8	**15**.12
4:7	**14**.173; **15**.44
4:9	**15**.15
4:10–12	**15**.12
4:10	**15**.14
4:11	**15**.139
4:13	**15**.15
4:14	**5**.171; **15**.15
4:15, 16	**15**.13
4:20–21	**15**.12, 17
4:20	**14**.227; **15**.32
5:1–2	**15**.*102–103*
5:1	**15**.13
5:2	**15**.17
5:3–4a	**15**.*103–105*

5:4	**14**.173; **15**.16
5:4b–5	**15**.*105–106*
5:5	**15**.13
5:6–8	**15**.*106–111*
5:6	**15**.9, 14
5:7	**5**.53; **15**.110
5:9–10	**5**.197; **15**.*111–112*
5:11–13	**15**.*113–114*
5:11–12	**15**.15
5:14–15	**15**.*114–116*
5:16–17	**15**.*116–121*
5:18–20	**15**.*121–123*
5:18	**14**.172; **15**.17
5:19	**15**.16
5:21	**15**.52, *123–125*

2 John

1–3	**15**.*137–140*
1	**5**.23; **15**.18, 138
4–6	**15**.*140–141*
4–5	**15**.130f
4	**15**.129f, 138
6	**15**.130
7–11	**15**.131
7–9	**15**.*141–144*
7	**15**.61, 129; **17**.62
8	**15**.130, 138
10–13	**15**.*144–145*
10	**15**.130, 138
12	**15**.129, 130, 138
13	**14**.160; **15**.130

3 John

1–4	**15**.*147–148*
1	**5**.23, 44

2	**15**.44
3–5	**15**.131
4	**11**.193; **13**.200; **15**.29
5–8	**15**.*148–151*
5	**15**.44
6–8	**15**.131
9–15	**15**.*151–154*
9, 10	**15**.132
11	**15**.44
12	**12**.214; **15**.132
13–14	**15**.129

Jude

1–2	**15**.*175–177*
1	**14**.293; **16**.25
2	**15**.140
3	**15**.158, 168, *177–179*
4	**10**.47; **15**.158, 160, 163, *179–181*
5–7	**15**.*181–186*
5, 6	**15**.158
7	**1**.371; **15**.158, 160
8–9	**15**.*186–188*
8	**15**.158, 160, 166
9	**14**.324; **15**.159, 166, 168
10	**3**.226; **15**.159f, *188–189*
11	**15**.159, *189–191*
12–16	**15**.*191–199*
12	**15**.161
13	**15**.28, 159
14–15	**15**.168
15	**15**.159
16	**15**.159, 161
17–19	**15**.*199–202*
17–18	**15**.168
18–19	**15**.159

18	**14**.175
19	**15**.165
20–21	**15**.159, *202–204*
22–23	**15**.160, *204–206*
24–25	**15**.160, *206–207*

Revelation

1:1–3	**16**.*21–27*
1:1	**16**.11, 24; **17**.228
1:2	**15**.24
1:3	**14**.249
1:4–6	**16**.*27–35*
1:4	**16**.11, 1i6, 155
1:5	**16**.92
1:7	**16**.*35–37*
1:8	**16**.*37–39*; **17**.173, 204
1:9	**15**.24; **16**.11, *39–42*
1:10–11	**16**.*42–44*
1:11	**16**.12
1:12–13	**16**.*44–46*
1:12	**16**.28
1:14–18	**16**.*46–53*
1:14	**17**.179
1:16	**16**.28; **17**.182
1:17	**17**.225
1:18	**2**.144
1:19	**16**.12
1:20	**16**.*53–55*
2–3	**16**.149
2:1–7	**16**.*57–71*
2:1	**16**.47
2:2	**17**.114
2:7	**16**.29, 84; **17**.229
2:8–11	**16**.*72–85*
2:8	**16**.47; **17**.225
2:10	**14**.162f; **16**.154
2:11	**16**.29; **17**.229

2:12–17	16.*86–99*
2:12	16.47
2:14	15.190
2:17	11.39; 16.29, 176; 17.229
2:18–29	16.*100–111*
2:18	16.47; 17.179
2:19	17.114
2:24	15.10
2:29	16.29; 17.229
3:1–6	16.*112–123*
3:1	16.31, 47, 155
3:4	16.154
3:5	16.98; 17.*95*, 196
3:6	16.29; 17.229
3:7–13	16.*124–135*
3:7	2.144; 16.47
3:8	16.149
3:12	11.39; 16.98, 176
3:13	16.29, 17.229
3:14–22	10.69; 16.*136–149*
3:14	16.92
3:15–16	8.165
3:16	10.69
3:17	2.218; 11.91
3:20	16.150
3:22	16.29; 17.229
4:1	16.*149–150*, 168
4:2–3	16.*150–152*
4:4	16.*152–154*; 17.170
4:5–6a	16.*154–156*
4:5	16.28, 31
4:6–9	17.170
4:6b–8	16.*157–163*
4:6	17.117
4:7	5.1
4:9–11	16.*163–164*
4:10	16.152; 17.170
5:1	16.28, *164–166*
5:2–4	16.*166–168*
5:5	16.153, *168–170*
5:6–14	17.170
5:6	16.28, 31, 157, *170–172*; 17.170
5:7–14	16.*172–183*
5:8	16.152, 153, 154, *174–175*
5:9–10	16.177–178
5:9	14.317; 16.34, 98, 157, *175–176*; 17.26
5:11–12	16.*178–180*
5:11	16.152; 17.168, 170
5:13–14	16.*180–183*
5:13	14.242
5:14	16.152, 157; 17.170
6:1–8	17.*1–9*
6:1–7	17.170
6:1–2	17.*3–5*
6:1	16.157
6:3–4	17.*5–6*
6:5–6	17.*6–8*
6:7–8	17.*9*
6:7	16.157
6:9–11	17.*10–13*
6:9	15.24; 17.40
6:10	4.220
6:12–14	17.*13–15*
6:15–17	17.*15–17*
7	17.103
7:1–3	17.*17–22*
7:2–3	17.67
7:3	17.171
7:4–8	17.*22–25*
7:9–10	17.*25–27*
7:9	16.98; 17.168
7:11–12	17.*27–28*
7:11	16.152, 157; 17.170
7:13–14	17.*29–34*

1 Matt, v.1	**3** Mark	**5** John, v.1	**7** Acts	**9** Cor
2 Matt, v.2	**4** Luke	**6** John, v.2	**8** Rom	**10** Gal, Eph

7:13	**16.**153	12:1–2	**17.***75–76*
7:15	**17.***34–36*	12:3–4	**17.***77–78*
7:16–17	**17.***36–39*	12:3	**17.**130
7:17	**5.**153; **17.**220	12:5	**17.**78
8–11	**17.**124	12:6	**17.**69, *79–80*
8:1–5	**17.***39–41*	12:7–9	**17.***80–83*
8:2, 6	**17.***41–43*	12:9	**17.**58, 62, 130
8:5	**17.**10	12:10–12	**17.***83–84*
8:7–12	**17.***43–45*	12:13–17	**17.***84–86*
8:7, 8, 10–11, 12	**17.**125	12:14	**17.**69
8:13	**17.***45–46*	13	**17.**62f, *86–92*, 184
9:1–12	**17.**125	13:1–5	**17.***92–94*
9:1–2	**17.***46–48*	13:1	**15.**63; **17.**131, 138
9:3–12	**17.***48–52*	13:3	**17.**138
9:11	**17.**47	13:5	**17.**69
9:13	**17.**40	13:6–9	**17.***94–96*
9:13–21	**17.***52–53*, 125	13:7	**17.**26
10:1–11:4	**17.**54	13:8	**17.**95, 196
10:1–4	**17.***54–55*	13:10	**17.***96–97*
10:1	**16.**167	13:11–17	**17.***97–100*
10:3	**16.**28	13:12	**17.**138
10:5–7	**17.***55–56*	13:13f	**17.**131
10:7	**17.**171	13:14	**17.**138
10:8–11	**17.***56–64*	13:18	**17.***100–102*
10:11	**16.**12	14:1	**17.***102–104*
11	**17.***64–66*	14:2–3	**17.***104–105*
11:1–2	**17.***66–69*	14:3	**16.**152, 176; **17.**118, 170
11:3–6	**17.***69–71*	14:4	**16.**157
11:7–13	**17.***71–72*	14:4a	**17.***105–107*
11:7	**17.**47, 62	14:4b–5	**17.***107–109*
11:8	**15.**185	14:6–7	**17.***109–110*
11:9	**17.**26	14:6	**17.**26
11:14–19	**17.***72–74*	14:8	**17.***110–111*
11:15	**17.**125	14:9–12	**17.***111–113*
11:16	**16.**152; **17.**170	14:13	**16.**27; **17.***113–114*
11:17	**17.**173	14:14–20	**17.***114–116*
11:18	**17.**171	14:18	**17.**10, 19, 40
12	**17.**62, *74–75*	15:1–2	**17.***116–118*

11 Phil, Col, Thes
12 Tim, Tit, Phlm
13 Heb
14 Jas, Pet
15 John, Jude
16 Rev, v.1
17 Rev, v.2

15:3–4	**17**.*118–120*	18:20	**17**.*165*, 168
15:3	**17**.173	18:21–24	**17**.*166–168*
15:4	**13**.83	18:21	**16**.167
15:5–7	**17**.*121–122*	19:1–10	**17**.167
15:6–8	**16**.28	19:1–2	**17**.*168–170*
15:7	**16**.157; **17**.170	19:2	**17**.171
15:8	**17**.*122–123*	19:3–5	**17**.*170–171*
16	**17**.*123–126*	19:4	**16**.152, 157
16:1–11	**17**.*126–128*	19:6–8	**17**.*171–174*
16:2	**17**.125	19:6	**16**.39
16:5	**13**.83; **17**.19	19:7	**14**.102; **17**.76
16:7	**17**.173	19:8	**16**.98
16:12	**17**.126, *128–129*	19:9–10a	**17**.*174–177*
16:13–16	**17**.*129–133*	19:9	**16**.27
16:13	**15**.63	19:10	**16**.12; **17**.224
16:14	**17**.173	19:10b	**17**.*176–177*
16:15	**16**.27	19:11–18	**17**.167
16:17–21	**17**.126, *133–134*	19:11–12	**17**.3
17–18	**14**.278; **17**.*134–136*	19:11	**17**.*177–178*
17	**3**.310; **17**.*135–142*	19:12	**16**.135; **17**.*179–180*
17:1–2	**17**.*142*	19:13	**17**.*180–182*
17:1	**17**.208	19:14–16	**17**.*182–183*
17:3	**17**.63, *142–143*	19:14	**16**.98
17:4–5	**17**.*143–145*	19:15	**17**.173
17:5–6	**16**.15	19:17–21	**17**.*183–184*
17:5	**15**.19	19:19, 20–21	**17**.168
17:6	**17**.*145–146*		
17:7–11	**17**.*146–147*	19:20	**15**.63; **17**.131
17:8	**17**.95, 96	20	**17**.*184–191*
17:12–18	**17**.*147–149*	20:1–7	**14**.237
17:15	**17**.26, 136	20:1–3	**17**.168, *191–192*
18–22	**17**.167	20:1, 3	**17**.47
18:1–3	**17**.*149–151*	20:4–6	**17**.168
18:4–5	**17**.*151–152*	20:4–5	**17**.*192–193*
18:6–8	**17**.*152–154*	20:4	**15**.24
18:9–10	**17**.*154–157*	20:6	**16**.27, 84; **17**.*193*
18:11–16	**17**.*157–164*	20:7–10	**17**.168, *193–194*
18:12–13	**7**.140; **12**.185; **16**.58	20:10	**15**.63; **17**.47, 131
18:17–19	**17**.*164*	20:11–15	**17**.*194–197*

1 Matt, v.1	**3** Mark	**5** John, v.1	**7** Acts	**9** Cor
2 Matt, v.2	**4** Luke	**6** John, v.2	**8** Rom	**10** Gal, Eph

20:11–14	**17**.168
20:11	**16**.98
20:12	**17**.95
20:14	**16**.84; **17**.47
20:15	**16**.123; **17**.47, 95
21:1–22:5	**17**.168
21:1	**2**.179; **16**.98, 176; **17**.*197–199*
21:2	**16**.176; **17**.*199–202*
21:3–4	**17**.*202–204*
21:5–6	**17**.*204–205*
21:5	**16**.98, 176
21:6	**5**.153; **17**.220, 225
21:7–8	**17**.*205–206*
21:8	**6**.189; **16**.84; **17**.227
21:9–27	**17**.*207–208*
21:9–10	**17**.*208–209*
21:9	**14**.102; **17**.76
21:11	**17**.*209*
21:12	**17**.*209–210*
21:13	**17**.*210–211*
21:14	**1**.360; **16**.13
21:15–17	**17**.*211–212*
21:16	**4**.180
21:18–21	**17**.*212–215*
21:19	**16**.151
21:22–23	**17**.*215–216*
21:22	**17**.173
21:24–27	**17**.*216–219*
21:27	**16**.123; **17**.95
22:1–2	**17**.*220–222*
22:1	**5**.154
22:3–5	**17**.*222–223*
22:6–9	**17**.*223–224*
22:6	**16**.12; **17**.171
22:7	**16**.12, 27
22:8	**16**.11
22:9	**16**.12
22:10–11	**17**.*224–225*
22:10	**16**.12
22:12–13	**17**.*225–226*
22:14–15	**17**.*226–228*
22:14	**16**.27
22:15	**3**.178; **11**.54
22:16	**1**.15; **16**.111; **17**.*228–229*
22:17	**17**.*229–230*
22:18–19	**16**.12; **17**.*230–232*
22:20–21	**17**.*232*
22:20	**14**.249

11 Phil, Col, Thes	**13** Heb	**15** John, Jude	**16** Rev, v.1
12 Tim, Tit, Phlm	**14** Jas, Pet		**17** Rev, v.2

D

INDEX OF SUBJECTS AND PLACES

Aaron's rod 13.96
Abaddon 16.181
Abiding, spiritual 6.175; 15.71f, 115
Abilene 4.3
Abomination 12.246
Abomination of desolation 2.306; 3.309f; 15.62f
Absolution 2.139
Absolutism 3.286
Abstinence 2.208; 12.79f, 120
Abyss, The 17.47f, 168, 191
Academics, The 12.140
Acceptance, duty of 8.113
Accuser, The 17.83
Achaea 3.12; 9.3
Acre 1.40; 3.52
Acropolis 7.134; 9.3
Acts, *Book of*
  'Gospel of the Resurrection' 7.27; 14.24
  'Gospel of the Holy Spirit' 7.18
  Introduction to 7.1–7
  Purpose of 7.193
  Sermons of 14.140f
  Size of 16.165
  'We passages' 7.6, 121
Adar 2.169
Adoption
  Roman law of 8.105–107
  Spiritual 8.107, 110; 10.79f; 12.9; 15.74
Adultery 1.136, 139, 145, 152; 2.199; 3.173, 238f; 4.211f;
  6.2; 8.176; 9.51f; 14.331
  and divorce 2.201f; 10.168f
  offerings for 5.202
  spiritual 6.28; 14.101f; 17.105f
Adversary, The 2.149; 3.22–24
Adversity 3.247
Afflictions 1.355; 9.170; 16.78
  spiritual 14.108
Africa 1.39, 73, 113; 3.361; 5.179
Aged, the 2.80
Age to come, The 1.373; 4.257; 5.168; 6.122, 197; 15.56, 80; 16.10f; 17.221
Agnosticism 5.55; 15.74
Agriculture 2.21, 73; 3.94–96, 157; 4.34; 5.167f; 17.167
Air, Prince of the 17.80
Akkar, Plain of 2.76
Alexandria 1.33; 2.81; 3.209; 14.4, 39
  and allegory 7.139; 9.15
  and Christianity 3.3; 7.101; 11.170
  greatness of 7.89
  and Jews 1.273; 7.139; 9.14f, 252; 11.59; 16.18
  library of 16.88
  scholarship of 13.107
Algiers 17.50
Allegory 2.55, 261; 3.90, 281; 10.41; 17.85
Alms and almsgiving 1.179, 185, 187, 233; 9.164f

Greek 14.75
Jewish 1.335; 3.30; 14.75
Altars 2.244
heavenly 17.10, 127
Amber 17.159
Ambitions 1.37, 90, 331, 396;
2.86, 173, 175, 228f; 3.147,
222, 224, 253, 329; 11.23, 31,
147, 150; 12.37; 14.91, 318;
15.57
America 1.117
Amethyst 17.159, 214
Amphipolis 7.128
Amulets 7.140; 15.125; 16.59,
97
Anarchy 9.265; 14.205
Anchor, symbol of 13.62
Ancyra 14.144
Anemones 4.165
Angels 1.69; 3.289; 10.92;
15.159, 166, 171; 16.167,
174f
archangels 8.17; 16.31
avenging 17.121f
of the churches 16.53–55, 104
contempt of 15.186–188
of death 2.339; 3.135; 13.134,
158
of doom 17.109f
fallen 3.34; 14.240, 321–323;
17.47
and Gnostics 11.119f
guardian 1.321; 2.180; 3.35;
4.161; 13.18; 16.31, 54
hosts of 13.17
immortality of 13.18f
and Jesus 3.24; 12.90f;
13.16–19
in Judaism 2.128; 4.250;

8.117f; 15.167
and the Law 10.29; 13.17;
16.24
of the Lord 3.22; 4.291
and lordships 8.117
and natural forces 17.127
of Peace 17.40
of the Presence 13.18; 16.31;
17.41f, 202, 204
of Punishment 17.53
ranks of 14.323
at resurrection 2.376; 4.291
'of service' 17.19
sin of 1.321; 14.321f; 15.183f
worship of 11.97, 135, 146;
16.173; 17.27f, 175f, 224
Anger 1.96, 136, 137–139;
2.47, 280; 3.236; 8.35;
9.264; 10.155, 159; 11.153;
12.65, 187, 236; 14.56
Animals, in Judaism 4.177
Anointed One, The 1.24, 29,
36; 2.137, 241, 254; 3.12,
297; 4.119, 252; 5.115, 154,
176, 237, 243, 245, 252; 6.53,
72f, 117f; 8.126; 10.86f,
107; 15.69f; 16.169; 17.60,
84
as King 4.26, 239f; 5.88f
Anointing of kings 15.69–71
Anthropomorphisms 5.29
Antichrist 5.223; 11.213; 15.14,
61–64, 119; 17.25, 55f, 57–64,
66, 70, 77, 90, 102, 118, 138f,
184
spirit of 5.13, 65; 15.64
Antinomianism 3.315; 11.66, 97,
98; 14.284, 297; 15.160–163,
172

---

1 Matt, v.1   3 Mark   5 John, v.1   7 Acts   9 Cor
2 Matt, v.2   4 Luke   6 John, v.2   8 Rom   10 Gal, Eph

Antioch in Pisidia 7.97, 101, 102, 106f, 119; 14.291

Antioch in Syria 3.209; 7.4, 5f, 88f, 97, 117, 119, 138; 10.18–20; 14.39, 79

Antipatris 7.167

Antisemitism, ancient 2.290; 4.85; 8.208f; 14.38, 148, 202

Antitypes 14.243f

Antonia, castle of 2.346; 7.157f tower of 3.324; 6.223

Anxiety 1.218, 255; 3.116f; 4.165; 9.213; 11.195; 12.132; 14.272

Apartheid 5.159

Apii Forum 7.190

Apocalypse, The See *Revelation, Book of*

Apocalyptic 1.7; 3.194, 305; 16.6–11; 17.117 literature of 5.7; 16.2–4 and prophecy 16.5f

Apocrypha, The 5.32

Apollonia 7.128

Apostacy 15.119

Apostates 1.121; 2.49; 6.174; 9.106; 13.57, 124; 17.112

Apostles, The 1.359–362; 3.144; 4.74f; 7.91; 9.134; 11.49; 12.158, 196–198; 14.17, 179; 15.132; 16.12, 25, 154 definition of 10.3, 145f; 12.195–197; 14.154f; 15.176 in Early Church 9.115, 184; 15.90 and elders 14.154 false 9.247; 249 female 8.212 respect for 7.44, 67

and the resurrection 7.17f; 9.78, 115

and the Sanhedrin 7.38f, 47f; 10.74f

Statutes of See Index VI

'super-apostles' 9.246, 261

support of 9.79

Teaching of See Index VI

Appian Way 7.190

Arabia 1.82; 3.52; 4.48; 7.73; 10.41

Arabs 1.93; 8.128; 9.173; 12.104; 13.143

Aralu 17.133

Aramaic language 5.29; 7.51; 14.37; 17.175

Ara Maxima, The 14.147

Archer, sign of the 17.215

Areopagus 7.131

Aretas 2.96

Aridity 11.166; 12.119

Aristocracy 10.45

Armageddon 17.132f

Armour, spiritual 10.181–184

Arrest, Greek law of 1.144

Arrogance 2.288; 8.37; 12.62, 185–187; 14.91f

Artaban 3.65f

Asceticism 9.55, 58f; 11.96, 98f, 135, 144f, 150; 12.5f, 30, 93f, 119–121; 15.9

Asher, tribe of 1.73; 3.178; 14.31

Asia 7.19, 121; 8.8; 12.155; 14.137, 144f, 160, 166; 16.11, 17, 28f, 58, 87

Asia Minor 2.218; 3.209; 5.17, 26; 7.5, 119; 8.209; 12.184f; 14.39f, 145, 160f; 17.86

11 Phil, Col, Thes
12 Tim, Tit, Phlm
13 Heb
14 Jas, Pet
15 John, Jude
16 Rev, v.1
17 Rev, v.2

Asiarch 7.3, 140
Aspasia 1.155
Ass, symbol of 2.243; 3.264;
    4.240; 6.118
Associations, Roman 12.165f
Assos 7.150
Assyria 1.58; 3.193; 11.111;
    16.8; 17.136f
Assyrians 1.73, 75; 2.281;
    5.149; 6.120; 7.65; 9.131;
    13.164; 14.37; 16.3; 17.53
Astrology 1.26; 7.66; 8.118;
    9.47; 10.35; 11.95f, 134, 137;
    12.182
Astronomy 5.57
Atheism 1.207; 8.49; 11.197;
    16.80
Athenaeum 12.124
Athens 1.154, 333; 2.80; 3.279;
    7.119, 130–133; 8.19; 9.1,
    49f, 119, 132, 164; 10.162,
    174; 12.38, 88, 210; 13.89;
    14.298
    Stoa Poikile of 3.279
Athenians 6.119; 8.202; 10.34,
    108f; 12.106; 17.103
Atonement
    Day of 1.142, 146, 233; 2.243,
        391; 3.58, 365; 4.223, 288;
        6.210; 7.182; 10.129; 13.3,
        18, 84, 96, 97–101
    Jewish 1.52, 142, 187f, 233;
        3.258; 4.266; 12.9, 18f, 43,
        127; 13.98–101; 16.177f
Attalia 7.97
Attalus 16.28
Augustan cohort 7.181
'Authorities' 10.182; 15.166
Authority 1.75, 133–135; 4.243f;

6.4f; 16.127f
Avarice 2.331f, 335
Azariyeh 6.102

Baal 1.58; 4.126; 8.120, 144;
    10.47
    prophets of 1.64; 4.48; 6.143;
        16.106
    worship of 2.134; 3.192;
        4.17; 16.105f
Baal-peor 16.67
Baaras 4.51
Babylon 1.13, 163; 5.149;
        14.277; 15.18–20, 131, 138;
        16.8, 36; 17.2, 88, 153, 161,
        211
    carpets of 9.2
    coverlets of 17.160
    deportation of Jews 11.93;
        14.37f
    doom song of 17.149, 150
    exile of Jews in 6.22, 117;
        11.111
    fall of 17.110, 128, 166
    symbolic use of 14.276–278;
        16.15; 17.63, 134, 136, 167,
        168, 209
Babylonians 2.281; 3.193;
        6.121; 7.11; 11.212; 14.37;
        16.3; 17.53, 80
    and astrology 16.153, 155
    and creation 17.58, 198
    empire of 5.185
    legends of 15.61; 17.77, 133
    religion of 16.153
Balaam 12.194
Balance, sign of 17.215
Balinas 3.192
Balsam 4.234; 9.2; 17.161

Ban, The 6.47; 8.124; 12.53

Banias 2.134; 3.192

Banishment 16.40–42

Baptism 5.84; 6.262; 7.69, 85;
    8.83f; 11.154f; 12.169;
    13.53f; 14.243–245, 247f;
    15.89, 109
  of adults 10.32; 12.135;
    14.306
  and anointing 15.70f
  and confession 3.14; 5.iii, 83;
    10.32
  for the dead 11.152f
  and enlightenment 15.119
  with fire 1.50f
  by immersion 8.208; 12.86
  of infants 8.83; 11.140; 13.53
  and instruction 8.89f
  'into Christ' 9.16; 14.67
  and kiss of peace 14.280f
  Jewish 1.59f; 3.14, 255; 5.79;
    7.69; 8.84; 10.31f
  of John 1.47, 50; 3.13, 15,
    17f
  new birth of 14.192
  oneness of 10.142
  ordained 2.278
  in Paul 10.174; 9.15; 11.139f
  and perfection 11.65
  and resurrection 12.174
  robes of 16.121
  and sealing 17.23
  sermon of 14.160
  symbolism of 5.180; 6.141f;
    13.56

Barbarians 10.113; 11.155

Barley 3.323; 9.80, 150; 17.7

Barley-bread 3.159; 5.5, 202

Barriers 10.113f; 11.155f;

12.64f

Baskets 2.127; 3.158, 184; 5.203

Basket, The 7.51; 12.85

Batanaea 3.53

Baths, public 1.144

Bear, symbolism of 17.88

Beast, The 17.47, 86–95, 138–
    142, 147, 184
  number of 17.100–102
  second 17.97f

Beatitudes, The 1.88–118; 4.5,
    76f

Beds, eastern 5.180

Beggars 7.32

Behemoth 1.216, 303; 17.77

Belief 3.227; 15.112
  and action 11.105
  certainty of 1.75, 352f; 8.181;
    9.130; 10.183; 11.41, 210;
    12.241; 13.128; 15.121–123
  and confession 8.139
  disturbed .3.123f
  and the Gospel 3.26
  impossibility of 3.317
  'in Christ' 5.44f, 135, 213;
    6.153
  Pauline 8.21
  Protestant 2.139
  purity of 12.153f
  restatement of 5.7
  unchangeability of 14.350
  uniformity of 12.241
  variety of 4.179; 14.73

Beloved Disciple, The 5.18–20;
    6.145

Benedictine Order, The 14.257

Benedictus, The 4.4

Benefactor, The 4.267

Benevolence 1.173; 10.164

Benjamin, tribe of 11.58; 14.31
Beroea 7.119, 129; 8.19; 11.47,
　　73, 86, 181; 12.22
Beryl 17.159, 214, 215
Bethany 2.238, 329, 331, 338;
　　3.263f, 269, 324; 4.142;
　　6.80, 102, 108f
Bethany beyond Jordan 5.6
Bethel 6.53, 79
Bethesda 5.177
Bethlehem 1.23-25, 31, 37; 3.65,
　　149; 4.21; 5.243, 252; 7.68
Beth-peor 2.159
Bethphage 2.238; 3.263, 324
Bethsaida 2.11-13; 3.27; 4.117;
　　5.6, 201
Bethsaida Julias 5.201, 206, 225
Bethulia 13.164
Bethzatha 5.177
Betrothal, Jewish 1.19; 4.12
Bible
　availability of 4.151
　criticism of 1.4; 10.64
　divisions of 3.299; 9.6, 223
　honesty of 7.44
　importance of 10.90
　inspiration of 4.8
　order of books 2.298
　power of 3.13; 8.178
　revelation and 6.195
　study of 8.195f
　understanding of 4.70f
　unity of 9.192f
　use of 5.198; 12.100
Binding and loosing 2.145f, 182,
　　189
Birmingham 15.162
Birth, Jewish 4.17
Bishops 12.3, 69-72; 14.139;

　16.54, 104
Bithynia 7.19, 121; 12.99;
　　14.137, 144f, 160f, 166; 16.17
Bitterness 1.110, 145, 174f, 202,
　　247, 392; 2.32, 119, 247f, 288,
　　340; 3.236, 243, 277; 4.27,
　　116, 168, 283, 285; 6.49;
　　9.34, 226, 239, 267; 10.90,
　　140, 157, 159; 11.80; 12.65,
　　128, 154, 162, 188; 13.132;
　　14.91f, 97, 173; 15.32
Black Sea 17.161
Blamelessness 10.78f; 11.43
Blasphemy 1.324; 2.315, 355,
　　357; 3.175, 279, 321, 351;
　　5.244; 6.76; 7.50, 61f;
　　12.187; 15.112; 17.89, 94
Blessings 1.370; 12.24; 16.180;
　　17.28
Blindness 1.349; 3.35, 189
Blood
　and covenants 2.342
　and Jerusalem Covenant 7.116
　sanctity of 2.112; 3.332;
　　17.10
　shedding of 13.107f
　sprinkling of 14.169f
　symbolism of 5.224; 13.131
　uncleanness of 1.346
Blood-feuds 1.164
Boasting 8.38; 12.185-187;
　　14.114
　in Christ 11.56; 16.83
Body 1.217; 3.42, 105, 315;
　　8.156; 9.55-57, 85f; 10.162f;
　　12.119
　Egyptian doctrine of 1.321
　and Gnostics 11.98; 12.7, 30;
　　15.11

1 Matt, v.1　　　3 Mark　　　5 John, v.1　　　7 Acts　　　9 Cor
2 Matt, v.2　　　4 Luke　　　6 John, v.2　　　8 Rom　　　10 Gal, Eph

and Greeks 5.64; 9.55, 58, 140, 204
intestines 11.18
spiritual 9.141, 157–159, 204f
temple of Holy Spirit 8.156f; 9.33f, 56; 12.96
as a text 14.308
Boils, plague of 17.125
Booths 2.169
Boredom 12.259; 15.100
Bottomless Pit, The 17.47
Bounty, The 3.13
Bow, sign of 17.4
Boy's Brigade 6.185
Branding 16.135; 17.99
Bread 1.23, 199; 2.79
bond of 9.91
breaking of 4.295; 7.149
daily 1.390
of God 2.127; 3.185; 5.215f; 16.95
of heaven 3.179
of Last Supper 4.265
of life 1.215; 2.124–128; 5.10, 216, 218
of the Presence 4.70
unleavened 2.79; 3.332
Britain 1.113; 2.87; 3.177; 9.121; 12.222; 17.140
Brotherhood, Christian 3.249; 9.13; 11.103f
Bull, sign of 17.214
Burden, definition of 1.310; 2.22; 4.60, 156; 10.52f
Burial, eastern 1.345; 17.197
of Gentiles 3.337
Jewish 1.313f; 2.372; 3.323f, 366; 4.289; 6.88
mistaken 4.111

Buskins 16 115

Caesar
household of 8.212; 11.87
symbolic use 3.284; 4.247
worship of 1.114, 391; 6.182f; 16.15–20, 90f; 17.63, 89, 93, 95, 98–100, 131f, 141, 184
Caeserea 2.135, 358, 363; 4.2; 7.138
Caesarea Philippi 1.65; 2.133–135, 157; 3.191f, 209, 251, 262, 324; 4.31, 112, 263, 280; 7.171; 14.5
capital city 6.238, 243
church of 7.6
fortress of 2.143
and Paul 7.73, 76
Roman H.Q. 7.79, 167
Calvary 2.160; 4.3; 6.251
Camel 2.217, 294; 4.229
Cana 1.41; 5.5f, 9, 91, 95–99, 174
Canaanites 1.73; 2.121; 13.90
Cannibalism 1.113; 4.258; 14.203; 16.80
Canon, The 14.5, 249
Capernaum 1.71, 74, 133, 301, 307f, 326, 331, 345; 2.11–13; 3.29, 39, 41, 46, 49, 52f; 3.176f; 4.49, 86; 5.106, 174, 201, 208
Cappadocia 14.137, 144, 160, 166
Cappadocians 12.242
Caria 16.28
Carmel, Mount 1.64; 3.52, 176; 4.48, 126
Carnelian 16.152; 17.214, 215
Carolina, North 3.13

Carousing 10.49

Carthage 2.364; 11.50; 13.192
    Council of 12.234

Carthaginians 6.250

Caspis 13.160

Cassia 17.161

Casting lots 7.17

Castration 10.44; 13.193

Catholic Epistles 14.137

Cayster, river 7.140; 12.184

Celibacy 2.208; 14.20; 15.9;
    17.106

Cenchraea 7.133, 138; 9.2, 186

Censoriousness 8.182f

Censuses 4.20f

Centurions 1.300f; 4.84; 7.79

Chalcedon 17.213

Chalcedony 17.213, 215

Chamber of the Silent 1.188

Chance 1.89, 207; 7.14

Character 1.242; 8.74; 17.114

Chariots 17.162

Charity 1.170; 3.229, 277; 4.109,
    209; 9.118; 10.139; 13.199

Charm 7.56; 9.121; 10.9

Chastity 1.155; 2.208; 3.237f;
    4.211; 7.116; 8.90; 9.43;
    10.46, 161f; 11.97, 150f;
    12.39, 76; 17.106

Cheerfulness 2.124

Cherubim 8.117; 13.17, 96f;
    16.157f; 17.171

Cherubs 16.157

Childbirth 1.320; 4.24f

Child exposure 10.176

Childlessness 4.10, 283; 9.61;
    10.41

Children 2.174–178; 10.175–
    178; 11.161f

and angels 3.35
'of the bridechamber' 1.335;
    3.59; 4.64
care of 1.399f; 2.81
'of God' 1.109; 15.73, 81f
and Greeks 8.39; 10.34;
    12.110
and Jews 10.33f; 12.199
and Romans 10.34

Chiliasm 17.184

China 17.160

Chios 7.150

Chislew, Month of 6.69

Choice 1.277; 8.29

Chorazin 2.11–13; 4.134

Chorus, Greek 8.202

Chosen People, The 1.15, 60;
    2.264; 4.25; 5.79; 6.63;
    7.4, 52f; 8.119, 145; 10.18;
    11.156, 192; 14.166, 167, 169,
    198f, 291; 17.84

Christianity 1.50, 88f, 111–115,
    120, 167f, 172f, 286, 357, 391;
    2.66, 77, 79–81, 138, 230f,
    267; 3.64, 99f, 145, 244f,
    262, 316; 4.15f, 43, 58, 101,
    120, 170, 208, 297; 6.288;
    8.139, 167; 9.32, 121; 11.13f,
    40; 12.40, 100; 14.59, 296,
    298

adventure of 1.374, 396f;
    2.323; 3.77; 4.194f, 270
apologetic of 5.132f, 173
basis of 2.219
the Christian 1.30, 291; 3.155;
    4.183, 295; 7.161f; 8.87;
    9.13f, 148–154; 12.160–163,
    190–194, 246–256; 14.173,
    267, 296; 16.22

and the Cross 1.95, 214, 287,
395; 2.107, 151f, 220; 4.121;
9.170, 200
and democracy 9.265; 10.45;
13.200
foolishness of 5.49; 9.16–20
growth of 3.125, 208f; 5.26;
8.213; 10.151; 14.36f
immortality of 12.168
Jewish 2.170; 5.10; 10.19;
14.22, 41; 15.6
name of 7.90
neutrality of 4.148
purifying influence 3.12f
revolutionary 7.128
and society 2.81, 83
task of 4.181f
universality of 12.23f, 55–57;
13.92f; 15.40; 16.178; 17.16
'The Way' 7.139
Christmas tree 1.35; 17.159
Christmonger 11.190
Christology 2.138; 4.120, 137;
5.224; 11.100
Chrysolite 17.214f
Chrysoprase 17.214
Church 1.6, 7, 43f; 2.89f; 6.273;
14.286; 16.104, 173; 17.170
assembly of God 12.88
attendance at 1.107, 121;
2.270
as body of Christ 2.183;
8.159; 9.95, 108, 112–116;
10.67, 92–94, 141; 11.120
as bride of Christ 5.143;
9.246; 14.102, 276; 15.131;
16.108; 17.76, 172–174, 208,
229
and buildings 9.167; 11.171f;

17.216
as a building 2.141; 8.192;
10.119
catholicity of 17.210f
a democracy 9.265; 13.200
divisions of 9.8, 13–16, 30, 34;
10.48; 11.182; 12.265;
14.225f; 15.200
flock of God 6.62f
function of 14.198f
growth of 3.110–112; 5.7;
7.9ff; 12.91; 14.145
house churches 11.73
household of God 12.88;
13.32
inclusivism of 1.266f, 288;
8.197–200; 9.34f, 100f;
16.154
importance of 4.181
indestructibility of 2.144
and Jesus 2.139–146; 11.120–
122; 17.85
leadership of 7.91; 8.162;
9.116, 166; 10.145–150;
12.69–86, 98, 99f; 12.101–
104, 117f; 13.194f; 15.194
membership of 2.155; 3.191;
4.131, 221; 12.118
nature of 2.142; 7.30f; 9.21;
14.195–197
organization of 9.133f;
11.129, 131; 12.3; 14.26,
139f
and Paul 8.159; 11.104
and Peter 2.139–146; 14.154
pillars of 14.10
services of 12.100; 16.26
as temple of God 9.33
unity of 2.311; 3.83; 6.65,

75, 190, 215, 217f; 7.92, 145,
148; 8.3, 196f, 198, 205; 9.9,
108, 113, 116, 157, 162;
10.114f, 116f, 119, 141–143,
149; 11.7, 30, 31, 33f, 71;
12.272; 13.144; 14.224–226;
16.61
  universality of 6.288; 7.145;
  9.35; 16.174
  weakness of 1.269; 2.166
  and women 9.96–100
  younger churches 12.2
Church of the Nativity 1.24f
Chuthites 5.150
Cilicia 7.73, 119; 9.2
Cilicians 12.242
Cinnamon 17.161f
Circumcision 4.24; 5.241f;
    7.69; 8.65f; 10.107; 11.135
  and the Church 7.112–118
  Ishmaelite 11.57
  and Paul 7.120; 9.251;
    10.16f, 43, 56; 11.55f, 138–
    140
  and proselytes 3.14
  spiritual 11.55
  symbolism of 8.125; 11.55,
    139
Citizenship 2.170f, 273f; 3.287;
    4.248; 8.173f; 11.69; 12.258–
    260; 14.159
  dual 9.206
  of the kingdom 11.29f; 14.201
  Roman 9.4; 11.20
  state and church 2.132; 3.287;
    8.170–174; 14.205f
Citrus wood 17.160
City of the gods 17.214
City of Palms 4.234

Class-distinctions 8.212; 10.19;
    14.47, 64f
Cleansing 2.110–117; 3.164;
    10.47; 14.107f
  spiritual 4.150; 6.19; 8.120;
    15.30f; 17.31f
  symbol of 7.69; 14.170
Cleopatra's Needle 14.250
Clothing
  aprons 7.143
  cloaks 1.167; 2.367; 3.142;
    12.219
  fine linen 1.239; 4.213;
    16.143f; 17.160
  girdles 1.367; 2.367; 3.142;
    4.285; 7.143
  leprous 3.144
  Jewish 2.367; 3.141f, 362;
    4.285; 6.253
  rending of 1.342; 3.134
  robes 3.130, 299f; 4.167, 205,
    285; 16.45
  shawls 4.113
  tassels 1.346f; 2.286f; 3.299;
    4.113
  'travelling-dress' 6.89
  turbans 2.367; 3.142; 4.202,
    285
  veils 9.97f
Clouds 2.161
Cocks 2.346; 6.229
  cock-crow, the 2.346f; 3.352;
    6.230
Coffins 4.62
Cohort 7.79
Coins
  Jewish 1.389; 2.273; 3.286,
    302; 4.171f, 241; 5.109
  Roman 17.99

Collection, The 7.51, 145, 147;
 8.2f, 205, 220; 9.162–165,
 228–232, 237, 262; 12.22,
 232; 14.14; 15.148
 collecting-bags 3.143
 collecting-boxes 4.254
Colosse 11.91f, 128, 171;
 12.184, 274; 16.28
 heresy of 11.92f, 94–97; 12.27
 Letter to 3.4; 10.61f; 11.91–
 101
Comas 1.345
Comfort 3.121f; 4.228, 254;
 9.129, 170f
Coming One, The 2.2; 3.266
Communism 4.81
Compassion 2.121; 4.140;
 11.34; 14.227
Compromise 1.70; 4.44; 7.156;
 13.73f; 15.145; 16.93, 102
Conceit 9.264f; 10.53; 12.126,
 191; 13.122
Conclusions 5.192
Condemnation 1.48; 4.135, 152;
 5.43, 46, 52, 67; 8.41, 51,
 69, 116; 11.112; 14.176
 Roman 3.358f
Confession 1.57, 142; 3.14f, 133;
 8.139; 14.131; 15.33, 68
 confessors 17.192f
Confidence 2.1, 3; 3.189;
 11.87f; 15.114
Conformity 14.326
Congregationalism 9.162
Conscience 2.96, 154; 3.48;
 4.115, 249; 6.192; 8.189f,
 194; 9.222; 10.131; 11.142;
 12.245f; 14.57
 branding of 12.93

cleansing of 13.104
 good 12.34
 of others 9.250
 petrifying of 10.153
 rejection of 12.53
 weak 9.73, 75
Conscientiousness 1.119
Consecration 2.202; 6.216
Constantinople 12.127
Contempt 1.139f; 5.193; 8.37,
 49f, 181; 10.122
Contention 8.179
Contentment 1.183; 11.84f;
 12.128–131, 132; 13.194;
 15.198
Contraception 11.200
Contracts 8.92f; 14.244
Convention 8.185; 9.99
Conversion 3.191; 6.41, 131;
 12.44f
Coptic Church 2.359
Coptic Gospels, The 5.96
Corinth 1.154; 7.119, 133f;
 9.1–4, 6, 58; 12.38
 bronze of 2.244; 17.161
 church of 9.7, 8, 13–16, 42,
 51–54
 gulf of 9.1
 industry of 9.125
 Letters to 9.5–8, 178, 237
 and Paul 7.133–136; 8.19;
 9.4f; 11.47
 synagogue of 9.16
 women of 9.99
Corn 17.6f
Corn-ships 7.184
Cornwall 2.373; 3.177
Costus 17.162
Courage 1.79, 229, 380, 390;

2.344–346; 3.341; 4.230, 234; 6.88; 7.19, 39; 8.206; 9.166; 11.30, 50, 129; 13.158; 14.301f, 303; 17.206

Courtesy 2.260; 3.182; 9.121; 10.17; 11.6

Courtship 2.204

Covenant 2.342; 3.339; 4.266; 9.104, 189; 10.109; 13.3f, 80, 90f, 106f; 15.74; 17.96
  ark of 13.96; 17.73, 121
  Book of the 9.189
  definition of 8.125
  new 3.339f; 4.266; 8.125; 9.189–191; 13.80f, 90–94, 185, 202; 16.161
  people of 11.57
  ratification of 14.170
  types of 7.116; 10.28; 13.90, 92–94; 16.161

Covenanters, The 1.213

Coverdale version 2.294

Covetousness 3.173f, 328; 8.176; 14.99, 259, 318, 333; 15.190f

Cowardice 2.258

Crab, sign of 17.215

Creation 1.22, 49, 52, 390; 2.200; 3.182, 240; 4.291; 5.30, 34, 183; 6.18; 9.157; 11.44; 12.30, 94; 13.35; 14.21f; 15.27, 56, 99, 140; 17.188
  animal 14.88
  culmination of 11.117
  and demons 3.34
  and Gnostics 11.97f; 12.27
  by Jesus See Jesus and creation
  myths of 15.61; 17.77, 133,

198
  new 2.309; 4.90; 11.121; 14.172, 342; 17.197–199
  out of nothing 5.41; 13.130
  reconciliation of 11.123f
  song of 16.180f

Creed, The 6.35, 9.137; 14.232, 236, 243
  basis of 8.139; 9.107; 12.135f, 153
  centre of 16.16
  in Early Church 10.141f; 11.39

Creeds 1.290, 339; 4.140; 8.116; 12.3f; 13.120
  in Judaism 3.295; 17.119
  singing of 12.90

Crenides 7.122

Cretans 12.237, 242f, 258

Crete 7.182; 9.21; 12.9, 71, 233, 234, 240f

Crises 8.74

Criticism 1.265; 9.181; 12.97f

Crowns 11.70, 193f; 12.211; 14.48f; 16.163
  of glory 16.83
  of life 14.48f
  of righteousness 16.83
  of victory 12.161

Crucifixion 1.395f; 2.363f; 3.360; 4.282f; 6.250f, 276; 13.197
  common death 2.165; 4.121
  cross-shapes 4.284
  origin of 6.250

Crumbs 4.213f

Cummin 2.293

Cup, symbol of 3.255

Curiosity 15.41

Cuthaeans 5.150

Cynics 5.46, 67f; 8.199; 12.241; 14.27, 315

Cyprus 1.89; 2.251; 7.3, 99f; 8.215f
  Church in 7.88, 97
  and Greek language 13.8

Cyrene 2.366; 3.361; 4.282; 7.88, 98; 8.215f; 14.39

Dagger-bearers 7.16, 158; 8.173

Dalmatia 12.265

Damascus 1.39, 73, 81, 331; 3.52, 124, 177; 4.48; 7.107; 9.255
  and Christians 7.70
  and Jews 14.39

Dan, tribe of 14.31; 17.25

Dark, darkness 5.45, 47–49; 11.112; 15.26f
  end of 17.198, 219, 228
  pits of 14.321
  plague of 17.125

Darnel 2.72f

Day, Jewish concept of 1.310; 2.223, 374; 3.37, 331; 4.289; 7.32
  religious observance of 8.180, 183f; 10.36

Day of the Lord 1.373f, 393; 2.302–304, 308f; 3.304, 318f; 4.257f; 6.184, 197; 7.25; 8.25, 108; 9.12, 37; 11.182, 204f, 212; 12.92, 182; 13.12, 57; 14.115, 343f; 15.39, 60; 16.3, 42; 17.16, 42, 69f
  of the Lord Jesus 9.12; 15.118
  The Day 9.32f

Day of Questions, The 4.243

Deaconesses 8.207f; 12.86f

Deacons 1.377; 9.163; 12.3, 84–86; 14.139; 16.12

Dead, Place of 2.143
  uncleanness of 2.295

Dead Sea 1.63; 2.157; 3.16, 149; 4.36, 43, 138; 15.195

Deafness 3.181

Death
  and Christians 8.117, 187; 16.27; 17.193
  conquest of 9.151; 13.153f; 16.10f; 17.197
  consequence of sin 8.80, 105; 14.248f
  in East 3.326; 5.55; 13.103
  fear of 9.140, 160; 11.203
  finality of 8.92f; 13.110f
  'in the Lord' 17.113f
  and Jesus 2.144, 371
  mystery of 13.135–138
  and Paul 11.27f; 12.209
  preparation for 9.110
  second 16.84f
  as sleep 1.344f; 4.110; 6.86
  spiritual 1.365; 5.192; 10.95f; 11.141; 14.248; 16.116
  'with Christ' 5.126; 11.182

Debts 1.170; 2.194f
  moral 1.221; 4.173
  of love 8.176

Decalogue, The See Ten Commandments

Decapolis 1.82, 363; 2.125f 128; 3.124f, 180, 184; 5.26

Deceit 2.292; 8.35; 11.96; 14.190

Decisions 1.315; 3.19; 13.30

Dedication, feast of 3.267; 5.2,

106; 6.69f

Defilement 3.171–175

Degeneration, spiritual 12.213

Deism 3.315

Deliverance 8.59; 9.23; 10.81f

Delphic oracles 14.349; 16.105, 114

Democracy 2.278; 3.227; 4.177; 9.265; 10.45; 11.182; 13.200; 14.206

Demons 1.289, 319–321, 366; 2.35, 112; 3.32, 34f, 71, 117–120, 225; 4.50, 54, 107f, 125f; 5.178; 9.72, 75, 91f; 10.92, 99; 11.96; 12.90f, 92; 15.89; 17.47, 176
    demon-possession 1.289, 308, 320–322; 2.35; 3.34–36, 71f, 115, 118–120; 4.50; 9.258

Dependence, spiritual 2.176; 9.198

Deposit, spiritual 12.4, 138f, 151–153

Depression 9.85

'Depths' 8.118

Derbe 7.97, 119; 11.47

Desert 1.46; 3.34; 17.143

Desire 1.136, 148, 272; 4.233; 8.28f; 10.100, 153; 11.84, 150f; 12.37; 53, 129, 189, 256; 13.40; 14.52f, 99–101, 187, 200, 329f; 15.57

Despair 2.61–63, 70; 3.97, 108, 136; 3.209, 217; 4.100; 5.55, 169; 10.109; 11.70, 82f

Destroyer, The 17.52

Devastation, The 1.63; 3.16; 4.43

Devil, The 1.106, 226; 3.22f, 330; 6.26–29, 147; 9.76, 195f; 10.157; 12.73f; 14.94, 106, 272; 15.77; 17.58, 80–82, 84, 186, 191f, 193f, 197
    devils 1.294; 2.35, 317; 3.32; 5.2; 9.72; 12.189
    Prince of devils 1.351; 2.36; 6.31

Dialogue—form 14.28

Diamonds 17.159

Diaspora 5.246; 14.21, 36–40, 166

Difficulties 2.167; 3.276; 9.170; 12.182

Dignity 12.253

Diligence 7.45

Dill 2.293

Dion 3.124

Dionysia 14.299

Discipleship 1.123, 199, 312, 361; 2.151–155, 177, 249; 3.75, 101; 5.74, 163, 196; 6.11f, 20–22, 133, 211f; 10.124f; 12.195

Discipline 1.175, 280, 292; 2.87, 173f; 3.59, 232, 234; 11.67, 150; 9.225; 10.177f; 12.161, 193; 13.175–179; 16.145f
    of Church 2.183f, 187f; 9.44–46, 96, 136, 267; 10.149; 11.131; 12.1, 116f

Discouragement 2.311

Diseass 3.23, 44

Disloyalty 1.388; 4.121; 6.142

Disobedience 1.386; 8.38, 53; 9.193; 10.100; 13.33, 46

Disorder 9.265

Dispersion, The   See Diaspora

Disputations 1.380; 11.43; 12.139f, 180

Dissension 8.218; 10.48

Divorce
and Christianity 2.200–205; 3.237–240; 9.62
Gentile law of 2.201
and Greeks 1.155; 2.81; 10.170
and Jews 1.18–19, 150–152; 2.195–199; 3.237–240; 4.211f, 283; 10.168f; 11.198f; 12.76f
and Romans 1.156f; 8.32; 10.170f; 11.199; 12.77f

Doceticism 5.13, 65; 15.7, 23, 180

Doctors, ancient 3.129; 7.3

Doctrine 1.20; 3.227, 314; 11.82
categories of 14.241f
development of 12.153
false 2.129; 15.199–202
in Paul 8.10, 15
and Scripture 1.387; 9.33; 11.136

Dogmatism 12.32f

Dogs 2.122; 3.178; 11.53f, 62; 17.227

'Dominions' 10.92

Doom Songs 17.149

Doors 4.145; 6.58f; 16.128f

Doubt 2.2; 3.116; 5.54f; 6.130; 8.181; 9.130; 12.65f; 15.86

Doves 2.245f; 3.273f; 5.110
symbol of 3.20; 5.83

Dragon, The 17.58, 62, 77, 80, 84–86, 98

Drugs 10.47

Drunkenness 5.97; 8.178; 9.53;

10.48f; 12.79, 237; 17.162

Dualism 12.62

Duty 1.41f, 188f, 243, 262, 317, 326, 353, 379; 2.277f; 4.109, 216, 220, 237; 5.52; 8.29, 161, 164, 190, 195, 221; 9.24, 94f, 163, 182, 232; 10.165; 11.80; 12.106, 171; 13.179–184; 14.204–211
of children 10.177; 12.187
civic 4.64
to the future 12.139
Greeks 8.202
and love 9.118f
parental 1.366; 10.177f; 12.106f
and privilege 8.161
Stoic 8.113

Dyeing 11.92; 16.102, 115

Eagle, symbolism of 5.1; 16.159; 17.45f, 85

Earnest, the 9.177; 10.87f

Earthquakes 17.13, 134

East Africa, Church of 3.15

Ebal, Mount 5.157

Ecclesiasticism 2.166

Eden, Garden of 1.388; 6.38; 8.95f; 9.246; 14.50; 15.164; 16.69, 70; 17.17, 98, 220, 221

Edessa 1.81; 14.4, 152

Edification 12.172

Edom 4.31; 17.150

Edomites 1.12; 8.128; 11.58

Education 3.17; 17.57
Jewish 14.37, 55

Eels 1.271

Effectiveness 9.261

Egnatian Way 7.127; 11.180

11 Phil, Col, Thes   13 Heb   15 John, Jude   16 Rev, v.1
12 Tim, Tit, Phlm   14 Jas, Pet   17 Rev, v.2

Egypt **1**.32-36, 39, 73, 329, 331;
 3.52, 91; **4**.20f, 48; **14**.38;
 16.8; **17**.2, 117, 160
 deliverance from **1**.390; **2**.160
 and Early Church **3**.3, 209
 'the granary of Italy' **7**.181
 symbolic use of **17**.71
Egyptians **1**.321; **2**.112; **17**.198
Eighteen, The **1**.192
Elder, The **15**.127
Elders
 Christian **1**.377; **5**.17; **17**.19,
  91, 111, 152; **9**.110; **10**.148;
  12.3, 69-84, 115f, 158, 234-
  240; **14**.21, 26, 129f, 140,
  154, 262-268; **15**.127, 133,
  137; **16**.12
 Greek **12**.70; **14**.263
 Jewish **1**.145; **2**.54, 143, 147;
  2.276, 281, 287, 362; **3**.163-
  167, 279, 346, 349; **4**.133,
  221, 243; **9**.49; **12**.70; **14**.21,
  26, 262f; **14**.154; **16**.153
 Twenty-four, the **14**.263;
  16.152-154, 163f, 174;
  17.170
Elect, the **14**.160, 165f
Elect Lady, the **15**.19, 129f
Election **8**.120, 122, 127, 131;
 14.169
Elements **16**.31
Emanations **5**.12, 40f; **11**.97,
 114; **12**.6, 27f; **15**.164
Emancipation, spiritual **15**.121;
 16.177
Emeralds **16**.151f; **17**.159, 213,
 215
Emmaus **4**.294
Emotions **2**.60: **4**.150; **11**.84;

 14.75f
 seat of **9**.218f
Emperor's Day, The **16**.43
Encouragement **8**.161; **13**.122
End, The See Last Things
Endor **4**.86
Endurance **9**.123, 170, 212f;
 11.210; **12**.135, 169, 197;
 13.173; **14**.176-178; **16**.39f,
 62, 131f
Engannim **5**.147
England **2**.372
Enlightenment **13**.56; **15**.119
Enmity **10**.47
Enthusiasm **1**.313
Envy **2**.288; **3**.175; **8**.35, 179;
 9.120, 263f; **10**.48; **13**.132;
 14.190
Ephesians, *Letter to* **10**.61-71;
 11.172, 174; **14**.139
 and *1 Peter* **14**.152-154
 and *Revelation* **16**.57-71
Ephesus **1**.378; **7**.3, 146f; **9**.6;
 10.148; **11**.91; **12**.33, 71,
 92f, 170, 184f; **16**.28, 58-61;
 17.206
 and Andrew **5**.21
 and Apollos **8**.209
 Bishop of **12**.275
 Capital of Asia **12**.155
 'Ephesian Letters' See amulets
 'Highway of the Martyrs' **16**.58
 and John the Apostle **2**.231;
  5.6f, 17, 20, 22, 27
 and John the Elder **5**.23
 Market of Asia **16**.58
 and Paul **5**.50; **7**.119, 121,
  138, 140-144; **9**.4; **11**.47
 provenance of John's *Gospel*

---

1 Matt, v.1   3 Mark   5 John, v.1   7 Acts   9 Cor
2 Matt, v.2   4 Luke   6 John, v.2   8 Rom   10 Gal, Eph

and *Letters* 14.161; 15.18f, 123f, 137
and Roma 16.17
and Timothy 12.89, 143, 184
Ephraim 6.106
Epicureans 3.125; 7.130, 132; 13.42f; 16.84
Epilepsy 1.321; 4.125; 9.258; 10.38
Epirus 12.9, 265
Equality 12.116
Escapism 2.167; 13.72f
Esdraelon, Plain of 1.71; 4.47; 17.132
E.S.P. 1.306
Essenes 1.161, 359; 8.182; 14.127
Eternal life 2.214, 216; 5.43f, 127–129, 136f; 6.207–209; 12.228; 15.113f
Ethics 1.118, 123, 163, 272–277; 2.172, 206, 310; 3.29; 4.79f; 6.26; 9.14, 64, 68; 11.29f, 12.40, 88f, 108; 14.72, 201f; 15.17f, 82, 88; 17.107
  Greek 9.37; 11.84
  O.T. 1.165
  of reciprocal obligation 1.274; 11.160f; 14.222f
Ethiopia 7.69
  church of 14.64
  eunuch of 7.19, 63, 68f
Eunuchs 2.207
Euphrates 1.113; 5.178; 17.52f, 128, 134
  valley of 12.184
Europe 7.5, 19, 119
Evangelicals 11.23f
Evangelism 2.173; 3.191; 5.173;

9.64, 84; 11.15, 24; 12.204, 229; 16.142
Evangelists 10.147
Evasion 2.291–293; 13.73
Evil 1.70, 245f; 2.118–120; 3.174; 4.150; 8.38, 98; 13.83; 14.50, 86f, 189f
  and Belial 17.59
  definition of 8.34
  fascination of 14.297; 17.147
  influence of 6.37f
  Man of 14.328–330
  origin of 1.226; 6.216
  power of 1.225, 351, 366; 11.212f; 15.89
  root of 12.131–133
Evil One, The 1.225; 3.174, 330; 6.216; 9.196; 15.51, 55, 122; 17.82
Evolution 4.137f, 175
Example 1.124
Excellence 11.80f; 14.301
Exclusivism, Jewish 1.266; 9.48
Excommunication
  Christian 9.44–46, 48; 15.118
  Jewish 3.165; 6.45, 47; 9.61; 12.53
Exhortation 8.161
Exile 1.13, 73; 2.136
'Exiles of Eternity' 14.167f
Exorcism 1.289; 2.37–39, 166; 3.35, 37, 78, 225; 4.50f, 129, 147; 7.144
  gift of 9.110f
  and prayer 3.219
Exorcists, Order of 3.35
Expediency 2.258
Experience 5.173; 12.32
Eyes 1.351; 3.231

---

generous **1.**245–248
evil **6.**42; **10.**24
Eye-salve **16.**138f

Factiousness **9.**264
Failure **3.**218f
Fair Havens **7.**182f
Faith **1.**69, 303, 340, 342; **2.**75,
    120–123, 167f; **3.**140, 216–
    218, 261f; **4.**112; **9.**143, 157;
    10.26, 183, 185; **11.**171, 186;
    12.3, 52, 134, 154, 180;
    13.53, 147; **14.**301; **17.**34,
    210
  aristocracy of **1.**304
  defence of **15.**177–179
  definition of **9.**78; **13.**128–130
  gift of **9.**109
  and love **9.**118
  and miracles **1.**350
  in Paul **8.**21f, 61–64, 140f;
    10.23, 43; **14.**349
  and prayer **3.**276f; **6.**180
  quaternion of **14.**287
  and thought **12.**33
  vicarious **1.**326; **2.**166; **4.**63
  victory of **15.**105
  and works **1.**290; **14.**22, 71–
    74, 76–79
Faith, The **8.**21; **9.**25f; **10.**141f;
    11.5; **12.**157f, 162; **13.**49, 53–
    55; **14.**182f
Falsehood **1.**286–290; **10.**155;
    12.194f
Family **1.**393; **3.**289f; **4.**145f,
    212; **8.**39; **12.**241
Famine **17.**6–8
Fasting **1.**44, 179, 185, 232–238
  Jewish **1.**233–236, 335; **3.**58f;

    4.66, 223; **13.**98
  pre-baptismal **13.**54
Fatalism **11.**96, 137
Fate **4.**250; **6.**212; **7.**49; **16.**167
'Father' **2.**287, 361; **8.**126
Fatherhood **10.**129f
Favouritism **14.**63
Fear **1.**386, 388; **2.**60; **5.**45;
    6.130; **8.**119; **9.**207; **11.**42f;
    12.127; **13.**38, 121; **17.**206
Fearlessness **4.**160f
Feasts **1.**111; **3.**300, 322–324;
    4.192f, 267; **5.**177, 203; **9.**100
Feet-washing **6.**137
Fellowship **1.**384; **2.**53, 142,
    146, 174, 189, 221; **3.**73,
    316; **4.**296; **7.**30, 111, 149;
    8.161, 195–198; **9.**10, 34, 99f;
    10.133; **11.**14, 64, 157;
    12.118, 278; **14.**195f, 208,
    281; **15.**17f, 21, 30
  apostolic **9.**145, 163
  with Christ **8.**81f, 93f, 105;
    15.35
  with God **5.**129; **13.**1, 106;
    15.29, 39; **17.**202–204
  with unbelievers **9.**221–223
Fight, Christian **12.**210–212
Fig trees **2.**251f; **4.**174f; **9.**80
  symbolism of **2.**251; **5.**93
Fig-mulberry tree **4.**234
Fire **1.**200f; **3.**234
  symbolism of **4.**169; **17.**117
Firkin **5.**98
Firmament **16.**155; **17.**14
Firstborn **4.**24; **8.**84; **11.**119;
    13.187
  slaying of **17.**125
First-fruits **2.**371; **4.**155; **9.**149–

| **1** Matt, v.1 | **3** Mark | **5** John, v.1 | **7** Acts | **9** Cor |
| **2** Matt, v.2 | **4** Luke | **6** John, v.2 | **8** Rom | **10** Gal, Eph |

151; 17.108
'of the seven kinds' 9.80
Fish 3.27; 5.202
Fishermen 1.78f, 332; 3.27
Fishes, sign of 17.215
Fishing 1.77f; 2.88f; 3.27; 6.281
Five Rolls, The 1.127
Flaccus 14.38
Flattery 11.189
Flavia 16.126, 135
Flesh 8.93, 101–103; 9.29f,
  239f; 10.100; 14.200;
  15.57
Flood, The 2.73; 14.339f
Flowers 1.257
Flute players 1.344; 3.134
Folly 3.175
Food 2.27; 3.158, 325
  fat 2.113
  heavenly 16.95
  and idolatry 9.71–76, 87–94
  meals 6.145; 8.178, 202;
    9.53; 12.209; 16.147
  pork 1.379
Food laws 2.113, 118; 7.81;
  8.137, 149, 179; 10.20;
  11.144, 146; 12.5, 244;
  13.196; 17.95
Fools 1.140
Forbearance 8.42; 9.75, 158,
  14.124
Foreigners 10.118
Forgiveness 1.52, 59, 95, 102,
  104, 199, 219–244; 2.173f;
  3.51; 4.19, 95, 226, 285f;
  5.71; 6.19; 7.29; 8.58f, 163;
  10.82; 11.112, 115, 158;
  12.263; 13.93, 105–108, 184;
  14.74, 134, 228; 15.53, 119

and confession 1.143
God's will 5.135
and health 1.327f; 4.62
and humiliation 3.15
Jewish 1.187; 2.193; 3.49
and others 1.222f; 2.193–195;
  4.216; 12.65
and repentance 2.44f; 3.81;
  4.298
Formalism 1.194; 12.65
Fornication 3.173; 7.116; 9.47f,
  51f, 56, 89, 265; 10.46;
  11.150f; 12.38; 16.107–109;
  17.111
Fortitude 3.341; 8.73, 166, 196;
  9.124; 11.109; 12.248;
  13.127
Forty days 3.21f
Forty, The 9.49
Four,
  horses 17.1–9
  living creatures 16.157–161
Fox, symbolism of 4.186
Frankincense 1.32, 391; 2.366;
  17.161f
Freedom 1.65, 97; 2.27, 263;
  3.287, 335; 5.67; 6.21–24;
  8.180, 190–194; 9.14, 55–57,
  73, 78, 93–95, 215; 10.45,
  46; 11.96, 112, 146, 189;
  12.9, 87; 14.207, 349
Free-will 1.14; 2.333; 4.91,
  295; 6.73, 212; 7.105; 8.29f,
  121, 143; 9.193; 11.216;
  15.99
in Judaism 4.250; 7.49
Friendship 1.227, 302; 2.53;
  6.178; 8.168; 11.193
See Guest Friendships

'Friends of the Bridegroom'
   5.143; 9.246
Fruits, spiritual 1.283–285;
   3.271; 6.174; 10.164; 11.107
Fundamentalism 11.136
Funerals, Jewish 4.86f; 6.88f
Futility 14.187

Gabbatha 5.6; 6.245
Gad, tribe of 14.31
Gadara 1.319; 3.124f
Galatae 16.88
Galatia 4.31; 7.5, 138; 10.44;
   12.184; 14.137, 144f, 160, 166
Galatians, *Letter to* 10.3–6
Galbanum 17.161
Galilee 1.39, 71–74, 80, 363f,
   395; 2.12, 95, 98f, 127, 194,
   343; 3.27, 37, 52, 53, 160,
   176, 210; 4.3, 31, 45, 129;
   7.5, 70; 8.173
  revolts in 2.180; 3.229; 4.45,
   172f, 278
  Sea of 1.72, 76f, 308, 316f;
   2.78, 125, 180; 3.115, 118,
   180, 184, 187; 4.56f, 105
Games
  gladiatorial 3.204
  Isthmian 7.134; 9.2, 20, 85;
   11.45
  Marathon, the 12.210
  Olympian 7.134; 9.2, 85;
   11.45; 12.211; 16.83
  Pan-Ionian 7.140; 11.45
  Roman 2.77
  of Smyrna 16.83
  Torch-races 8.202
Gate, Eastern 2.142f
Gaul 2.97; 3.153; 14.144;

   16.89; 17.92
Gaulonites 3.53
Gaza 3.52; 7.68
Ge 3.175
Gehenna 1.47, 139, 140f, 304,
   388; 2.182f; 3.231f; 6.90;
   12.67; 17.12, 47
Gehinnom 2.206; 5.162
Genealogies 1.12; 5.7; 12.6,
   26, 264
General Epistles, The 14.137
Generosity 1.245–248; 8.161;
   12.23, 278f
Geneva Version 1.245
Gennesaret 3.115; 4.56
Gentiles 1.6, 17, 73, 82, 363;
   2.34, 114, 121f, 126f, 131,
   187, 189, 224, 243f, 266, 270;
   3.177; 4.6
  conversion of 1.301–304; 2.71,
   145; 3.283; 6.133, 283;
   7.19, 88, 112–118; 8.53, 121–
   123, 147–150; 10.126; 12.23f;
   14.291f; 15.169; 17.216–218
  and Jews 1.370; 2.80, 290;
   3.178; 4.48, 140; 5.79;
   10.107–110; 15.45; 16.7f
  and Luke's Gospel 4.3
  reception into Church 7.4,
   62f; 14.10
  uncleanness of 2.110, 295;
   3.13f, 69, 143, 166; 6.235
Gentle, gentleness 1.98; 9.238;
   10.51, 137; 11.19, 75, 158;
   12.83, 135, 181, 259; 14.58,
   231
Gerasa 1.320; 3.124; 4.107
Gerasenes 3.184
Gergesa 1.320

Gergesenes **1**.319

Gerizim **2**.359; **5**.116, 157
  temple of **5**.150

Germany **1**.113; **14**.221

Giants, The **3**.175

Gibeonites **13**.90

Gifts (talents) **1**.66f; **2**.67, 91;
  3.219; **4**.97; **8**.91, 159f;
  9.12, 116, 127; **10**.81–83;
  11.127; **12**.60–62, 94f;
  14.255f; **17**.219
  Spiritual **9**.95, 108–112, 117,
  133f, 136; **10**.143–145; **14**.45;
  15.90

Gifts, giving **1**.169–172, 187–
  191, 357, 366; **3**.302f; **4**.178,
  191, 255; **5**.161; **9**.164,
  228–230, 232f, 234–237, 261f;
  14.44f; **15**.151

Gihon **6**.43

Glass **16**.156

Glastonbury Thorn **2**.372, 289f

Glory **5**.68–70; **15**.166
  crown of **16**.83
  'to give glory to' **6**.48

Gluttony **17**.157

Gnat **2**.294

Gnosticism **5**.12f, 18, 40f;
  6.257f; **10**.163; **11**.68f, 97–
  99, 113–120, 130, 134f, 136,
  144–146; **12**.6–8, 27–31, 119,
  192f, 244; **13**.197; **14**.284;
  15.5–12, 66, 76f, 78f, 93, 108,
  163, 171, 180; **17**.106
  dualism of **12**.62
  and matter **5**.12, 40; **6**.259;
  11.97, 114, 144; **12**.6, 27
  scriptures of **12**.199
  and sin **15**.164

  and spirit **11**.97, 114; **12**.30

Goat, sign of **17**.215

God
  access to **10**.117, 127; **13**.1f,
  102
  almighty, the **16**.38, 162;
  17.173
  alpha & omega **17**.204
  arms of **17**.85
  army of **13**.17
  assembly of **12**.88f
  authority of **6**.6
  the beginning **17**.204, 226
  the Blessed One **14**.90
  breath of **7**.20
  calling of **10**.77; **15**.177
  care of **1**.217, 389f; **2**.99, 173;
  4.161; **6**.161
  children of **5**.60–63
  city of **17**.207–216
  comfort of **2**.224; **11**.83
  compassion of **2**.127, 225;
  6.98
  consuming fire **14**.188f;
  17.117
  council of **16**.153
  creator **1**.97; **7**.132; **8**.27;
  11.158; **12**.94; **16**.141, 164;
  17.110
  decree of **17**.97
  the end **17**.204f
  existence of **1**.206–208
  eternity of **14**.38, 163
  family of **3**.112; **8**.107, 124;
  10.117f; **13**.17; **15**.78, 102
  fatherhood of **1**.200, 202–204;
  2.176, 349f; **3**.249, 344; **4**.74,
  143, 222, 226; **5**.51, 73, 138;
  6.27, 64f; **8**.107, 113f, 132f,

164; 10.35, 128–131, 142; 11.162; 12.261; 13.42; 15.73f

fear of 6.212

forbearance of 8.41f

foreknowledge of 14.169

forgiveness of 3.51f; 4.205; 10.54

foundation of 12.176

friend of 6.178

fullness of 10.65; 11.118f, 137

generosity of 1.247; 2.225; 3.282; 10.25, 76, 77

glory of 2.161, 191, 196; 3.238; 5.9, 68–70; 6.39, 100; ·7.164; 8.125; 11.41; 17.35f, 72f, 122f, 169, 202f

grace of 1.198, 287, 300; 2.31, ·268; 5.62; 6.39; 7.114; 8.5, 13, 27, 139; 9.160, 174, 211; 10.30, 94f, 127, 163; 11.17, 19, 53, 63; 12.24; 13.93, 182; 14.177; 15.96, 180, 206

greatness of 17.120

hand of 14.271

holiness of 1.62, 203, 208, 388; 2.6; 3.315; 4.225; 5.112, 214; 8.25; 9.89, 132, 174; 10.130; 13.42; 15.26, 33, 127; 16.152, 156, 162; 17.123

of hope 11.82

house of 16.153

household of 12.88; 13.119

image of 11.116–118

infinite 13.51

initiative of 5.86; 11.214

of Israel 2.126

jealousy of 14.104

joy of 4.202

judge, the 1.137, 146; 2.75, 263, 309, 324–326; 3.250; 4.220, 246; 5.187; 8.33; 9.190, 193; 11.149, 197; 12.121, 179; 13.187; 14.112, 115; 15.176, 185; 17.2, 16, 44, 57, 169, 194

justice of 1.55, 208; 2.6; 3.282, 316; 8.52, 138; 13.93

kindness of 4.201; 8.41f

kingship of 1.202, 388; 2.100, 169; 8.73, 222; 10.108; 12.17; 14.166; 15.24; 17.119

knowledge of 6.208f; 8.114; 10.91; 14.294f; 15.17, 40–43, 54

life-giver 1.256; 2.144; 5.44, 64; 9.140; 15.113

the light 6.13; 15.25f; 16.151

'the living God' 5.43; 17.21f

Lord of hosts 16.39

Lord Sabaoth 16.39

love of 1.208, 214; 2.6, 185f, 278, 367; 3.277, 316; 4.6, 114, 203, 205, 272, 288; 5.73, 137, 214; 6.55, 85, 201; 8.75–77, 112, 115–119, 153–155; 9.12, 147, 160, 190, 193; 10.9, 10, 82, 119, 124, 130, 163; 11.51, 78, 122f, 125, 187, 216; 12.29, 36, 148, 230, 261; 13.13, 58f, 93, 117, 119, 146; 14.216, 253; 15.24f, 97, 203, 207; 17.97, 142, 169

is love 9.34; 10.104; 15.17, 98

of love 11.83

loyalty of 9.199
majesty of 13.186; 16.151;
   17.28
mercy of 1.14, 54f, 56, 309;
   4.90; 6.24, 274; 7.35; 8.41f,
   57, 85, 107, 138, 151–153;
   9.33, 89, 193; 10.22, 43;
   11.56, 142; 12.24f; 13.43;
   14.240, 307; 16.152, 176
names of 1.205f; 5.30, 60f;
   6.210–211; 16.97, 135;
   17.138, 169, 180
nature of 5.161; 13.27;
   15.13, 25
omnipotence of 1.390; 16.162
omniscience of 16.172
oracles of 8.52; 13.188
patience of 2.263, 299; 3.282;
   4.246; 8.41f; 10.51, 139;
   11.83; 14.348
of patriarchs 3.290
of peace 8.219; 11.82f, 13.201
peace of 4.182; 7.72, 206;
   11.77f, 159; 13.35
people of 5.59; 8.133; 12.257;
   14.197, 267f
perfection of 10.28, 104, 136
power of 1.49, 69, 204; 4.44,
   182, 233; 5.37, 180; 6.39;
   7.42; 8.199; 9.200; 10.91f;
   11.78; 16.179; 17.54, 128,
   169
praise of 4.4
presence of 1.208; 3.210;
   5.69f; 9.132f; 10.142; 13.18,
   66, 78, 119; 16.155; 17.215f
promises of 8.68; 9.176f;
   13.154; 17.29, 205f
purposes of 1.14, 16–17; 2.70,

351; 3.11; 5.190, 231; 6.73,
   132, 211f; 7.14, 23, 26f, 104;
   8.12, 112f, 114, 120f, 127,
   129f, 132f, 152; 10.13, 31;
   73f, 77, 79, 86, 126; 11.66,
   191, 213; 12.148, 229–231;
   14.124, 185, 194; 15.177;
   16.167; 17.13, 56, 109, 123,
   147–149
reason of 5.30f
rest of 13.35f
the rock 2.140
saviour 12.18f, 29, 230;
   15.207; 17.169
seed of 15.78f
the seeker 16.147
self-sufficiency of 3.226;
   9.188; 11.85
servant of 3.281; 6.177f;
   11.10
the shepherd 6.53f; 14.215f;
   17.37f
sorrow of 4.91
sovereignty of 8.129–131;
   9.144; 11.213
spirit 5.161
splendour of 15.26
suffering of 9.18
sympathy of 13.42f
terrors of 17.126–128
throne of 1.52; 16.150f
titles of 2.277; 9.188; 11.82
transcendence of 5.29; 13.16;
   16.24, 175; 17.175
treasure of 5.59
triumph of 11.213; 12.183;
   15.59; 17.147, 194
trust of 12.153
trustworthiness of 12.170

true **16**.127

unchangeableness of **14**.54; **16**.30

unity of **8**.60; **10**.142f; **12**.62; **15**.165; **17**.195

vengeance of **17**.165

vision of **1**.105, 184f; **9**.193 256; **14**.179; **15**.75; **17**.222

voice of **3**.20; **6**.126; **13**.188; **16**.44, 50; **17**.104, 126

'seven voices of' **17**.55

will of **1**.211–214; **2**.70, 87, 348, 369; **4**.271f; **5**.165f; **6**.104, 180; **8**.28; **10**.75, 76, 83f; **11**.78, 85, 108, 139; **12**.164; **13**.74; **14**.36, 69, 252; **15**.115

wisdom of **1**.213; **5**.33, 214; **11**.78; **13**.141; **16**.179; **17**.28

work of **5**.9, 183; **11**.41

wrath of **1**.46; **2**.251; **3**.48; **4**.49, 89, 186; **8**.21, 23–27, 41, 69, 153; **9**.193; **10**.101; **11**.60, 152; **16**.152, 157; **17**.3, 53, 111, 117, 122, 123– 128, 134, 182f

God-fearers **2**.290; **7**.69, 79, 106f; **16**.79f

God-haters **8**.36f

Godlessness **12**.189–191

Godliness **11**.168; **12**.61, 97, 134

Gog **17**.133

Gold **1**.32

street of **16**.74

Golden Age **1**.373; **3**.24; **4**.257; **5**.185; **6**.59, 122; **9**.18; **17**.1, 221

Golden calf **7**.60

Golden Rule **1**.273, 275f; **4**.77– 80

Golgotha **2**.366; **3**.366; **4**.3; **5**.6; **6**.251

Goodness **1**.21, 100–102, 124– 126, 180, 181, 399; **2**.43f, 118–120, 297; **3**.25, 169, 213, 243, 245; **4**.160; **6**.62; **8**.15, 29, 42, 65, 164; **10**.9, 51; **11**.19, 157; **12**.35f, 179, 186, 260f; **13**.83, 142; **14**.229; **15**.202f

gospel of **2**.377

haunting **3**.152f; **4**.269; **8**.99, 146; **12**.44

inadequacy of **1**.137; **3**.107; **4**.184, 208

and rabbis **4**.227

triumph of **9**.147

Good Samaritan **4**.5, 138–140; **12**.201

Goodwill **1**.173

Gospel, The **2**.6; **3**.9, 24–26; **5**.137; **7**.23f; **8**.10, 13f, 18ff, 22; **10**.3f, 10; **11**.17, 20, 41, 107, 190; **12**.143, 145–150, 164f; **15**.24f

commands of **16**.120

everlasting **17**.109

and Law **1**.131–133

social gospel **3**.42; **4**.34; **14**.130

truth of **3**.25

universality of **5**.151; **11**.116

word of **15**.24f

Gospels, the

early forms of **1**.1–4; **3**.5; **4**.2f; **12**.219

importance of **12**.200

symbolism of **16.**160f
synoptic **1.**1–4; **2.**299; **3.**1f;
 5.3, 10
Gossip **1.**141; **12.**86f; **14.**111,
 190f
Goths **3.**204
Grace **2.**214; **4.**137; **5.**66, 71f;
 7.56f; **8.**67f, 73; **8.**82f;
 9.121, 259; **10.**9, 21, 36, 57,
 75f, 91, 104f, 163, 185; **11.**12,
 103, 107, 175; **12.**23, 95, 223,
 266; **14.**105, 294; **16.**29;
 17.232
 free grace **8.**88, 180; **9.**39;
  10.10
 gospel of **12.**147
 means of **17.**34
 word of **15.**24
Grace, mealtime **1.**192; **2.**100,
 270; **3.**338; **4.**118, 218
Gratitude **2.**100; **4.**191, 217;
 5.206; **11.**132; **13.**198;
 17.169
Great Harlot, The **17.**143–145
Great-heartedness **9.**40
Greatness **1.**278, 398f; **2.**230,
 232f; **3.**222, 254–257; **4.**127f;
 6.139
Great Road to the East **4.**48
Great Way of the Sea **4.**48
Greece **3.**209; **5.**26; **7.**133, 147;
 16.36
Greed **9.**47f; **12.**237
Greeks **1.**17, 172; **2.**122, 290;
 3.194; **5.**7f; **6.**119f, 252;
 7.11, 52; **8.**15, 17f, 19;
 10.86; **11.**45, 155; **12.**96,
 140; **16.**3
 language **1.**87, 101, 173, 272;

 3.8; **4.**7; **5.**27, 39; **6.**271;
 8.22; **10.**39; **11.**35; **12.**9,
 230f; **14.**28; **15.**34, 50f, 171;
 16.30, 34
 tragedy of **10.**54
Greetings, eastern **1.**369f
Grief **1.**93
Grumbling **9.**89; **15.**197f
Guest Friendships **12.**82; **13.**191;
 15.149
Guidance **1.**213; **7.**19; **9.**28;
 15.26
Guile **3.**174
Guilt **10.**102

Habit **1.**237; **10.**98; **11.**42;
 13.61
Hades **2.**142–144; **6.**35; **14.**236f,
 321; **16.**70, 181; **17.**197
Hallel, the **2.**342; **5.**249; **17.**169
 The Great **2.**342; **3.**338
Hallelujah Chorus **6.**195
Halley's Comet **1.**26
Halo **16.**84
Hammurabi, code of **1.**163
Hand-washing **1.**126; **2.**114,
 362; **3.**164, 337f; **4.**155;
 5.98f; **14.**107
Hanukah, feast of **3.**267; **17.**69
Happiness **1.**89; **4.**103; **10.**166;
 11.72; **12.**129f
Hardening, spiritual **4.**153;
 8.121, 132f, 145f, 152;
 10.152–154
Harlotry, spiritual **17.**142
Harps **16.**174
Harvests **2.**222f; **3.**323; **9.**150
 spiritual **1.**47f, 356f; **2.**62, 71;
 3.94, 108; **4.**100, 132f; **5.**166–

169; 17.114–116
Thanksgiving 5.248; 7.21
Hate, chapel of 10.89f
Hatred 8.35; 12.188; 15.32, 48f
Hauron, Mount 3.115
Head of Days 16.167
Healing 1.325, 345; 4.115f; 6.164; 9.109f; 14.129f
  Jewish 1.129; 2.30; 3.67; 4.60, 177; 6.45
Health 1.236; 2.31; 11.24
Heart 1.242; 2.50f; 3.35, 231; 4.153; 5.250
  new 5.131
Heaven 1.203; 2.277; 3.291; 4.224, 251, 299; 6.152–156; 7.13; 9.177; 11.215; 13.186; 16.71, 150, 154–156; 17.180
  court of 16.149
  Jewish 1.225f; 2.179; 3.20
  in N.T. 13.41
  primaeval war of 17.80
  seventh 6.38
Heavens, the 9.256; 17.15
Hebrew 9.252
  language 1.8–9; 5.27; 11.59
  parallelism 1.211, 267; 3.232; 4.54; 5.128; 7.12
Hebrews, Letter to 13.1–9, 59, 63
Hebron 1.68; 6.53; 7.68
Heifer, red 2.239; 13.103
'Heights' 8.118
Helios 2.369
Hell 1.52, 140f; 3.231f, 315; 6.35, 91; 9.137; 10.167; 14.236, 321
  everlasting 2.182

Hellenists 3.267; 5.7; 7.76; 14.40
Helplessness 1.91
Herbs 2.293, 340; 3.333, 338; 4.147
Heresy 3.314f; 5.11; 9.120; 11.123; 10.48; 12.4f, 26, 31, 92; 13.190; 14.316; 15.92–94; 16.66–68, 117; 17.62
Heretics 12.3, 31f, 178, 195, 265, 310; 15.63, 204
Hermetic mysteries 5.126, 222
Hermits 1.149
Hermon, Mount 1.77; 2.157; 3.115, 210; 7.71
Herodians 2.273; 3.69, 229, 285
Heroism 1.379f
Hierapolis 5.23; 11.91f, 128, 171; 12.274; 14.162; 16.28, 139, 142
High priesthood 1.29; 2.243, 247, 327, 371; 4.32; 7.39; 13.84f, 97–103, 116
  clothing of 2.168; 4.213; 6.254; 13.98f; 17.121, 211, 214
  pronouncements of 6.105
  and Sanhedrin 2.353; 4.276
Hinnom, valley of 2.182f; 3.231
Hippos 3.124
History 1.16, 260; 4.7f; 8.153; 9.88; 14.340f; 15.144
  facts of 4.297; 9.130
  and Jesus 4.137f; 8.222; 12.230; 15.93
  purpose in 2.312f; 3.11, 322; 4.261; 6.155f; 7.23f, 104, 132; 8.222; 10.83–85, 107f; 16.24; 17.13, 56, 143

Hobbies 13.73

Holiness 2.270; 4.44; 8.89;
9.10; 10.154; 11.124; 12.146;
13.181f; 14.188, 189f, 199
beauty of 17.222
spirit of 9.216
way of 6.157

Holy 8.94; 10.77f; 11.10;
12.65; 15.176f

Holy City, The 2.225; 4.180

Holy Grail, The 2.372; 4.290

Holy Land, The 5.59

Holy Spirit, The 1.20–23, 48–50,
201; 2.39, 41–44, 83, 156;
3.6, 17, 140; 4.8, 13, 26, 68,
82, 145, 286; 5.154, 227;
7.5, 66, 141f; 8.101–104, 110;
9.106; 10.23, 141; 13.55f;
14.141, 313; 15.15, 89, 101,
108; 16.43f
Comforter 1.200; 5.5; 6.166f;
7.10
coming of 5.82–85; 7.10, 12,
18f; 9.205; 14.175, 250;
15.70f
and Docetics 5.13
earnest of 9.177
eternal 13.105
filling of 10.166
fruit of 10.49–52
gifts of 6.284; 16.31f, 116
grieving of 10.158; 13.125
and Jesus 3.20f, 79f; 5.5, 52,
53, 250; 6.273f; 7.29, 42;
9.17, 157; 10.145; 11.25;
12.90; 15.108f
Jewish doctrine of 1.48f;
4.161; 5.83f; 6.30; 13 166
liberty of 9.194

personal 5.252
power of 12.262f
and prayer 8.111; 15.203
revealer 9.27f
and Scripture 5.22f, 24, 185;
14.180, 313f
sealing of 10.87; 17.23
sevenfold 16.31f, 116, 155
sin against 2.41–45; 3.80f;
4.161; 16.12
symbolism of 16.160
teacher 6.170
temple of 8.156f; 9.33f, 56;
12.96
of Truth 4.161; 5.24, 53, 67;
6.18, 194–196
and unity 11.33f
of wisdom 10.90
witness of 6.188; 8.107
work of 6.192–194; 7.19f,
142; 9.189f; 10.35; 14.169,
171; 16.22; 17.222
and worship 11.56

Home-life 1.112; 5.100f; 9.70;
11.199; 12.250

Honesty 1.119; 14.202

Homosexuality 8.32; 9.53;
12.38, 97; 15.42, 185; 17.140

Honey 3.16; 9.80

Hope 2.63; 3.108, 136; 4.27f,
57, 190, 287; 8.108–111, 166,
196, 198f; 9.124, 169; 10.91,
110; 11.25f, 83, 106, 125,
186f; 12.19–21, 154, 263;
13.61–63, 127, 128–131, 149f;
14.172, 183; 17.26
and character 8.74f
and faith 2.124; 8.21
gospel of 3.25

and love 9.124
oneness of 10.141
and religion 5.160
Horeb, Mount 2.159
Horns 16.171; 17.60, 94, 138
Horses 2.243; 3.264; 4.240
 white 5.178; 17.167, 179
Hosea, *Book of* 13.13
Hospitality 1.261, 397f; 3.143,
 326; 4.145, 265; 8.220; 9.15;
 12.81f; 13.161; 14.254
 duty of 7.123; 8.167; 12.238;
 13.190f; 15.148–150
 laws of 1.371; 4.94; 5.97, 101
 See Guest Friendships
'Hospitals', ancient 16.89
Houses 1.122, 239f; 2.46f;
 3.44, 47, 331; 4.62, 145f, 202,
 264f; 7.81, 149; 14.89
Households 1.383; 8.213
Humble, The 1.91
Humility 1.97, 297; 2.173, 175f,
 283f, 297; 3.219, 242; 4.136,
 185, 189; 6.110; 8.17, 164;
 10.135–137; 11.158; 14.35,
 105f, 109f, 228, 270f
Hunger 1.99, 355; 5.212
Husbands 10.173f; 14.222–224
Hybca 14.221
Hymns, early 10.164; 12.89–91,
 169f
Hymns of the faith 1.274
Hypocrisy 1.197; 2.46; 3.168;
 4.160; 12.85f; 14.190
Hypocrites 1.158, 188; 2.288
Hyssop 3.337; 6.259

Iconium 7.97, 107f, 119;
 12.232

Idealism 10.98, 103; 12.180;
 17.200
 platonic 13.88; 16.55
Idleness 2.51f; 12.113f
Idolatry 1.397; 3.238; 4.211;
 5.161; 7.116; 8.28; 9.47f,
 52, 71–76, 89, 92; 10.47;
 11.152; 15.123f; 16.106f;
 17.25, 44, 53
Idumaea 2.194; 3.70; 12.156
Ignorance 3.57; 8.142; 14.186f
 wilful 5.48, 194; 9.136
Illumination 1.50
Illyricum 7.148
Imitation, spiritual 10.160f;
 15.35
Immorality 1.324; 8.178; 9.47;
 11.182, 199; 12.5; 13.182;
 14.319; 15.180
Immortality 3.25, 289; 4.287;
 7.9f; 9.125; 12.148, 175;
 13.55
 conditional 1.387
Impatience 2.3; 8.180; 11.180
Impiety 12.37
Impurity 10.47; 11.188; 12.245;
 14.43
Inaction 2.13; 4.214
Incendiarism 1.113, 376; 16.81
Indecency 2.198; 3.239; 4.211f
Incense 4.10; 16.174; 17.40,
 99, 161f, 211
Incest 9.42, 43–46; 12.54
Independence 3.330; 9.235;
 11.84
India 14.221; 17.161
Indian's Tomb, The 9.119
Indifference 2.12; 5.232, 235;
 6.254; 16.142

Indiscipline 12.37

Individualism 2.174; 9.139

Indulgences 3.99

Infidelity, spiritual 1.386; 2.49; 16.108

Infirmity 9.198

Influence 13.182

Ingathering, festival of 5.248

Ingratitude 2.108, 237; 4.218; 12.188; 17.28

Innocence 10.97, 102; 11.43f; 12.20, 245; 15.53

Inns, ancient 4.21; 12.82, 110, 238; 14.254; 15.149

Insanity 2.199; 4.107

Insecurity 12.20

Insincerity 4.160

Insolence 8.37; 9.265f

Inspiration 6.195; 14.180
  biblical 4.8

Instincts 15.188f

Insults 1.118, 139–141, 166f, 179; 2.122; 9.251; 10.159; 12.187

Intellectualism 11.23f; 12.4f, 127

Intemperance 12.80

Intercession 15.116f

Inter-testamental literature 14.30f

Intolerance 3.226; 5.193; 11.191

Invalids 1.351

Iron 17.161

Irony 14.29

Irreverence 12.37

Irritability 4.188; 10.155

Isauria 14.144

Ishmaelites 11.57

Islam 9.118

Isles of the Sea 4.48

Israel 1.13, 176; 2.142; 3.214; 8.124–126; 11.58, 119; 15.181f
  bride of God 2.49; 5.143; 6.28; 9.246; 14.101f; 16.108; 17.76, 172
  new 14.21, 41, 166, 286; 17.24
  of God 14.41, 166
  son of God 3.71; 8.124
  ten tribes of 3.193
  true 3.178; 8.122
  vine of God 6.172

Israelites 9.252; 11.58

Issacher, tribe of 14.31

Italy 13.6; 14.145

Ituraea 2.95; 4.3, 31

Ivory 9.2; 17.161

Jacinth 17.214

Jacob's Well 5.147

James, Letter of 14.1–33

Jamnites 12.157

Japan, church of 16.147

Jaspar 16.151f; 17.159, 213, 215

Jealousy 1.244; 2.93; 3.328; 5.193; 8.35; 10.47

Jehoshaphat, valley of 17.116

Jeremiah, book of 3.134

Jericho 1.29; 2.219; 3.259f; 4.138f, 234, 239; 5.250; 13.160f

Jerusalem 1.15, 29, 37, 45, 58, 63, 69, 122; 2.346, 348, 358; 3.27, 175, 197, 231, 343; 4.4, 8, 129, 138f, 172f, 239, 271, 296; 5.6, 120, 178; 6.43, 221, 239; 7.12, 119, 138;

14.40; **17**.116, 142

church of **3**.4; **7**.5, 6, 95, 101;
   7.145; **8**.2; **9**.228, 236

conquests of **2**.281; **3**.193

council of **2**.145; **7**.19, 112–
   118; **14**.10, 23, 264, 292;
   15.169; **16**.67

fall of **1**.383; **2**.28, 267, 300,
   302, 305–308; **3**.68, 306, 309–
   311, 321; **4**.173, 241, 258;
   13.167; **14**.38

gate of **4**.229

mountains of **2**.182

new **3**.197; **13**.145, 186; **16**.8f,
   98, 128, 135, 176; **17**.199–
   202, 212

at Passover **2**.238; **3**.324

and the prophets **2**.299

Jeshimmon **1**.63; **3**.16; **4**.43

Jesse, stump of **1**.40

Jews

defined **7**.51; **8**.47, 66, 127

dispersion of **1**.383

and Gentile **1**.17; **4**.133; **5**.55;
   7.52f, 80, 82, 107; **8**.41, 137;
   9.49; **10**.4f, 18, 85f, 92;
   11.54; **12**.32; **14**.26, 62

and Gnosticism **10**.99

history of **2**.134

ingathering of **16**.8; **17**.18f

pride of **11**.155

problem of **8**.5, 6, 119–123

rebelliousness of **8**.173

religious genius of **10**.86

sins of **11**.191f

Jezreel, plain of **4**.47

Job, *book of* **1**.181; **3**.134

John, *Letters of* **5**.23f; **14**.137;
   15.3–20, 123, 127–136; **16**.165

John, *gospel of*

authorship **5**.15–24, 53

and crucifixion **6**.292f

discourses of **5**.164f, 185;
   6.16, 86

and Ephesus **5**.6

and Gnosticism **12**.27

introduction **5**.1–24, 42, 51,
   66, 76, 107, 185; **16**.165

and Jews **5**.76

judgement in **5**.43, 138–140;
   6.193f

and life **5**.42–46

and light **5**.42, 45f, 48, 54

and love **6**.85, 169, 177; **15**.44

and miracles **6**.39

oral preaching **5**.3

order of **5**.176; **6**.108

paradoxes of **5**.138

prologue of **5**.1–75

and resurrection **5**.43

size of **16**.165

symbolism **4**.2; **5**.1; **16**.160f

and truth **5**.1, 9, 53f, 66–68

'witness' in **5**.19, 51–53, 76

words of Jesus **5**.133, 185

and the world **6**.18

Jordan, river **1**.58, 69, 82, 308;
   2.11, 134; **3**.52, 192; **5**.201

and Jewish hopes **3**.185

Jordan valley **1**.76, 316; **2**.157

Jotapata **3**.134

Joy **1**.89f, 95, 116, 337; **2**.267,
   376; **3**.60; **4**.66, 103, 230;
   6.177, 198, 214, 220; **7**.65;
   8.192; **10**.50; **11**.13f, 50–52,
   71, 75, 109f, 189, 195; **12**.163;
   14.48f, 174; **15**.13, 21; **16**.10

The Epistle of **11**.8

---

and wine 5.97
Judaea 1.39, 73; 2.95, 194;
    3.16, 52f; 4.31; 6.53
  church of 7.5
  and Pilate 2.358f; 4.3
  and Syria 4.20
Judah
  and Benjamin 11.58
  Lion of 2.234; 5.1
  tribe of 2.49; 17.25
Judaism 6.157; 8.48f, 50, 136f;
    12.7, 244; 14.146, 156f
Judaizers 10.4, 16; 14.26
Jude, *Letter of* 15.157-73
Judgement, The 1.7, 137, 287;
    2.74f, 155; 3.108, 304; 4.26,
    89, 108, 169; 7.132; 8.187;
    11.24, 213; 13.55, 110;
    14.71, 345; 16.7, 22, 132;
    17.66, 114-116, 168, 192f
  Books of 17.196
  certainty of 2.309; 6.85; 8.21,
    29, 42; 9.12, 132, 206;
    13.125f; 17.123
  final 9.37; 14.175; 16.85;
    17.194-197
  a fire 4.169
  of love 15.175
  and Messiah 1.322; 6.135
  seat of 8.188
  second chance 4.174f, 287;
    6.7
  standards of 3.250; 4.175;
    8.45f
  threefold 9.35-38
Judgement Court, The 1.138
Judgement of others 1.246, 261-
    265, 334; 2.74f, 188; 9.48;
    14.110-112

Jupiter 1.26
Jupiter Capitolinus 2.170, 273
Justice 1.131, 158, 164; 2.83;
    8.22, 34; 11.79f; 12.117, 239,
    257; 14.116-118; 17.178
  'at the gate' 2.143
  Greek 8.94f; 9.206, 238;
    11.75f
  Roman 4.246, 280; 7.172;
    8.188
  social 4.242
Justification 8.22f, 57, 72; 17.31
  by faith 8.58
  and James 14.7
  and sanctification 8.77
Just One, The 7.161

Kanatha 3.124
Katakekaumene, plain of 16.125
Kavella 7.122
Keys 2.144-146; 16.48
Khan Minyeh 1.74
Kidneys 5.250; 16.110
Kidron,
  brook of 5.6; 6.221
  valley of 1.68; 4.44; 6.43
Kindness 1.103, 241; 3.113, 228;
    4.142; 8.42, 170; 9.120, 165,
    216; 10.51, 159f; 11.157;
    12.259
Kingdom of God 1.8, 67, 92,
    162, 210-214, 258, 304, 360;
    2.8, 39, 41, 74, 78f, 81f, 83,
    156, 207, 223-226, 266, 289,
    342f; 3.106f, 177, 232, 242,
    246, 248, 255; 4.5, 54, 103,
    122, 135, 148, 165, 179, 184,
    227; 6.64; 7.111, 127, 134;
    9.159f, 217; 11.15, 112;

12.36, 198; **14**.347; **15**.56;
16.40, 94, 123, 129; **17**.187,
196
and children 2.174–178
citizens of 2.289; **11**.29f
consummation of 1.212
entry into 2.84; **4**.229
feast of 4.195
imminence of 1.364, 381f;
2.137, 155f, 315; **3**.208
and Jewish hope 3.17, 188
and love 4.193
mystery of 3.91f
proclamation of 1.370; **7**.5,11
and repentance 1.352
signs of 4.220
sons of 1.304
stewards of 2.145
word of 15.24
yoke of 2.17
Kingdom of heaven 1.92; **2**.7f,
76, 87ff, 139–146, 169, 173,
217–219; **3**.111, 241; **4**.179,
181f, 228; **5**.127; **8**.192
Kingdom of priests 16.35, 178
King's College 12.176
King's Highway 1.45
Kingship 3.71; **4**.267; **11**.58;
15.69
spiritual 3.82f
Knowledge 1.291; **3**.104f;
8.100; **9**.109, 215; **10**.35, 82;
11.63, 99, 130; **14**.302; **15**.10
gift of 9.118
and Greeks 5.55; **8**.159; **9**.37
growth in 13.50
O.T. 8.114
responsibility of 6.186
self-knowledge 8.159; **9**.132

sexual 6.209; **15**.185
way of 5.197; **11**.18
Kranion 4.3
Krenides 11.3

Lake of Fire 17.47
Lambeth Conference 1.392
Lamentations, *Book of* 3.135
Lamps 1.85; **4**.167
Lamp of Israel 1.122
Lampstand 1.122; **2**.244
Landlords 4.208
Language, eastern 4.216; **11**.155
Laodicaea 3.320; **11**.91, 93;
12.184; **16**.28, 47, 137–139
Church of 2.218; **10**.68f;
11.127f, 171; **12**.273
and Jews 16.139
Letter to 16.136–148
Lost letter to 10.172–174;
12.273, 274
Last days, The 3.306; **14**.174;
15.59f; **16**.7, 22; **17**.5, 17
Last hour, The 15.59f
Last Supper, The 1.113; **2**.128,
338–343, 348, 372; **3**.347;
4.264–267; **5**.1, 19, 48, 204;
6.272, 292; **7**.95; **10**.84
Last Things, The 1.8; **8**.151;
14.250; **16**.167; **17**.13, 29, 55
as Terror 17.15–17
Last Trumpet, The 10.165
Laughter 4.66, 195
Lausanne 2.359
Law, and Greeks 1.144; **12**.35
Law, Jewish 1.6, 47, 52, 80, 126–
131, 134, 166, 208, 268, 284,
337, 356; **2**.8f; **3**.31, 163,
293, 4.59–61; **5**.120f, 197;

8.126; 13.66; 14.69
books of 1.347
burden of 2.17; 10.6
ceremonial 1.286; 2.290;
4.250
of freedom 14.7
function of 10.29
and Gospel 1.131–133
homes of 1.242
inadequacy of 1.366–368;
10.20f, 26; 11.61–63
and the Kingdom 3.17
oral 1.127, 129; 2.114, 128;
3.32, 164, 289; 4.250; 8.44–
46
personified 1.52
and religion 10.36
royal 14.68
scribal 1.127; 2.128; 3.57
simplicity of 2.117
son of 4.29; 10.33f
study of 5.124
tables of 13.96
use of 8.57
and wisdom 5.154
written 2.114
yoke of 2.17
Law, moral 1.201, 208; 10.55
Law, Roman 2.74, 372
Lawlessness 1.221; 8.90; 12.37
Lawless One, The 11.212
Laying-on of hands 7.66f;
12.117f; 13.54f
Lazar-houses 3.45
Learning 1.97; 3.114; 4.29;
13.48
discipline of 17.224
Leaven 1.7; 2.79, 130–132, 339;
3.187f, 225, 332; 4.50, 180–

182, 262; 9.45; 10.44
Lechaeum 7.133; 9.2
Legalism 1.128, 311f; 2.132,
189, 209f; 3.32, 168; 4.157,
159, 178; 5.121; 8.64; 9.160;
10.24, 37, 42; 11.96, 189;
12.6, 7
and Jesus 8.138, 140f; 10.26,
115
Legalists 2.282, 292; 8.180;
9.15
Leontopolis 14.39
Leopard, symbolism of 17.88, 93
Lepers 1.293, 296, 365; 3.238
cleansing of 1.299f; 14.170
Leprosy 1.295–299; 3.35, 43–46;
4.217f
Lesbos 7.150
Letters, ancient 8.x–xi; 10.62;
11.12
of commendation 8.207;
9.185
of credit 16.138
Leviathan 1.216, 303; 4.192;
17.58, 77
Levi, tribe of 14.31
Levites 1.26; 2.293; 4.155, 224;
5.76f; 6.36; 9.80; 13.8, 76;
17.34
Libations 1.111f; 11.46
Liberality 1.245
Liberation 8.59; 10.81f
Liberty 1.117, 168; 7.105;
8.179, 192f; 9.76, 134, 214;
11.68f, 189; 12.192; 13.196;
14.207; 16.68
of conscience 3.287
law of 14.60, 70
of speech 3.227; 11.26;

15.114
of truth 14.133
and vigilance 12.51
Licentiousness 10.47
Life 1.22, 160, 182; 2.91;
 3.314; 5.216–218; 14.87f
 Book of 16.123; 17.95, 147,
 186, 196
 crown of 1.183; 16.83f
 development of 9.157
 fountain of 17.220f
 from God 1.49
 laws of 2.66f
 natural 8.24–40, 104, 178f
 necessities of 9.213
 storms of 1.318f; 2.105f
 symbolism of 6.89
 tree of 16.69; 17.221f
 uncertainty of 14.113
 value of 1.396f; 2.152–154
 word of 15.25
Life after death 2.275; 6.91f
Life to come 1.47; 3.288, 290;
 6.95; 9.155; 11.64; 15.99f
Light, The 1.122–125, 243; 2.7;
 3.97; 11.112; 15.28–30;
 17.209
Lilies 4.165
Lion, symbolism of 5.1; 16.159;
 17.88, 215
Litany, river 1.71
Liturgies, Greek 8.202f
Locusts 3.16; 17.48–52
 plague of 17.125
Loneliness 1.117, 350, 355;
 3.251f; 6.190; 8.119
Lord's Day 1.286; 7.27; 8.184;
 16.42f
Lord's Prayer 1.92, 102, 198–

232; 2.86; 3.232; 4.54f, 143f;
 5.127f; 7.11; 8.16, 175;
 9.182, 196; 17.82
Lord's Supper 1.215, 266f;
 2.66; 5.225; 6.262; 7.149;
 9.95; 14.148; 15.109; 16.95
 in *Didache* 7.91
 institution of 9.103–105
 name of 9.102
 symbols of 9.104f
Lord's Table 1.215, 266; 2.103,
 291; 9.73, 105; 11.156;
 14.280; 15.109
 fencing of 1.266; 10.118
Lost, The 4.235
Lots, casting of 7.17
Louisiana 3.13
Love 1.124f, 172–178, 182, 224,
 302, 354, 400; 2.4, 123, 330;
 3.292–296, 327; 4.124, 189;
 8.190, 218; 10.49f, 88, 139f;
 11.129f, 159, 186; 12.98, 134,
 180; 13.190; 14.172f, 188,
 209, 227, 252f; 15.82, 92,
 97f; 16.64
 brotherly 8.164; 14.304f
 claims of 4.217
 debt of 8.176
 extravagance of 2.329
 & family 12.188
 Hymn of 9.95, 116–126
 immortal 3.292
 in Judaism 1.388
 kiss of 14.279–281
 and Law 1.131; 9.238f
 law of 14.60
 motivation of 1.132f; 8.163;
 9.76, 166; 14.102f
 and obedience 2.53

and tolerance 4.130f; 5.18;
  9.116; 12.33
triumph of 9.147
Love Feasts 1.113, 166, 376;
  6.184; 7.149; 9.95, 99f;
  10.18; 11.189; 14.148, 203;
  15.192f, 194; 16.80
Loving-kindness 1.171; 12.24
Loyalty 1.111, 392, 395; 2.310;
  3.235; 4.103, 121, 162; 6.50;
  7.41; 8.21; 10.51, 88; 11.46,
  131; 12.99, 134, 154, 160;
  13.127, 151, 189; 14.35;
  16.82, 131; 17.97, 98, 102,
  173, 205
  conflict of 3.287f
Lucerne 2.359
Luck 9.47
Luke, *Gospel of*
  introduction to 3.2; 4.1–6,
  120; 5.22; 7.161; 16.165
  symbol of 5.1; 16.160f
  universalism of 4.179
Luna 14.147
Lust 1.147; 2.119; 8.34;
  12.180; 14.51
Luxury, ancient 9.2; 14.119,
  221f
Lycaonia 9.2; 11.92; 14.144
Lycia 14.145; 16.28
Lycus Valley 11.91, 128; 16.137
Lydda 7.77
Lydia 11.93; 16.125
  and Jews 14.40
  King of 16.113
Lying 1.158; 12.39
Lyons, Bishop of 5.20
Lystra 7.97, 109, 110, 119;
  11.47; 12.21; 17.110

Maccabees 3.124, 172; 4.248;
  5.150; 7.94; 12.149; 13.174;
  16.171; 17.11, 26, 60
  coins of 6.172
  wars of 2.136f; 3.68; 5.82;
  13.164, 166
Mace 17.162
Macedonia 4.4; 7.138, 147;
  11.179
  Empire of 5.186
  'Man of' 7.121f
Machaerus 1.71; 2.1, 38, 93;
  3.149; 4.36, 89
Maeander, river 7.150
  valley 12.184
Maecenas 12.166
Magi 1.25–27
Magic 2.37f; 3.37; 7.66
Magistrates, Roman 4.222;
  8.106
Magnesia 16.28
Magnificat, The 4.4, 15f
Magog 17.133
Magus 1.26
Makaria 7.99
Malaria 1.308
Malea, Cape of 9.1
Malice 11.153
Malignity 8.36
Malta 7.187f
  fever of 1.307f
Mammon 12.138
Man 1.13–14, 21, 97, 100f, 136,
  178, 378; 2.40, 278; 3.25,
  108; 8.33, 55, 99, 110, 185f;
  9.29f, 47; 13.39f
  brotherhood of 1.202; 11.71;
  12.63
  glory of 1.225; 13.23

Greek belief **12**.175; **14**.93; **15**.201

Heavenly Man **6**.244

image of God **3**.287; **15**.75

Jewish belief **8**.98f; **14**.50

needs of **5**.71

perversity of **2**.9; **3**.152f

soul of **1**.217; **3**.42; **6**.38; **9**.28, 55, 120, 137–140, 201; **13**.39; **14**.93; **15**.11, 201

spirit of **5**.161; **6**.99; **9**.55; **11**.163; **13**.39, 129; **15**.11, 201

supremacy of **9**.28; **16**.159

symbolism of **5**.1

true **3**.139; **13**.84

will of **3**.140; **10**.98, 103f, 131

Manger **4**.21

Man of God **12**.134

Man of Lawlessness **3**.310

Man of Sin **11**.212; **15**.63; **17**.61

Manna **1**.67, 218; **4**.144; **5**.215f; **9**.88, 230; **13**.96

hidden **16**.94

Manuscripts, uncial **2**.27

Marazion **2**.373

Marble **17**.161

Mark, *Gospel of*

Earliest Gospel, **3**.1; **9**.115

Introduction to **3**.1–9, 192, 251, 253, 328, 345; **5**.1; **16**.165

and Peter **2**.345; **3**.4–5, 7–9, 136, 157, 353; **5**.10; **6**.101; **11**.170; **14**.278, 308f

realism of **3**.6; **5**.22

and Rome **3**.361; **4**.283; **8**.215

symbol of **4**.2; **5**.1; **16**.161

Market days **1**.235; **4**.223

Market-place **2**.223

Markings **17**.102–104

Marriage, Christian **1**.157, 377; **2**.203, 206, 209f; **10**.168, 174f; **11**.162f

desertion in **2**.199

fidelity **1**.155; **4**.211; **8**.178; **10**.171

infidelity **3**.240

and Jesus **1**.150; **2**.201f; **17**.106

love **10**.173f

mixed **9**.63, 71

and Paul **9**.57–64, 69–71; **10**.171–173

re-marriage **9**.71

symbolism of **17**.172f

Marriage, Greek **1**.153; **3**.289; **10**.174

Marriage, Jewish **1**.18–19, 150–152, 320; **2**.196f, 202f; **3**.237f, 240; **4**.211; **11**.198f

a civic duty **2**.196; **9**.60f

dowry **12**.77

inter-marriage **5**.149

levirate **2**.276f; **3**.289; **4**.41, 249

made in heaven **12**.76f

mixed **12**.237

Marriage, Roman **1**.156f, 377

Mars Hill **7**.131; **9**.23

Martyrs **1**.116, 378f; **2**.230; **7**.13; **11**.66; **12**.169; **16**.70; **17**.10–13, 25–27, 118, 171, 192f

Materialism **2**.132, 154; **4**.116; **9**.28, 47

Matthew, *Gospel of*

date of **1**.382; **2**.68, 153, 170,

214, 229, 267, 273
introduction to 1.1–9, 324;
  2.207; 3.2, 55; 5.3, 22
Jewishness of 1.127
symbolism of 4.2; 5.1;
  16.160f
use of O.T. 1.36, 39, 40, 75;
  2.337; 4.3, 137
Meanness 9.182; 14.265f
Mecca 3.274
Medes 1.25; 6.121
Media 5.156; 17.88
  Empire of 5.186
Mediators 10.30; 12.62f
Medicine 1.26
Mediterranean Sea 1.7; 4.48
Meekness 1.96; 10.137
Megiddo 17.132f
Melancholy 9.219
Mercenaries 14.39
Mercy 1.103–105, 131, 163, 165;
  2.295; 8.162f; 11.157; 12.23–
  25; 14.70f, 198
  personified 14.28
  and wisdom 14.96
Merit
  doctrine of 1.187; 8.67
  treasure of 1.47
Meshech 17.194
Mesopotamia 11.93; 14.38
Messiah 1.5, 44, 58, 60, 67;
  2.33, 147, 241f, 279; 3.72;
  5.26; 7.23; 17.228
  age of 14.140; 17.187f, 199
  banquet of 1.67, 216, 303f;
  4.192; 17.174f
  community of 16.129
  false 1.69; 2.33; 3.185;
  5.115; 9.18

forerunner 2.136f, 159
Jewish doctrine of 1.267, 216,
  303f, 322, 349; 2.6, 48, 129,
  164f, 235, 279f, 303; 3.24,
  147, 188, 193–199, 210, 222,
  265–268, 297–299, 310;
  4.18f, 26, 38, 54, 169f, 250;
  5.7, 52, 77, 108, 114f, 155,
  206f, 215, 243; 6.117f, 197,
  210; 10.86; 14.178, 347;
  16.2f, 6–11, 33, 69, 94, 110,
  169; 17.13, 177f, 181, 206
  as judge 9.50
  kingdom of 16.9
  and living water 5.251
  mother of 17.75f
  names of 1.52; 3.267, 297
  at Passover 2.136; 3.338
  as Shepherd 17.38
  suffering 2.148; 7.27, 37, 129;
  9.17f; 17.188
  titles of 2.2; 3.196, 261; 298,
  6.13; 11.119
  travail of 3.194f; 16.6; 17.75
Methodists 4.56, 130
Middle age 12.214
Midianites 9.88
'Mights' 8.117; 10.92
Miletus 7.138, 150; 16.28
Military Service 4.20
Millenarianism 17.184, 189–191
Millenium 17.73, 186, 188–191
Millstones 2.179; 3.229
Mind, the 3.124; 11.79–81;
  14.84
  adventurous 1.337–340; 3.61,
  67f; 4.270
  and the body 3.48
  and prayer 9.129

questioning 2.102; 4.124;
10.90; 16.117

shut 1.361; 2.59f, 323; 4.68,
100; 5.131, 192, 198; 6.21,
170, 245; 12.101; 13.49

and truth 1.338–340

and universe 1.207

Ministry, Christian 1.121; 4.115;
9.84; 10.90; 12.100f, 128, 217

in Early Church 9.134;
10.146f; 11.171; 15.132–
136; 16.12

Mint 2.293

Miracles 1.289, 300, 304–307,
350; 2.171, 237; 3.218;
4.57; 5.119; 6.100, 101;
7.32f, 193; 9.109f

Mirrors 9.125; 13.95; 14.59;
17.140, 159

Misenum 7.190

Missionary task 1.356f; 2.291;
6.67; 11.44; 16.129

Mites 3.302; 4.171

Mithradates 14.144

Mithraism 5.222; 17.33

Mitylene 7.150

Moab 2.159

Moabites 9.88

Mohammedans 1.194, 196, 233;
3.168, 291; 9.118

Molech 1.58, 141; 2.183; 3.231;
7.60

Monarchy 10.45

Money 1.252; 2.84; 4.164f

love of 3.328; 12.131–133,
184

money-changers 2.244f;
4.241; 5.109f

Monks 1.149

Monotheism 3.295; 6.161

Months, Jewish 2.169; 6.69;
10.36

Morality

of world 8.26f; 11.152;
13.108; 17.86

pollution 12.37f; 14.173

sexual 3.240; 15.199f

Moravian Church 14.131

Moriah, Mount 3.308

Morning Star, The 16.110f

Mote 1.85

Motherhood 12.68f

Motives 1.185, 342; 2.173;
9.37, 174f, 209; 12.120, 252f

Mourning 1.93, 233, 343f; 3.132–
135; 4.86f; 6.88f

spiritual 14.108f

Murder 1.135f, 379; 3.173, 238;
7.166; 8.35, 176; 12.38

and the Jews 2.297f; 4.211

Muslims See Mohammedans

Mustard 2.75f; 3.109f; 4.178f

Myra 7.181

Myrrh 1.32; 17.161f

Mysia 7.19; 16.28

Mystery 2.64, 66; 3.91; 5.226;
9.26, 94, 125, 170; 10.83;
16.53; 17.109, 143f

'Secret' 11.126, 130

Mystery Religions 2.65f; 3.91;
5.126f, 222; 8.84f; 10.113;
12.67f, 262; 14.25, 295f, 310f;
15.42, 70; 17.33

Mysticism 6.175; 9.256

Nablus 5.147

Nain 4.86

Names 6.5, 210; 13.60; 15.87

---

1 Matt, v.1   3 Mark   5 John, v.1   7 Acts   9 Cor
2 Matt, v.2   4 Luke   6 John, v.2   8 Rom   10 Gal, Eph

Jewish **1**.205; **2**.177; **3**.225; **4**.17, 24, 143; **5**.62f, 90; **6**.87; **7**.100; **11**.38; **15**.53; 16.98f
New ones **16**.95, 176
Roman **8**.212
Naphtali, tribe of **1**.73; **14**.31
Nationalism, Jewish **1**.330, 359; **2**.332; **3**.356
Nature **1**.260; **7**.109; **8**.27, 45, 108f; **10**.66f; **14**.87f; **16**.159, 162f, 173, 181; **17**.19, 43f, 46, 86, 170f
Nazarenes **1**.40; **7**.169; **14**.316
Nazareth **1**.38–42, 73; **2**.17, 78f, 91f; **3**.18f, 128, 138–140, 177; **4**.21, 46f; **5**.92
Nazirites **7**.138, 155; **12**.119; **14**.10
Neapolis **7**.119, 122
Nebo **2**.136, 159
Needle's Eye, The **2**.217; **4**.229
Nehardea **14**.37
Neighbour **4**.140
Nemesis **10**.54, 82
Neocaesarea **16**.126, 135
Neroneas See Caesarea Philippi
Neutrality **2**.39–41
New Age, The **13**.189; **15**.16; 16.69
New Birth **4**.130; **5**.124–132; **9**.145; **12**.262; **14**.21, 54, 171–173; **15**.78f, 102f
  of baptism **14**.192
  Greek **5**.126; **8**.85
  Jewish **5**.126
New heavens and earth **8**.108f; **16**.98, 176; **17**.168, 197f
New song, the **16**.98, 175f

New Temple **5**.114; **17**.212
New Things **16**.176; **17**.204f
New World **3**.304; **5**.154; **17**.195
New Year, Jewish **13**.98
Nicaea **16**.17
Nicanor **2**.136
Nicanor's Gate **2**.244
Nicolaitans **16**.66–68, 92f
Nicopolis **12**.9, 265
Nile, river **2**.65; **17**.128, 198
Nineveh **2**.129; **17**.142, 150, 167, 211
Nirvana **9**.204
Nisan **2**.340; **4**.262
Nisibis **14**.37
North Africa **17**.160, 162
Novelty **11**.52; **12**.31, 180
Nunc Dimittis **4**.4, 26

Oaths **1**.158–162; **2**.116; **3**.170; **14**.126f
  binding **2**.292
Obedience **1**.21, 92, 183, 209, 212, 289f, 292; **2**.53, 153, 259; **3**.233f, 242; **4**.150, 226; **5**.128, 217; **6**.21, 169, 211; **7**.48, 71; **8**.93, 171–174; **9**.194; **12**.159f, 255; **13**.33f, 114f, 199; **14**.35, 100, 169f, 188, 199, 293, 347; **15**.17f, 29, 35, 59, 77, 103f
Offerings **2**.245; **9**.80f; **13**.116; **14**.233; **15**.37
  of the poor **4**.24
Oil **3**.146; **15**.70; **17**.6f
Oligarchy **10**.45
Olive tree **8**.147–151; **9**.80
Olives, Mount of **2**.342, 348; **3**.274, 339, 343; **4**.241, 271;

11 Phil, Col, Thes
12 Tim, Tit, Phlm
13 Heb
14 Jas, Pet
15 John, Jude
16 Rev, v.1
17 Rev, v.2

5.14; 6.221
Olympus 17.133
Onycha 17.161
Opal 17.159
Ophites 15.164
Optimism 2.230; 3.304; 6.32
Opportunity 2.330; 6.40, 87;
    8.165; 11.24; 13.50; 16.149
Order 1.207; 5.57
Orontes 7.89, 97
Orphic religion 14.25, 87f;
    16.29f
Orthodoxy 3.316; 4.140; 11.105,
    113; 12.4, 31; 14.349;
    16.62-64, 117
  frozen 11.132
  Jewish 3.48; 4.140
Ostia 17.164
Ovens 1.121, 257; 4.165
Overseers See elders
Ox, symbolism of 5.1; 16.159

Pacifism 1.175
Pain 1.201, 354f; 2.39
Palaia Kaumene 17.45
Palestine 1.72, 298f, 307f; 3.37,
    46, 52, 53, 124, 208; 5.59,
    146f; 6.237f; 7.11, 15;
    17.5, 116
Palm, sign of 17.26f
Pamphylia 3.3; 7.97
Pan 2.134; 3.192
Panias 2.134; 3.192
Panium 2.134f
Pantheism 15.161
Papacy 2.139; 15.63; 17.100
Paphos 7.97, 100
Papyrus 1.330; 7.86; 8.x; 9.223;
    11.142; 15.127; 16.165f

Parables
  defined 2.54-56, 261; 3.85,
    90, 281; 4.146
  of dragnet 2.78; 12.179
  of the friend 4.4, 222
  of great feast 1.333
  of hidden treasure 2.79, 83-86
  of the Kingdom 2.79
  of last judgment 1.179f
  of the leaven 2.79
  of the lost sheep 4.200
  of the mustard seed 2.78
  of the pounds 4.172
  of the prodigal son 3.14; 4.5;
    16.116
  of the rich man 4.5
  of the sheep and goats 17.195
  of the sower 2.55-63, 78;
    4.98-102; 14.57, 189
  of the talents 1.184; 2.84,
    321-324; 4.172
  of the ten virgins 14.300
  of the unjust judge 4.4
  of the wheat and tares 2.78;
    12.179
  of the wicked husbandman
    2.69; 3.89f; 14.166, 194
Paradise 1.52; 4.286f; 6.34,
    153f; 9.257; 13.134; 16.69f,
    84, 122; 17.199, 220
Parchment 16.88
Parent-slayers 12.38
Parthia 15.63; 17.63, 147
Parthians 3.103, 320; 15.18;
    17.4, 53, 129, 141, 184
Partnership 11.17
Passion 1.137; 3.231; 4.106;
    9.158; 10.159; 11.151; 12.191
Passover 1.41; 2.79, 238f, 245,

296, 328, 339–342; 3.260,
270, 331–334, 336–339; 4.4,
9, 29, 232, 241, 262f, 265;
5.106, 108, 177, 201, 228;
6.115, 146f, 235; 7.21, 94,
148, 150; 9.149f; 10.36;
13.158; 14.185
and Bethany 3.264
Christian· 9.44
and Elijah 2.136; 3.147
and Greeks 6.119
Lamb of 2.339, 341; 5.80f;
6.259, 261; 14.244
the Last 3.331–334
and Messiah 2.136; 3.338
and the Preparation 2.374
at spring-time 2.105, 252;
3.160f
and trials 2.353; 4.280; 6.241
Pastoral Epistles, the 12.1–13
Pastors 10.147f; 11.194–196
Paternity 10.129
Patience 1.78f; 2.63, 167; 3.108,
113; 4.220; 8.42; 9.119f,
216; 10.50, 138; 11.75, 83,
108, 158; 12.135, 196; 13.46,
144f; 14.43, 124f, 303
Patmos 5.17; 16.14, 40–42, 50,
156; 17.127
Patriarchs 8.149; 13.148;
16.154; 17.170
Testament of See Index VI
Paulinism 8.44; 9.204; 11.11;
13.1
paradox of 10.104f
pillars of 8.19–23
quintessence of 10.70f
Peace 1.97, 108, 112, 158; 3.213,
236; 4.230; 5.87, 93; 6.171;

7.114f; 8.169f, 191f, 199;
10.50, 76, 140, 185; 11.12,
206; 12.23f, 180; 13.72–74;
14.95, 294; 16.29; 17.5
angel of 17.40
Gospel of 3.25
King of 13.69
kiss of 1.113; 4.94; 8.169;
9.63, 168; 11.189; 14.148,
279–281
meaning of 4.19; 10.9
and Messiah 5.77
The Peace 9.168
and righteousness 13.72
way of 10.26
Peace-makers 1.108; 3.140f;
13.180f
Pearl 2.86f; 17.159
Pella 1.82; 3.124; 17.85
Peloponnese 9.1
Penitence 1.95, 142, 234; 6.274;
14.347; 17.34
and forgiveness 3.81
Pentateuch, The 1.127; 2.275f,
277, 281; 3.31, 163, 289
and Samaritans 5.159
Pentecost 2.42, 145, 156; 3.80;
5.83, 252; 6.115; 10.36;
15.109
Day of 7.18
Feast of 3.323; 4.9; 5.177;
7.21, 150f, 157
People, importance of 1.251;
2.173; 3.64; 4.174, 177;
8.12; 14.208
People of the land 3.56; 4.199;
5.253; 13.93
Peroea 1.82; 2.95; 4.31
Perfection, moral 1.177; 9.26;

10.79; 11.65f, 69; 12.204; 14.44

and martyrdom 11.66

symbol of 17.211

Perfectionism 15.79–81

Perfume 2.329; 6.109

Perga 3.3; 7.97

Pergamum 16.28, 58, 87–90
Letter to 16.67, 86–99
library of 16.88

Perjurers 12.39

Persecution 1.115–118, 179, 241f, 372–378, 382–384; 2.8; 3.99, 250; 4.193, 258; 8.167f; 9.106f; 13.6, 57; 14.247, 257f; 16.40, 79; 17.127, 137, 145
courting of 9.119
of Early Church 1.112–114, 375, 376f, 393; 2.153, 304, 310; 3.306, 312–314; 6.181f; 7.62f; 9.63; 11.51; 12.58f, 167; 14.148, 156–158; 16.80
salt of 3.234

Perseverance 1.79; 13.127

Persia 2.364; 16.36; 17.88
Empire of 1.25f; 5.186

Persians 1.25f, 168; 2.281; 3.193f; 6.121; 7.11; 15.55; 16.3
beliefs of 3.22f
and crucifixion 6.250

Persistence 2.123; 4.222, 232

Personalism 13.60

Pessimism 3.108, 159, 189, 217, 304; 5.55; 6.213; 10.91; 12.154

Pessinus 14.144

Pestilence 17.9

Peter, Letters of 14.137–163, 275f, 283–289
and Ephesians 14.154

Petra 1.82

Phaeno 13.192

Pharisees 1.43, 129, 325, 351, 356, 359; 2.30, 128f, 196, 200, 214, 261, 272f, 275–278, 279, 294, 374; 3.63, 69, 73, 163, 185, 187, 237, 285, 288, 300, 349; 4.4, 61, 65, 70, 73, 155f, 185f, 199, 206, 210, 244, 250, 275; 5.77, 79, 120, 233f, 249, 253; 6.45, 47–49, 93, 104, 212; 7.49; 8.13; 10.114; 11.60
and the church 7.113
and fasting 3.59
heresies of 14.316
origins of 2.282
and religion 2.132
and Sadducees 2.128f, 131, 275; 4.250; 7.165; 12.175
and the Scribes 2.147
sin of 2.291; 4.223f
types of 2.282–284; 4.185

Philadelphia 3.124; 16.28
Letter to 16.124–135

Philemon, Letter to 11.172; 12.269–276; 16.165

Philippi 2.135; 7.119, 122f, 128; 8.19; 11.3f, 9, 31, 73

Philippians, Letter to 11.3–8

Philosophy 1.26; 11.96, 134
Mother of 15.41

Philistines 3.22

Phoenicia 3.176; 9.2; 17.160

Phoenicians 1.72f; 2.121, 125

Phrygia 7.138; 10.44; 11.93;

14.40, 144f; **16.**28, 125, 137, 139

Piety **1.**185, 325; **12.**239; 14.303f

Phylacteries **2.**286; **3.**295; **4.**140; **17.**99

Pilatus, Mount **2.**359

Pilgrims **3.**273; **13.**149; **14.**144, 167; **16.**91
  Jewish **3.**324

Pillars **16.**134

Pisidia **14.**144

Pitiless **8.**39

Pity **1.**103, 354; **4.**214; **11.**157; 14.96, 227

Plagues **2.**339; **17.**14, 44, 71, 124f, **17.**125–128, 130, 134

Platonism **8.**173f; **12.**2, 88; **16.**55; **17.**199

Pleasure **1.**94, 238, 240, 391; **2.**207; **4.**195; **6.**23; **8.**28f, 31, 96, 189; **9.**52, 76; **10.**100; **12.**161, 188, 191; **13.**129, 184; **14.**98–101, 331

Plutocracy **10.**45

Poetry **5.**22, 27

Polygamy **12.**76

Pomegranate **9.**80

Pompeii **3.**320, 359

Pontifical Letters, The **12.**1

Pontus **8.**209; **14.**137, 144, 160, 166

Poor, The **1.**90–92, 241; **3.**6, 326; **4.**5; **14.**61, 66f

Possessiuns **1.**239f, 249–254; **2.**215f; **3.**122, 244, 247f; **4.**164f, 194, 206, 228f; **9.**120, 235; **12.**129f, 185; **14.**255f

Postal system, Roman **10.**62;

16.101, 129

Poverty **1.**90–92; **2.**208; **3.**122f; **12.**130; **14.**66f; **16.**78

Power **3.**219; **8.**200; **9.**110

Powers **8.**117f; **9.**92; **10.**92, 182; **11.**96

Praetorium **3.**359; **7.**167
  guard of **7.**193; **11.**20f

Praetor Urbanus **8.**188

Praise **8.**47, 197; **17.**169

Prayer **1.**179, 191–232, 270–272; 357; **2.**123f, 190f, 255–257, 350; **3.**38, 40f, 155, 275–278; **4.**5, 13, 53, 143f, 146; **6.**48; **8.**16, 111f; **9.**13, 173; **10.**184; **11.**13, 77f, 108f, 166f, 196; **12.**56–60, 64–66; **13.**199f; **14.**131f, 252, 279, 346f; **15.**115f, 203; **16.**129, 152f; **17.**34, 39–41
  constancy of **4.**221–223; **8.**166
  Jewish **1.**80, 185, 191–198, 261f, 335; **2.**80; **3.**104, 135f; **4.**64, 223f; **7.**123; **10.**32f, 128, 184; **12.**95, 156f; **13.**47f; **14.**89f, 131f
  laws of **6.**179–181
  morning **6.**176
  as sacrifice **17.**40f

Prayer-shawl **2.**287

Preaching **1.**75f, 79, 312, 352; **2.**69f, 108, 145; **3.**140, 245, 370; **4.**81, 134; **8.**137; **9.**39; **11.**53; **12.**31f; **14.**181f, 256, 307f, 336f, 347
  apostles' **7.**22–24, 33–36; **9.**17, 25, 32; **14.**140f
  defined **7.**67; **9.**176

equipment of 9.216f
gift of 9.111, 117f, 127–130
Greek 14.27–29
and healing 4.115f
Jewish 4.81, 160; 14.29f
the preacher 1.44f, 106, 285,
   385; 2.61, 91f, 289; 3.131f;
   9.24, 117f, 179, 208; 13.49;
   15.148
as proclamation 12.258
and virtue 12.52
Predestination 6.73; 8.114
Prefect 11.21
Prejudice 1.21, 50, 243, 338;
   2.60, 289; 3.127; 4.99, 124;
   5.193; 9.33, 192
Presbyters See Elders
Prestige 1.189, 285; 4.128;
   11.32
Pride 1.97, 137, 140; 2.14, 60,
   119, 288; 3.15, 128, 175,
   250, 330; 4.15f, 27, 135f,
   190, 223f; 5.193; 8.37, 53f,
   169; 9.34f, 38–40, 127, 182,
   197f, 232, 240, 244, 266;
   12.5, 73, 186f; 14.105f;
   15.58, 184; 17.80, 152–154
Priestesses 1.154
Priests 1.12; 2.211; 5.76f;
   6.104; 9.81; 12.109; 15.69;
   16.153; 17.34
   chief 1.29f; 2.261, 275, 374;
   3.346, 349; 4.243; 5.233f,
   253; 7.38; 14.263
Priesthood, Christian 12.1;
   14.199; 16.35, 178; 17.193
   Jewish 2.17, 217; 4.9, 275;
   5.77; 11.10; 13.45–47, 68,
   74, 78; 14.170

Principalities 8.117; 9.92; 10.92;
   11.96
Privilege 1.371, 383; 2.12, 61,
   108, 224, 263; 4.134, 151,
   245; 5.200; 6.186; 8.43, 52,
   173; 9.77, 122, 197; 10.124f;
   14.199; 15.72–74
Procurators 2.357
Profanity 12.37f
Profligacy 12.235
Progress, spiritual 13.50–55;
   14.299–307; 15.46, 77;
   17.105
Promise 1.48; 3.25; 8.126
   and fulfilment 9.176f
Promised Land, The 13.33, 35–
   37, 153f; 14.42, 173f
Property, Law of 4.204
Prophecy 1.5–6, 16, 36, 38, 43;
   2.8f; 3.17; 5.50, 157
   and fulfilment 5.115; 7.23,
   27, 105; 9.17; 10.96
   gift of 8.161; 9.111, 117f, 128
   interpretation of 14.311–314
   personified 1.52
   symbolism of 2.240–243, 253,
   341; 3.264, 270, 339; 4.239;
   7.154; 13.13
Prophetesses 16.105
Prophets 1.20, 80, 116; 2.5;
   3.16; 4.51, 245; 5.83, 145;
   8.12; 11.10; 12.227; 13.12–
   14; 14.180f, 293; 15.132–135,
   170; 16.25; 17.143, 171
   anointing 15.69
   clothing 1.282
   in Early Church 1.282; 4.134;
   7.91f, 98; 10.146f; 12.49,
   123; 14.79; 15.90; 16.12f;

17.127
false 1.281–288; 2.258; 3.49;
    4.220; 5.77; 6.48; 7.91f;
    10.147; 14.312, 314–318;
    17.47, 130–132, 184
and the Law 1.127; 2.282
Promised one, the 4.115;
    5.78; 6.72; 9.18
Propitiation 8.58
Proportion, sense of 2.293f;
    4.188f; 10.90f; 12.253;
    14.58, 77, 329
Proselytes 1.59f, 273; 2.290,
    359; 3.14; 5.79, 126; 7.69,
    106; 8.65; 9.106; 10.31,
    111; 12.194, 262; 14.38,
    79, 149; 16.80
Prosperity 1.181; 2.251; 3.246;
    4.210f; 9.173; 12.185; 13.126
Prostitution 1.154, 156; 3.152;
    9.52; 10.169f; 12.67; 17.137,
    144
Proverbs, Book of 5.31
Providence 10.142; 13.15; 15.99
Proxenos, The 15.149
Prudence 1.256, 379; 2.47, 330;
    9.215; 12.80, 239, 247, 251,
    257
Pseudonymous Writings 14.30f,
    32, 288
Psoriasis 3.44
Psycho-analysis 9.86
Ptolemais 1.40
Ptolemies 14.39
Publicans 1.329f; 3.53
Punishment 1.138, 175, 180,
    386; 2.179, 182, 323; 3.228–
    230; 4.214; 17.153
    double 17.153

death-penalty 2.179, 357;
    3.229; 6.233; 9.257; 16.90
everlasting 2.182
future 3.85f; 16.145
Jewish 3.113; 9.253
restorative 9.44–46, 182
Roman 2.179
and sin 2.98; 8.42
Purification 1.50f; 3.12, 234;
    4.24f; 6.107; 14.246f
Purim, feast of 3.183; 9.228;
    11.58
Puritans 2.372
Purity 1.119; 2.208; 3.236;
    9.42, 174, 185, 215, 221;
    11.19, 43, 80, 153f, 198–200;
    12.99, 104; 13.102, 193;
    14.61, 106–108; 15.75, 76–78;
    17.105
    of heart 1.51, 105–108; 2.16,
    119; 9.193; 12.33f
    symbolism of 16.122
Purple 14.221; 17.160
    symbolism of 4.213
Purpose 1.177f; 5.35
Purses 1.367
Puteoli 7.190
Pythagoreans 8.182; 12.262;
    13.197

Quakers 1.161; 2.52f
Quiet in the Land, The 4.26;
    5.86
Quietness 17.143
Quiet Times 1.194; 3.123;
    4.261, 298

Ra 3.71
Rabbis 1.86, 296f; 3.241, 279,

345; 4.94, 96, 115, 140, 253f,
275; 9.110, 251; 14.80
authority 1.134; 4.243f
disciples of 2.249; 4.273, 276
and Messiah 2.303
and sacrifice 13.199
sayings of 1.22, 52, 54, 56f,
110, 134, 139, 147, 151, 158,
159, 191, 236, 261, 268, 270,
304, 367, 379, 390, 393, 398;
2.18, 26, 48, 84, 144, 145,
188, 206, 225, 269, 303, 330;
3.17, 32, 47, 57, 104, 153,
231, 238; 4.10, 70, 118, 191,
209, 211, 216, 227, 253; 5.79,
83, 87, 97, 124, 126, 183, 213,
220, 243; 6.2; 8.70f, 187;
9.125, 136, 235; 10.168;
11.54; 12.76f, 129, 280f;
13.18, 47; 14.51, 69, 81, 85,
113, 127, 131, 134, 331, 347;
15.37, 45; 16.29, 48, 84, 95,
134; 17.221, 227
teaching of 2.236; 3.52, 85, 222,
260, 278, 331; 4.48, 81, 143,
230, 265; 8.55; 9.130; 10.27f,
40f; 13.67f; 14.132
titles of 2.287, 361; 3.32, 300
trade of 1.284, 366–368;
3.300; 4.254; 7.135; 9.79;
11.218
Racial memory 1.252
Rain 14.121
Rainbow 8.125
Ram, sign of 17.214
Ramadan 1.233
Ramah 1.38
Ransom 3.258; 8.59; 10.81;
16.34

Ranters, The 15.161f
Rapacity 8.34f; 9.53
Raphana 3.124
Readers 16.26
Reason 1.137; 10.131; 14.337
Rebirth   See New Births, Renatus
Rebukes 12.102f
Received Text, The 15.111
Rechabites 12.119
Reciprocity, ethical 1.274;
2.160f; 14.222f
Reconciliation 2.189; 9.211;
10.67, 92, 117; 11.12, 122–
125; 13.187
word of 15.25
Red Sea 2.87
Redemption 3.217; 4.24; 5.133;
8.59; 9.57, 65, 152; 11.111,
115; 12.30; 13.104, 109;
15.99; 16.34; 17.31
Reed 2.5; 17.66
Reformation, spiritual 12.122
Reformation, The 1.357, 385;
3.61; 13.39; 14.77
Scottish 12.167
Reincarnation 8.182; 12.262;
14.88; 17.141
Religion 1.97, 107, 286–288,
323, 325, 354, 359; 2.4, 118f,
163, 166, 214, 278, 294, 296;
3.40, 64, 69, 122f, 168f, 214,
271; 4.8, 15, 156, 182; 8.50,
100; 9.46f; 10.10, 36f, 90,
151; 11.107; 13.1, 66, 77f,
102, 112, 138; 14.61f, 297,
304; 15.31, 39, 203; 17.110
duties of 1.187, 334f; 5.160
Jewish 1.128f, 185; 2.109,
115, 284–287; 3.165

1 Matt, v.1	3 Mark	5 John, v.1	7 Acts	9 Cor
2 Matt, v.2	4 Luke	6 John, v.2	8 Rom	10 Gal, Eph

Negative 2.51f, 284f; 4.149f;
9.68
Prophetic 10.37
Remnant, The 8.53, 120, 122,
144f
'Removing mountains' 2.167;
3.276
Rents 4.208
Reparation 1.57
Repentance 1.51–58, 76, 95, 234,
352; 2.44f; 3.14, 17, 26, 144;
4.298; 7.28f, 35, 179; 8.42;
9.17, 227; 13.53, 134, 184;
14.141; 15.37; 16.65f, 120;
17.72
baptism of 4.37
'nine norms of' 1.54
Resolution 8.100
Respect 2.285; 14.62f
Respectability 3.244
Responsibility 1.252, 371; 2.12,
60, 108, 173, 178–181, 263;
3.105, 247f, 4.134, 151, 246;
5.200; 8.52; 9.122; 14.207,
254–256
Restitution 4.235
Restoration 1.143
Rest 13.33–40; 17.114
Resurrection 3.368; 5.193;
9.150; 11.203; 12.174; 13.55;
14.175; 16.9, 27, 110f;
17.168, 192
of body 3.221, 290f; 9.137,
141; 12.6, 30f, 175; 16.123
empty tomb, the 2.377; 4.291;
9.143
Jewish 2.128, 275f; 3.289;
4.250f; 12.175; 13.111
Retaliation 1.165–169

Retribution 3.280
Reuben, tribe of 14.31
Revelation 2.130; 5.73–75, 156,
198; 6.169, 194–196; 7.35;
11.192; 12.41; 13.11f, 14,
20, 22; 15.42, 203; 16.21f,
23f, 45, 155; 17.26, 56f
Book of 5.82; 16.1–20, 26,
28, 35, 41, 47, 97, 98, 165,
170, 176; 17.100f, 173, 195,
229, 230
Revelry 8.178
Reverence 1.131, 206–210, 297,
388; 2.163, 285; 5.112;
7.30; 9.207; 12.61f, 134;
14.188, 209, 231; 16.30, 51,
156; 17.138, 169
Revival 12.263; 15.157
Revolution, French 1.42
Rewards 1.179–185, 397–400;
2.317; 3.228–230; 16.82–84
Rhone 2.359
Riches 2.218f; 3.246; 12.137f;
14.27, 48, 66f
Rich young ruler 2.213; 5.19;
17.107
Ridicule 8.181
Righteousness 1.44, 101, 187;
8.5, 191; 9.22, 217; 10.164,
183; 11.54, 62; 15.84
age of 16.11
and almsgiving 9.164f
of Christian 1.132; 12.178,
180; 14.172; 15.17f
crown of 16.83
and Greeks 8.91
and Holy Spirit 6.193
King of 13.69
and Messiah 5.77

11 Phil, Col, Thes   13 Heb   15 John, Jude   16 Rev, v.1
12 Tim, Tit, Phlm   14 Jas, Pet   17 Rev, v.2

and peace 13.72
primary virtue 12.134
way of 13.74
and wisdom 14.45
word of 15.25
Rights 1.167f
Rings 4.205; 14.64; 17.23
Ritualism 1.43; 11.145
Roads 3.17; 5.79; 6.138f
  to the East 1.40, 73
  of the Sea 1.39; 3.52
  from the South 4.48
Robbery 9.52, 53
Rock 2.140; 5.251; 12.18
Rod 6.55; 17.66f
Roman Catholic Church 2.139;
  3.61, 99; 6.65
Romans, Letter to 8.1–10;
  10.44; 16.165
Rome 1.113; 2.135; 7.89; 8.1;
  14.159; 17.63, 139, 164
  army of 1.300f; 6.229; 8.49
  as 'Babylon' 14.277f; 15.19f;
    16.15; 17.63, 134, 136, 149–
    151, 166–168
  bishop of 2.139; 12.222
  Church of 1.120, 381f; 3.209;
    8.1, 15, 207, 211; 9.186;
    14.160
  citizens of 7.126, 163
  colonies of 7.123; 11.3f, 30,
    69
  doom of 17.110f
  emperor 1.114; 3.100
  empire of 1.25, 40; 3.100,
    287; 7.11; 12.231; 16.3,
    14–20, 36; 17.88, 101
  fear at 12.190, 219
  fever of 11.49

fire of 12.167
immorality of 8.32
and Jews 9.167; 11.59
laws of 6.252; 10.86; 17.219
luxury of 5.212; 8.31f;
  14.221; 17.154–157, 158f
people of 3.194
polytheism of 17.138
prisoners of 7.95
provinces of 3.284; 9.209f
as Restrainer 11.213
riots of 7.147, 169; 8.30f
sayings of 1.119
standard of 2.358; 4.280
Rust 1.239; 14.28

Sabbath 1.126, 128, 286; 2.19–
  23, 290, 374f; 3.31, 39, 63f,
  67–69; 4.70, 289, 291; 5.6,
  30, 181f, 238, 241f; 7.15;
  10.36; 16.93; 17.95
  and circumcision 4.24
  and Gentiles 8.48f
  and Jesus 2.26, 28; 4.187;
    6.44f
  journey on 3.263; 4.156
  law of 1.309f; 2.21–27, 30f,
    208, 372; 3.39; 4.60, 177;
    5.121f; 8.137, 180; 12.264;
    14.69; 17.19
  meals 3.37; 4.187, 213
  offerings 2.24
  rest of 17.188
  tyranny of 8.184
Sabbatic years 10.36f
Sacraments 2.103, 296, 342;
  4.265, 295; 6.262; 9.42, 91–
  93, 110, 168; 12.261; 13.198;
  14.130, 245; 17.34

---

1 Matt, v.1	3 Mark	5 John, v.1	7 Acts	9 Cor
2 Matt, v.2	4 Luke	6 John, v.2	8 Rom	10 Gal, Eph

Sacrifice
  and almsgiving 9.165
  Christian 1.115, 396; 2.87,
    151; 3.230f; 4.230; 8.58;
    10.25, 78, 117, 125, 161;
    11.16, 44, 46, 65, 86, 126;
    12.43f, 160, 208f; 13.151,
    195–199; 14.196f; 17.11, 31,
    108, 127
  heathen 9.71–76, 80, 91;
    13.197f
  Jewish 1.80, 119, 131, 142;
    2.245; 3.234; 5.112; 10.161;
    13.45, 78, 102, 113
  for proselytes 3.114
  Samaritan 5.157
  substitutionary 1.143
Sacrilege 13.125
Saddle, The 4.285
Sadducees 1.43, 355, 359;
    2.128f, 147, 211, 275–277,
    278; 3.288–291, 349; 4.249–
    251, 275; 5.86, 234, 249;
    6.93, 104, 113f; 7.37; 8.205;
    9.137; 16.84
  heresies of 14.316
Saffron 17.161
Sagan, The 4.273; 7.37
Saints 1.116, 354; 2.52; 7.77f;
    9.25; 10.150; 11.10; 12.45,
    83; 13.194; 15.4, 122, 176f;
    16.70
Salamis 7.97
Salt 1.85, 118–122; 3.234f;
    4.197f
  bond of 9.91
  and Christian life 3.233
  'of the covenant' 3.234
  at Passover 2.340; 3.333

Salvation 1.217; 3.25f, 213,
    226, 248, 256; 3.248; 4.220;
    5.7, 137, 190; 7.24; 8.13,
    19–21, 121, 134f; 9.39, 143;
    10.43; 11.40–44; 12.146;
    13.20f, 48; 14.174; 15.9,
    40, 100f; 17.28, 227
  chain of 1.398–400
  cost of 3.259; 6.161
  gift of 9.12; 10.56, 104;
    11.53
  and Gnostics 11.115f
  helmet of 10.183f
  the purpose of God 8.153;
    12.230; 14.180f
  universal 17.216
  wells of 5.249
  wholeness of 4.148; 7.178;
    10.163; 11.24f; 12.30f;
    14.175f
  word of 15.24
Salvation Army 3.54; 4.52;
    6.124; 9.208
Samaria 1.73; 2.95, 194; 4.31,
    129
  and Christianity 7.4f; 12.62f,
    64f, 88; 15.89
  and Dispersion 14.37
  and Pilate 2.359; 6.240
  Woman of 1.363; 5.5, 15,
    52f, 147–161; 9.132
Samaritans 1.363, 370; 4.5, 6,
    129, 139f, 217; 5.16; 7.4,
    62f, 64f; 14.37
  and Jews 5.6, 149, 157; 6.31
  Pentateuch of 5.159
Samos 7.150
Sanctification 2.202; 3.337;
    8.91

and justification **8.77**

Sandals **2.367; 3.17,** 142; **4.94,** 285; **5.98; 6.139; 10.183**

symbolism of **4.205**

Sanhedrin **1.12,** 36, 140; **2.258,** 343; **3.279,** 312; **4.247f,** 275–277; **5.123; 6.103f,** 260; **7.38; 9.186**

administrators of **14.263**

apostles of **7.177; 13.30**

composition of **2.147,** 353; **3.346; 4.133**

and divorce **3.239**

local **3.312**

and orthodoxy **5.77; 17.131**

police **3.346; 7.70**

procedure of **4.276; 7.164**

and Romans **3.349; 7.61**

trials in **2.353f; 3.348f**

Sanity **14.251**

Sapphire **17.213,** 215

Saracens **4.111**

Sard **17.214**

Sardian **16.151f**

Sardis **9.89f; 12.184; 16.28,** 113–115, 126; **17.214**

Letter to **16.112–123**

Sardonyx **17.159,** 213, 215

Saronic Gulf **9.1**

Saturn **1.26**

Saturnalia **17.159**

Scapegoat, The **13.100f; 14.244**

Scarlet **17.160**

Sceptics, The **8.159**

Schism **14.316**

Schoenus **9.2**

Scoffers **1.158**

Scorpion **1.271,** 17, 51

Sign of **17.215**

Scourging **2.363; 3.358; 6.244,** 250; **7.163; 9.253f**

Scribes **1.29f,** 128, 133f, 294, 328, 354; **2.90f,** 116, 165, 227, 280–282; **3.31,** 164, 279, 293, 299f, 346, 349; **4.156f,** 243, 275

Scribes and Pharisees **1.6f,** 8, 46f, 132, 286, 333f, 337, 355; **2.16,** 18f, 22f, 27, 30, 32, 35f, 44, 46, 50, 54, 109f, 113, 116–119, 121, 125, 147, 211, 280–284, 298, 323; **3.56,** 58, 76, 79, 165–167, 177; **4.65,** 91, 100, 161, 187f, 199; **5.86,** 122, 199; **6.1f,** 4f, 15, 165, 169; **14.263; 15.104**

woes against **2.288–299**

Scripture **12.198–202; 14.337;** 17.34

and Jesus **2.118; 15.112**

and Jews **1.127; 10.40f;** 13.67f; **16.26**

and Paul **8.55; 9.88f,** 223; **10.27f, 12.177**

Scruples **8.180,** 182, 194; **9.73**

Scythia **17.159**

Scythians **11.155; 16.97; 17.194**

Scythopolis **1.81; 3.124; 5.147**

Sea **2.179; 9.254; 17.198**

Seals **5.145; 8.87; 9.78; 13.14;** 14.244; **16.166; 17.1ff,** 18, 21–23, 66, 99

Sealing **10.87; 12.177; 17.23**

Seasons **10.36**

Secret See Mystery

Sectarianism **2.291; 12.265**

Secularism **4.81**

Security **5.86f; 6.59; 14.228–**

230; **16**.61; **17**.103
Seed **15**.78
Seemism **15**.7
Seleucia **7**.97; **14**.39
Seleucids **14**.39; **16**.87
Self-centredness **1**.202, 219, 396;
    3.335; **4**.164; **9**.22; **10**.48;
    12.236; **14**.329
  -control **1**.96f, 237; **2**.208;
    10.52, 138; **11**.67, 75, 85f;
    11.45; **12**.80, 144f, 239, 252;
    14.302f; **15**.188f
  -deception **1**.244; **4**.95; **15**.32–
    34
  -denial **2**.151, 173, 175, 182;
    3.232; **4**.121; **11**.150; **12**.161
  -esteem **1**.230; **2**.32, 325;
    3.112; **4**.190; **5**.193; **12**.180
  -examination **1**.244; **3**.175,
    261; **9**.249f; **10**.90, 135;
    13.1
  -pity **13**.178
Selfishness **1**.254, 323; **2**.103,
    205, 210, 219, 326; **3**.236;
    6.114; **7**.125; **9**.121f, 232;
    10.46; **11**.15, 23, 38; **12**.184,
    259; **14**.118–120, 227, 329;
    15.57, 190, 193f
  in marriage **2**.205
  in prayer **2**.190; **6**.180
  in worship **9**.130
Sensationalism **4**.44
Senselessness **8**.38
Sensualism **9**.52
Sephoris **4**.121
Septuagint, The See Index VI
Seraphim **8**.117; **13**.17; **16**.157f
Seraphs **16**.158
Serenity **1**.256; **10**.75; **14**.75,

272
Sermon on the Mount **1**.5, 9,
    33, *83–294*, 358, 372; **2**.206;
    476; **5**.160; **8**.6; **12**.201;
    14.22, 25, 126; **15**.83; **17**.153
Sermon on the Plain **4**.76
Serpent **8**.96; **16**.89f
  The Ancient **17**.80, 82, 98
  The Crooked **17**.58
Servant of the Lord **1**.310; **4**.38
Service **1**.97, 149, 169, 179, 225,
    248f, 308f, 310, 361, 392,
    400; **2**.25, 90, 186, 226, 230,
    232, 279, 323f; **3**.29, 38, 69,
    123, 203, 257f, 301; **4**.52,
    97, 118, 121f, 128, 132, 210,
    264, 267f; **5**.87, 142; **6**.124,
    136–140, 190, 217; **7**.78, 111;
    8.157, 159, 161, 202f; **9**.114,
    163; **10**.99, 124, 149; **11**.103,
    187; **12**.52, 148, 173; **13**.61;
    14.199, 255f, 293; **16**.25
Seven **1**.170; **5**.103; **7**.87; **8**.107;
    13.36; **16**.11, 28f, 172;
    17.117
  Spirits **16**.31f, 116, 155
Seven, The **7**.19, 52, 64
Seventy, The **4**.133, 135
Shadow and reality **11**.79;
    ˙**13**.2f, 88
Shamelessness **3**.175; **8**.179
Sharon, plain of **3**.52
Sheba, Queen of **2**.50; **4**.151;
    14.42
Shechem **5**.6, 150
Sheep **2**.184; **6**.56
Sheepfolds **6**.58
Sheol **6**.91; **9**.137; **16**.9, 181;
    17.184

Shephalah 17.38
Shepherds 1.281f; 2.184f;
    4.22f, 200; 6.52–57; 14.215f
  false 6.61; 15.194
  Messianic 17.38
Shunem 4.48, 86
Sicarii, the 3.356
Sichem 5.150
Sicily 17.103
Sickness 1.44, 327; 3.49; 14.131
Sick-visiting 1.261; 6.90
Sidon 2.84; 3.177, 180
Signs 2.48f, 128–130; 3.185
Silk 17.160
Siloam 4.173; 5.6, 249; 6.42f
Silver 17.158f
Simony 7.67
Simoon, The 14.47f
Simplicity 1.41f, 243, 399f;
    2.14, 102, 212, 248–250, 325;
    3.8, 16, 38, 144, 247; 4.23,
    137; 8.161f; 9.23f, 130, 240;
    9.82, 114, 115, 134; 14.204,
    301
  of the Gospel 5.137; 11.96
  of the Law 2.117
Sin 1.14, 95, 141, 219–222, 287;
    3.26, 147; 4.44, 245f; 5.42;
    8.54f, 96; 10.29, 95f; 12.282;
    13.21, 45; 14.114, 230–233;
    16.116f; 17.17
  consequences of 6.38f; 7.29;
    8.186; 9.150f; 10.54; 13.77;
    17.9
  and death 8.80
  death of 6.94; 15.77f;
    17.198
  deliberate 1.142; 2.263f, 300;
    6.151; 8.194

essence of 3.330; 8.28, 95;
    9.22, 181; 10.20; 12.37;
    14.107, 233f
  hardening of 4.153; 10.152f
  of ignorance 13.45
  influence of 2.178–181;
    4.215f; 9.219; 12.207;
    14.333; 17.142, 169f
  law of 8.90f, 110
  mortal 15.117–120
  original 3.187f; 8.55; 14.51–53
  personification of 14.28
  post-baptismal 13.56, 58;
    15.119
  pre-natal 6.37, 49
  of presumption 13.46
  satanic 3.23, 80
  sense of 1.219; 5.156; 6.192f;
    8.29f, 99, 146, 163f; 9.132;
    10.82, 162; 12.19f, 78;
    13.123f; 14.327
  and sickness 3.47–49; 4.62;
    5.183
  slavery of 8.89
  and suffering 1.327; 3.47f;
    4.62, 173; 6.37–39; 9.170,
    172; 11.110; 14.246f, 273
  total depravity 4.204
  types of 3.173, 230, 357;
    8.37; 12.36–40; 13.4, 125;
    15.33
  unforgivable 2.41–45; 3.79–
    81; 4.161f; 17.225
  universal 8.54; 14.82
Sinai, Mount 5.69; 16.94, 155;
    17.200
  covenant of 8.125
Sincerity 1.272, 289; 4.235;
    8.218; 12.34, 204

1 Matt, v.1	3 Mark	5 John, v.1	7 Acts	9 Cor
2 Matt, v.2	4 Luke	6 John, v.2	8 Rom	10 Gal, Eph

Sinope 14.145, 160

Sion, Mount 1.68; 2.305; 17.102

Sirius 1.26

Sirocco 17.19f

Six 5.103

Skull, place of 6.251

Slander 1.158, 325; 3.175; 4.148; 8.36; 9.259f, 264; 11.153; 12.116f, 189; 14.111

Slanderer, The 1.226; 3.22; 12.74, 189

Slavery 1.248f, 301f, 377; 2.223; 4.84f, 178, 209f; 8.89; 9.21f, 10.179f; 11.155; 12.39, 121f, 270; 14.208, 210; 17.162f
  and Church 1.377; 12.121–123; 14.210–213
  emancipation 12.271
  and Jews 2.80; 4.205; 14.38
  treatment of 9.40, 52; 12.39; 16.135; 17.99

Sling 6.55

Sloth 5.160

Smyrna 1.115; 14.162f; 16.17, 28, 73–76, 127
  Letter to 16.72–85

Snobbery 1.140; 8.38, 169; 9.118; 11.97; 12.28; 14.63f

Sobriety 12.79f, 247; 14.108, 183, 251f

Socnopaeus 14.263

Sodom and Gomorrah 1.371; 2.12; 9.221; 14.327f; 15.158, 184–186; 16.121; 17.71, 112

Solidarity, spiritual 8.79f, 103; 9.151

Solitude 3.214

'Son of' 1.109

Son of Man 1.312, 380–382; 2.26, 42, 49, 165, 234; 3.220f; 4.70, 222, 235; 5.185f, 192; 6.121f, 128; 7.14; 9.144; 13.23; 16.36, 45

Son of Perdition 11.212

Sons of God 1.109, 226; 3.22, 71; 4.103; 5.61f, 127; 8.133; 11.119; 14.322; 16.153; 17.80f, 89, 205

Sons of Thunder 5.16

Soothsayers 7.66

Sop, The 3.338

Sophists 9.19; 12.124, 207

Sorcery 1.34

Sorrow 1.93, 355; 3.116; 4.27, 87, 106, 124; 6.130, 269; 9.171, 213, 226f; 11.203; 14.174; 16.10; 17.105, 198

Spain 8.3f, 204; 12.10–12, 283; 14.9; 17.92, 158, 161
  Armada of 13.161
  Inquisition 6.190; 9.120

Sparrows 1.389

Sparta 1.333; 2.80; 3.223; 9.1; 12.196; 13.148; 14.195f
  elders of 12.70

Spartans 12.151; 14.261

Speech 4.83; 11.153f; 12.6, 112; 14.55f, 81–83; 17.129f

Sphinx 1.202

Spice 17.161

Spikenard 17.161

Spirit of God See Holy Spirit

Spirits, evil 1.320; 2.50–52, 112, 166, 359; 3.289; 4.250; 5.1; 6.258; 7.144; 8.101–103;

9.75; 10.182; 11.96, 134;
12.92

unclean 3.32; 4.148; 7.46;
17.129f

Spittle 3.181, 190; 6.41f, 45;
9.258

Stable 1.24–25

Stacte 17.161

Stars 1.26; 8.118; 11.96, 134f,
137; 16.153, 155; 17.14
of Bethlehem 1.31

Steadfastness 14.303; 17.97

Sterility 2.199

Stewardship
Christian 9.36; 14.255
eastern 4.168; 5.99; 14.255

Stoics 1.274; 2.313; 3.11, 279;
4.25, 79, 87, 103, 261, 285f;
5.197; 6.23; 7.104, 130, 132;
8.4, 28, 33, 45, 159, 189;
9.140, 235; 10.48, 108, 142;
11.84f; 12.75, 128, 146, ?75,
262, 265; 13.42, 87, 137,
157, 177; 14.27, 60, 75, 299,
341; 15.79; 16.159

Stones, precious 17.159, 212–215

Stoning 6.234; 7.61f

Strife 2.247; 8.35, 169; 9.30,
263; 10.47; 14.97, 225f
final 17.5f

Striking 9.251; 12.83, 237

Stripping 16.143

Stumbling 1.148; 2.180; 9.74,
94; 11.19

Sublime Porte 2.143

Submission 1.32, 209; 5.165;
10.51; 14.219

Suffering 1.111–116; 9.171, 214;
11.14, 17, 126; 13.165–171;

14.229f, 246f, 258–260;
16.62; 17.113
law of 14.273f

Suicide 6.17; 12.146

Sun 1.119; 12.100; 16.14

Sunday 3.64; 4.149, 291; 7.27;
8.184

Sunday Schools 12.73

Superstition 5.160f; 8.185;
9.47

Swiss Confession 12.55

Sychar 5.6, 14, 147, 167

Symbolism 1.25

Sympathy 1.104; 4.87; 13.192;
14.75f, 226f

Synagogues 1.80, 121, 188,
296; 2.290, 346; 3.30–32, 67,
300, 312; 4.45f, 48, 262;
8.60; 9.162; 12.70, 85;
14.129, 223, 263; 16.26;
17.119
Christian 14.21, 26
The Great 2.281f
and the Law 1.134; 3.295
prayers of 1.53f, 192f; 6.190f;
17.200
ruler of 1.80, 341–343; 2.92;
3.30f, 126f; 4.111
seats of honour 3.67; 4.156
teaching of 3.323; 4.262;
14.29f

Syria 1.72, 81, 363; 2.282, 359;
3.12, 124, 143; 4.20; 6.238;
7.73, 119; 9.5; 14.38

Syrians 1.73; 2.134; 4.5, 248;
17.103

Syro-Phoenician 1.363; 5.175;
6.63f

Syrtis Sands 7.183

Tabernacle 2.23, 161; 3.210;
  5.69; 13.94–97; 16.44; 17.10,
  121, 202
  brazen altar 13.95
  court 13.95
  golden lampstand 13.96
  heavenly 13.103
  holy place of 13.96
  laver 2.244; 13.95
  mercy seat 13.96
  sacrifices 13.113
  shewbread 13.96
  veil of 13.96
Tabernacles, feast of 3.323;
  4.9; 5.2, 4, 15, 177, 230, 247f;
  6.10f, 115–117; 7.21; 10.36
Tabor, Mount 2.157; 3.210
Talents 2.194, 321–324; 3.203;
  7.45; 13.11
Tallies 12.82
Tanners 2.197
Tarbert 9.1
Tares 2.72f
Tarichaea 1.77; 3.27, 159
Tarshish, stone of 17.214
Tarsus 7.76, 136, 159; 11.59
Tartarus 3.175; 14.321
Tavium 14.144
Taxation
  Palestinian 2.168, 272; 3.285;
    4.20, 64, 234, 247
  Roman 1.157, 329f; 8.175
  Temple 2.168, 244; 3.273;
    4.172, 241; 5.109; 14.172,
    241
Tax-collectors 1.5, 329f; 2.187,
  189; 3.53; 4.64, 224
Teachableness 14.56–58
Teaching 1.284; 2.55; 3.112f,

  244; 4.81; 9.25f, 84; 10.146;
    11.53; 12.31f, 82f, 96
  duty of 9.179; 12.204–206,
    207f; 13.49
  in Early Church 7.98; 9.115,
    208; 10.147f; 14.26, 79f;
    16.12
  false 8.218; 12.53, 92, 126–
    128, 173f, 240–242; 14.80,
    175, 318f; 15.5–7, 31f
  gift of 8.161; 9.130
  Jewish See Rabbis
  teachers 12.144f, 180f, 252–
    254; 13.146f; 14.91–93
Telepathy 5.175
Tell Hum 1.74
Temper 1.139; 4.106; 9.122;
  10.48, 155; 11.153
Temple celestial 1.52; 17.35
Temple, of Jerusalem 1.28, 32,
  68f, 80, 101, 189; 2.23, 244,
  304f, 353; 3.30, 143, 210, 258,
  272f, 307; 4.46, 223, 300;
  5.6; 6.11, 70; 7.32, 46;
  17.68, 213
  altar of incense 17.40, 211
  Beautiful Gate 2.244; 3.302;
    5.6
  captain of 4.273; 7.37
  courts of 1.143; 2.243f, 247,
    336f; 3.272f, 302; 4.10, 254;
    5.113, 243; 6.10, 120, 226;
    7.36; 10.111; 14.234f; 17.34f,
    67
  destruction of 1.383; 2.170,
    267, 273; 3.321
  of Ezra and Nehemiah 5.150
  gifts of 1.171; 3.302; 4.254
  Golden Vine 4.258; 6.172f

Hall of Hewn Stone 2.353;
  3.349; 4.276
Holy of holies 2.243, 371;
  3.63, 365; 4.288; 13.62, 96;
  16.94; 17.212, 221
Holy Place 2.23, 243; 11.10
inspectors of 5.110
Mount of 1.368
police 2.335, 351; 5.245;
  6.222
Royal Cloister 3.278
Royal Porch 1.68; 2.305;
  3.308; 4.44
profanation of 2.241; 3.267
sacrifices 1.142f; 2.26, 168;
  3.332f; 4.10, 22f, 242; 5.81
shewbread 2.23, 244; 3.63
of Solomon 5.69; 16.45;
  17.10, 203, 212
Solomon's Porch 1.68; 2.305;
  3.278; 4.44; 5.6
treasury 2.168, 245; 6.10, 70,
  239
Trumpets, The 3.302; 4.254;
  6.8
Water Gate 5.249
veil of 2.371; 3.365; 4.288
Temples, pagan 15.124
Temptation 1.199, 224–232,
  380; 2.80, 180; 3.130, 189;
  4.105f, 125, 144, 215, 270;
  8.221; 9.76, 90; 10.183;
  11.42, 71; 12.251; 14.42–44,
  50f; 15.54f, 76, 106; 16.119
avoidance of 9.59, 257
laws of 6.111
types of 9.89f
Tempter, The 1.64, 66; 2.148;
  3.199; 17.82

Ten 16.79
Ten Commandments 1.127, 130f,
  221; 2.115, 214, 281, 285;
  3.31, 163; 4.59f; 5.69; 8.52;
  9.190; 12.38, 187; 13.20;
  14.21, 60
Ten Tribes (lost) 5.149; 14.37;
  16.3
Tension 8.199f
Tent of witness 17.121
Testimony See Witness, Christian
Thanklessness 12.187
Thanksgiving 4.118; 10.167;
  11.77f, 132; 12.58
Theft 3.173; 8.39, 176; 9.52
Theocracy 2.272; 10.108
Theology 1.291, 342; 3.29;
  5.56f; 9.130, 161; 10.45;
  11.108f; 12.127; 14.140;
  15.88; 17.219
Theosophy 11.99
Thermai 11.180
Thessalonians, Letters to 11.179–
  183
Thessalonica 2.83; 4.182; 7.119,
  122, 127, 128; 11.73; 12.205
Thessaly 4.31
Thirst 1.99, 188
spiritual 5.153; 17.22
Thomist Church 6.277
Thought 1.136; 3.124; 4.150;
  11.210; 14.77
Thousand 17.192
Thrace 5.178
Thracians 16.97
Three 17.117
Three Taverns 7.190
Thrones 8.117; 16.148
Thyatira 16.28, 66, 101f

Letter to 16.100–111
Thyine 17.160
Tiber 2.359; 17.91
Tiberias 1.77, 308, 317; 2.105; 3.146
Sea of 4.56
Time 3.368; 4.171, 266; 6.83; 8.177; 9.206; 14.342; 17.55, 198
Timothy, Letters to 12.1–13
Tirabatha 2.359
Titans 14.321; 17.101
Tithes 1.286; 2.293f; 4.155, 224; 9.80; 11.10; 13.75f
Tolerance 1.338; 2.41; 3.110f, 226; 4.130; 5.252; 8.170; 10.89f; 12.104, 259
Tombs 1.320; 2.296; 3.324, 368; 4.291; 6.99, 266
Tongue, The 14.82–88
Tongues, gift of 7.21f, 66; 9.96, 111f, 117, 127–130, 131; 15.90
Topaz 17.214f
Topheth 1.141; 3.231
Touchiness 12.181
Trachonitis 2.95; 3.53, 115; 4.3, 31
Tradition 1.231; 3.316; 6.25; 9.135, 142; 11.81f; 15.178
of the elders 2.114; 3.163–167
oral 15.199
Tralles 16.28
Transfiguration, Mount of 2.157, 162f, 348; 4.123; 5.89; 6.127; 11.166; 14.269, 310–312; 17.54, 71
Transgression 8.69
Travel 1.44, 320; 4.29, 145;

5.153, 203; 9.167; 12.231
Tray, The 7.51; 12.85
Treachery 12.190
Treasure 1.238–243
Tree, symbolism of 4.179
Trent, Council of 14.5f, 9
Trepanning 3.33f
Trespasses 10.95f
Tribulation 4.259; 8.166; 9.213f; 16.39f
The Great 17.17f, 21, 23, 29
Tribunal, The 8.188
Tribute-money 2.272–274; 3.284f; 4.247–249; 8.175
Trimitaria 16.138
Trinity The 1.199f; 3.72; 6.284; 7.12, 18; 15.110; 16.30f
Tripoli 4.282
Triumph, The (Roman) 9.39, 183, 198; 11.143; 16.122; 17.178
Troas 7.19, 119, 122, 138; 16.28
Trouble 8.73; 9.212; 12.213
Trouble-makers 1.110
Trumpets 17.42, 125
Trust 1.91, 218, 258; 5.217; 6.152; 8.5, 21; 11.56; 12.138, 150–152; 13.33f; 17.169
of children 2.176; 3.242; 4.226
Truth 1.20–21, 49, 79, 82f, 158, 265–267, 337; 2.16, 63, 69, 291; 3.87, 99, 101f, 190, 315; 5.46, 68, 213; 6.29; 7.45; 9.123, 132; 10.155, 164; 11.82, 154; 12.89; 14.133; 15.29f; 16.23

11 Phil, Col, Thes
12 Tim, Tit, Phlm
13 Heb
14 Jas, Pet
15 John, Jude
16 Rev, v.1
17 Rev, v.2

belt of 10.183
criteria of 15.71
fundamental 11.52f
recognition of 2.43f; 4.99,
   244; 5.196
touchstone of 2.42; 6.21
triumph of 1.385; 2.377;
   9.146f; 12.168; 15.95
vastness of 3.226; 4.130, 179;
   5.72, 160
word of 10.87; 14.54; 15.25
Tubal 17.194
Tunic 1.167; 3.141f; 4.285;
   16.138
Turkey 2.143
Twelve, The 1.84, 86, 332, 359–
   362; 2.133; 3.8, 43, 144,
   158, 222, 269, 328f; 4.4, 75,
   115, 117, 119, 127, 133; 5.17,
   89; 10.7, 145; 14.17; 15.169f,
   171; 17.170
Twelve Tribes 14.21, 31, 40f;
   137; 17.24f, 210
Twins, sign of 17.214
Two ages, The 1.372f; 4.257;
   6.197; 7.25; 8.25, 118;
   9.196; 11.203; 12.92, 182;
   13.12, 57; 14.343; 15.60,
   80; 16.3, 22, 132
Two worlds, The 5.8; 13.87
Tyndale Version 2.294
Types 14.244
Tyre 3.176, 180; 7.138; 17.142,
   154, 158, 164, 166f
   King of 16.151
   and Sidon 2.12, 120f, 125,
   128; 3.70, 176; 5.2, 26;
   7.96
Tyrians 2.121

Tyropoeon Valley 3.308

Uganda, Church of 9.249f
Unbelief 6.131–133
Uncertainty 1.353; 3.116;
   13.128
Unchastity 1.151, 379; 3.238;
   4.211
Uncial scripts 6.290
Uncircumcized 11.55, 139
Uncleanness 1.303f; 2.110–117,
   295f; 3.129, 165f; 4.24f,
   156; 5.99; 6.106; 8.90;
   9.265f; 11.150f
United Church of South India
   3.62; 13.144
Universalism 1.17; 4.179;
   11.123f
Unleavened Bread, Feast of
   2.339; 3.323; 4.262
Urim and Thummim 13.99
Uselessness 1.48, 121; 2.183,
   254, 263, 322f; 3.272; 4.175,
   198; 6.174; 8.55; 12.245f;
   15.195

Valhalla 3.291
Valley of Hinnom 1.141
Veil, spiritual 9.192f
Vellum 11.142
Vendetta 1.164
Vengeance 1.163; 8.170; 17.41,
   148, 153
Venus 7.100
Vesta 14.147
Vesuvius 3.320; 17.45
Vice 3.173, 175; 9.56
Viciousness 8.35
Vienne 2.359

| 1 Matt, v.1 | 3 Mark | 5 John, v.1 | 7 Acts | 9 Cor |
| 2 Matt, v.2 | 4 Luke | 6 John, v.2 | 8 Rom | 10 Gal, Eph |

Vigilance **1**.65; **9**.89f; **14**.272

Villainy **8**.34

Vineyard **4**.245; **6**.173f
of God **2**.261f

Violence **2**.351; **12**.122, 237;
17.97

Virgin, sign of **17**.215

Virginity **9**.66f; **17**.106
Jewish **1**.19; **2**.196; **4**.12

Virgin's fountain **6**.43

Virtue **1**.96, 278; **8**.164; **9**.40;
11.157; **12**.39, 61f; **13**.46;
14.300–305
healing **1**.308

Visions **1**.243–247; **11**.145f

Votive shields **6**.239f

Vows **2**.208; **7**.166

Vulgate, the **6**.291; **15**.111

Wady Hamam **2**.72

Wages **1**.99; **2**.245

Wailing **1**.344; **3**.134; **6**.96f
women **4**.111

Wallet **3**.142f

Wantonness **10**.47, 153

Warfare, Christian **1**.393;
10.181–184; **12**.159–160

Washings **2**.114, 362; **3**.13f

Watchers, The **14**.322f; **16**.175

Watchfulness **2**.317; **4**.260f;
16.118f, 120

Water **1**.188, 322; **2**.340; **3**.331;
5.98, 129, 153f, 178, 249;
17.125, 221
living **5**.152, 250; **17**.220

Water-carrier **17**.215

Way of the Sea **1**.73, 330

Way of the South **1**.39

Weak, The **2**.80

Weakness **1**.365

Wealth **1**.239f, 249, 252; **3**.244;
4.165, 228f; **12**.132, 137;
13.62; **14**.115f

Weddings, Jewish **1**.19, 335;
2.266, 319; **3**.59; **4**.66; **5**.96f,
143f; **9**.246

Wells **4**.188

Westminster Confession **1**.53;
5.56

Wheat **2**.73; **9**.80

Whisperers **8**.36

White **16**.98
day **16**.97
horses **5**.178; **17**.167, 179
ones **16**.31
robes **16**.121–123; **17**.26, 29f,
121
stone **16**.95–97
throne **17**.194

Wickedness **3**.174f

Widows **9**.62; **12**.3, 105f, 109–
115
Jewish **1**.19; **4**.12, 254; **12**.105

Wilderness **1**.63; **3**.16, 23;
4.43; **17**.143

Wind **17**.19f

Wine **1**.391; **2**.340; **3**.333;
5.97; **10**.49; **12**.79f; **17**.6,
162
-presses **2**.261f; **17**.116
-skins **1**.338; **3**.61

Wisdom **1**.273; **2**.10; **5**.33;
7.56f; **9**.109; **10**.82f; **11**.108f,
129; **14**.93–97, 295
gift of **14**.45
and Greeks **9**.19; **15**.79
O.T. **11**.117
personified **1**.52; **5**.31

Wisdom literature 5.31–34;
    14.25
Wise Men 1.9, 25–27, 30, 31–33;
    3.64
Witchcraft 10.47
Witness, Christian 1.391f;
    4.109, 251; 6.49, 188, 235;
    ·7.12f; 9.210f; 10.14; 11.26,
    167f; 16.92; 17.80, 176, 193
    law of 1.367; 2.353; 12.116;
    15.111f, 180; 16.140; 17.101,
    111f
    Tent of 17.121
Witnesses, The Two 17.66, 70f
Women 1.16f, 151, 153; 2.80,
    197, 283, 329, 366; 3.126,
    238f; 4.4, 95, 110, 211; 5.6,
    151, 162; 6.89; 9.98, 136;
    10.168f; 11.161; 12.66f;
    14.148, 218, 220–222
    and Church 8.208, 211f;
    9.96–100, 136; 10.173; 11.73;
    12.66–69, 86f; 13.9; 14.217–
    222
    emancipation of 12.192
    equality of 14.223
    and Greeks 2.80; 4.4; 7.133;
    9.136; 11.161; 12.67, 87, 250
    hair of 4.95; 6.110; 14.322f
    in Rome 12.67, 77f; 14.218f
Wonder 4.226; 5.71f; 9.11
Wool 9.2; 11.92
Word, The 5.25–40, 75; 8.112f;
    10.184; 14.191; 17.181f
Word of God, The 1.215; 2.59f,
    92; 4.99, 134; 5.28–30;
    12.167, 173; 13.39f; 14.57;
    15.24, 79
Words 1.391; 2.46f; 12.126,

170f; 13.38; 15.24
Work 1.106f, 111, 118, 119, 184,
    218, 278–280; 2.31f, 172, 225,
    263, 323; 4.167, 237; 8.214f;
    9.215; 10.158, 181; 11.164f,
    186, 200–202, 217f; 14.196,
    213f; 16.62, 160
    and Greeks 9.79, 249
    and Jews 1.128f, 310; 2.22,
    223, 282; 3.63, 293; 4.60, 69f,
    156, 177; 6.160f; 8.64
Works 1.187, 191, 235; 5.213f;
    8.102, 180; 10.105; 12.23;
    14.316; 15.37; 17.114
World, The 1.22, 236, 242, 391;
    2.154; 5.42; 6.167, 181, 214;
    7.109; 8.157; 9.44, 196;
    10.182; 13.137; 14.86f, 102f;
    15.16, 56f, 95; 17.82
World to come 1.134; 3.250;
    4.253; 13.56f
Worldliness 3.247; 14.103
Worms 1.141
Wormwood 17.44
Worry 1.254–261; 4.165; 8.200;
    11.77
Worship 2.66, 117, 271; 3.103f;
    4.28, 180; 5.112f; 7.30f;
    8.126; 9.95f, 130, 132; 11.38,
    56; 13.61, 102, 120f; 16.160;
    17.109f, 222
    in Early Church 7.149;
    9.134f; 11.159; 14.127
    false 5.159–161; 12.241
    Jewish 2.117, 295f; 3.275,
    293
    and women 9.95–100
    true 5.158f; 8.155–157; 14.61f
Writing, ancient 1.279; 4.115;

7.35f, 86; 8.ixf, 46, 165;
9.33; 11.142; 14.137; 15.147
pseudonymous 14.288; 15.172

Yemen 17.162
Yoke 2.17

Zanzibar 17.161
Zeal 8.165; 11.60; 14.91

Zealots, the 1.359; 3.74; 4.75;
6.59, 248; 8.173; 14.229;
17.68
Zebulun, tribe of 1.73
Zion, Mount 3.272; 10.143
Zodiac 16.158; 17.75, 214f
Zoroastrianism 4.263; 5.47;
9.196; 15.55; 17.59,
130

INDEX OF PERSONAL NAMES

Aaron **1**.12; **2**.276; **4**.40; **12**.194

Abbot, E. A. **3**.287

Abbott, T. K. **11**.155

Abednego **1**.117

Abel **2**.298; **8**.213; **15**.189

Abgar **1**.81

Abiathar **16**.133

Abijah **16**.121

Abishai **1**.225; **3**.22

Abraham **1**.12, 47, 55, 62, 224; **3**.62, 87; **4**.40, 54, 185; **5**.14, 90; **6**.24–26, 34–36; **7**.55; **8**.6, 12, 47, 62–71, 101, 116, 120; **9**.221; **10**.6, 24, 27f, 33, 41; **11**.38f, 55, 57f, 138; **13**.62, 142–145, 191; **14**.29, 35, 42, 200, 327; **16**.9, 25, 38, 52, 98, 121, 134; **17**.11, 26, 151, 188, 200, 205f, 226

  covenant of **8**.125; **10**.28; **17**.205f

  descendants of **9**.252; **10**.28; **14**.41

  faith of **13**.144, 152; **14**.78

  friend of God **6**.178

  and Gentiles **8**.41

  and Gerizim **5**.157

  and Kingdom of God **1**.210

  legends of **13**.142–144

  and Melchizedek **13**.69f

  and Messiah **6**.34f

  promises to **10**.41f; **13**.146f

  and rabbis **2**.140

  seed of **15**.78

  sons of **1**.60; **4**.33; **8**.65f,. 120; **10**.6

Abrahams, I. **2**.246f

Abram See Abraham

Achaicus **9**.6, 8, 166

Achan **1**.239; **6**.48; **8**.79; **14**.115

Acher **9**.256

Achilles **3**.335; **4**.246; **7**.39; **12**.26; **13**.110

Acilius Glabrio **8**.210

Acland, Lady. **7**.18

Acton, Lord **3**.286

Adam **4**.40; **6**.251; **8**.79–81, 95f, 103, 110; **9**.150f, 157; **16**.69; **17**.199

  covenant of **16**.161

  and Eve **2**.200; **9**.246; **14**.52; **17**.17, 98

  legends of **13**.131; **14**.50f, 53; **16**.38

  Life of Adam and Eve See Index VI

  rib of **9**.98

Adonai **6**.210f

Adonis **1**.25

Adrian **12**.124

Aelian **9**.2

Aeneas **7**.77; **12**.61

Aesculapius **1**.289; **9**.110; **12**.18; **14**.89, 95

Aeschines **1**.78; **12**.106; **15**.36

Aeschylus **8**.202; **9**.150; **10**.82; **11**.203; **13**.48, 110; **14**.143, 298; **16**.113

Afranius Burrus **17**.91

Agabus 7.19

Agamemnon 10.148

Agate, J. 1.348; 10.158; 11.210; 14.350

Agatharchides 2.29

Agesilaus 12.196

Aglaitidas 13.176

Agrippa 3.312; 7.4, 173–176, 178; 9.106; 14.40

Agrippina 8.32; 17.90–92

Ahab, King 12.102; 16.105

Ahasuerus 17.23

Ahaz 1.141; 3.231

Ahaziah 17.132

Ahijah 2.240; 3.339

Ahriman 3.23; 5.47; 9.196; 17.59, 130

Ahura-Mainyu 15.55

Ahura-Mazda 15.55

Aidan 8.16

Akiba, rabbi 1.152; 2.198; 3.239, 293; 4.212; 9.256; 10.169

Albert, King 4.161

Albinus 14.12

Alcibiades 5.140; 9.132; 12.205; 13.142; 14.114, 120; 15.85

Alcimus See Eliakim

Alexander, the apostate 12.53

Alexander, coppersmith 12.219

Alexander the Great 1.39, 98, 154f; 2.84; 3.124, 202; 7.122; 8.165f; 11.137, 179f, 186; 12.26; 14.39; 16.87, 115; 17.88

Alexander, of Herod 1.29, 36; 3.149

Alexander Philalethes 16.138

Alexander, rabbi 1.327; 3.187

Alexander Severus 1.274

Alexander, of Simon 2.366; 3.361; 4.283; 8.216

Alexandra 1.29, 36

Alexandrai, rabbi 14.131

Alford, Dean 11.175

Aliturus 6.183; 14.149

Allen, W. C. 2.40

Allenby, E. 1.39

Allshorn, F. 1.83, 124; 2.25; 4.53; 10.40; 12.103

Alypius 8.177f

Ambrose 4.209; 6.290; 11.31f; 12.35, 205f

Ami, rabbi 1.327

Amnon 12.79

Amos 1.193; 13.13

Amplias 8.9

Ampliatus 8.212

Amram 13.155

Anacreon 1.256

Ananias, high priest 7.164

Ananias, prophet 7.72, 75, 77, 161

Ananias and Saphira 12.44, 54, 82

Ananus 6.233; 14.12

Anaximenes 3.359

Andreas 17.225, 227

Andrew, apostle 1.77; 3.54; 5.5, 21, 23, 88, 91, 202, 204f; 6.120; 8.221; 14.162; 15.175

Andrew, Father 1.208

Andrews, C. F. 6.81

Andromache 12.26

Andronicus 8.212; 10.145; 14.17

Andronicus Rhodius 14.58

Anilaeus 14.38

Anna 4.4, 27f; 16.105

---

1 Matt, v.1   3 Mark   5 John, v.1   7 Acts   9 Cor
2 Matt, v.2   4 Luke   6 John, v.2   8 Rom   10 Gal, Eph

Annas 3.274; 4.3, 32; 6.225
  bazaars of 2.246; 6.226
  booths of 4.242
Anthony, saint 1.149
Antisthenes 8.199; 9.37
Antiochus Epiphanes 2.28, 241,
  282, 306; 3.172, 267, 310;
  6.69; 8.137; 13.30, 166f,
  183; 14.202; 15.62f; 16.137;
  17.26, 60f, 62, 69, 79
Antiochus the Great 11.93; 14.40
Antiochus of Sardis 16.115
Antipas 16.92
Antipater 1.29, 36; 3.149
Antiphanes 12.35
Antistius Vetus 14.219
Antoinette, Marie 1.42
Anton, P. 12.2
Antoninus 3.85; 6.37
Antonia 12.200
Antony 7.168; 11.3; 12.78
Apelles 8.213
Aphrodite 1.154; 7.134; 9.3,
  52; 10.162; 12.38, 67; 16.75;
  17.144
Apicius 17.156
Apion 14.202
Apollo 1.289; 7.89; 10.34;
  15.124; 16.75, 89
Apollonius 2.80, 16.75
Apollos 7.138f; 8.209; 9.14f,
  36, 38f, 165; 11.103; 12.68,
  266; 13.9; 16.60
Apphia 12.277f
Apuleius 5.73, 127
Aquila and Priscilla 7.136, 139;
  8.7–9, 208–211; 9.5, 167f;
  11.172; 12.68, 221f; 13.9;
  16.60

Aquinas 2.119; 8.35; 9.174;
  12.2, 80
Archelaus 1.39; 2.95; 3.150,
  284; 4.31, 35, 237; 6.237;
  7.93; 14.38
Archelaus of Macedonia 9.260
Archippus 11.174; 12.159, 273,
  277f; 16.139
Aristarchus 7.181, 192; 9.229;
  11.169
Aristeas 1.134
Aristides 6.185f; 13.142, 192;
  15.85; 16.73f; 17.155
Aristion 5.23; 14.162f
Aristippus 14.84
Aristobulus 1.29, 36, 74; 3.149f;
  4.35f; 5.123; 7.93; 8.213
  household of 8.9
Aristophanes 13.191; 16.88;
  17.130
Aristotle 1.96, 302, 375; 2.246;
  3.246; 8.ix, 28, 36, 37, 45;
  9.40, 79, 109; 10.52, 82, 113,
  137, 179; 11.34, 158, 179;
  12.35, 39, 45, 61, 80, 83, 104,
  107, 186, 235, 236, 238, 240,
  259, 271; 13.174; 14.40, 58,
  84, 95, 186, 211, 300, 302;
  17.211
Armitage, A.H.N.G. 5.22, 100
Arnobius 8.172
Arnold, M. 1.216; 3.132, 235,
  251; 5.212; 9.123f, 198;
  11.79; 13.120; 14.96, 128;
  17.198
Artemas 12.265
Artemis 1.196; 7.140f, 146;
  12.89; 16.89
  Temple of 16.59

Artemon 8.ix
Arthur, King 2.372; 10.125
Asclepios 16.75, 91
  A. Soter 16.89
Asher, *Testament of* See Index VI
Ashmedai 6.31
Asidaeus 14.38
Asquith, C. 13.122
Asquith, M. 3.140, 144
Assael 3.34
Astor J. J. 1.348
Athanasius 13.5; 14.5; 16.161
Athenagoras 8.172; 13.12;
  14.280
Athene 10.174; 16.89, 91
Attalus II 16.125
Attalus III 14.145; 16.87
Augustine 1.133, 228f; 2.140;
  3.161, 294; 4.63, 193; 5.13,
  64, 86, 138, 155; 5.14; 6.81,
  290f; 8.96, 168, 177f, 190;
  9.18, 39, 192; 12.44, 263;
  13.8; 14.4, 207, 279, 323;
  15.6, 18, 41, 93; 16.119, 161;
  17.37, 130, 190f
Augustus, emperor 1.27, 29;
  3.71, 229; 4.31, 85, 237;
  5.98; 6.238; 7.123; 9.249;
  10.171, 180; 11.21, 137;
  12.78; 13.177; 16.17f, 99;
  17.89, 139, 146, 161
Aulus Fulvius 13.177
Aulus Plautius 12.223
Aurelius Archelaus 9.185
Aurora 1.271
Avery, M. 1.318; 5.209
Azai, rabbi ben 9.69, 256
Azariah 1.365
Azazel 14.322f

Bacchus 10.9
Bacon 6.242; 13.135
Bagehot, W. 12.204
Bailey, P. J. 12.171
Bain 1.348
Balaam 3.22; 14.332; 15.159,
  164, 190; 16.66f, 92; 17.81
Balak 14.333
Baldwin, S. 1.324; 3.223; 13.200
Ball, R. 15.162
Balthasar 1.31; 3.65
Barabbas 3.173, 356–358
  Jesus B. 2.361; 6.248f
Barachios 2.298
Barak 4.47; 13.163; 17.132
Barclay, F. 4.153
Bar-Jesus See Elymas
Barnabas 1.109; 3.3, 361; 7.19,
  75f, 90, 98f, 117f; 10.139,
  145; 12.44
  apostle 14.17
  Letter of See Index VI
  and Hebrews Epistle 13.8f
  and Paul 7.96–101, 117, 118;
  8.13; 10.19; 11.170; 12.21,
  217, 232; 17.110
Barrett, C. K. 6.166
Barrie, J. M. 1.41, 149, 229;
  2.250; 4.39, 168, 265; 8.64;
  9.121, 171; 11.72; 12.210;
  13.122, 138; 14.113, 273
Bartholemew 5.94f
Bartimaeus 3.260
Barton, B. 3.12f, 257; 4.267
Baruch
  Apocalypse of See Index VI
  Book of See Index VI
Basil 9.264, 265; 10.48, 135, 153
Basilides 12.8

Bathsheba 1.17; 3.85

Baxter, R. 15.161

Beare, F. W. 14.138, 142

Beatus 16.31

Becker 10.175

Beckwith 17.142

Bede 4.127

Beethoven 1.213; 7.189; 8.73, 166; 10.126; 13.117

Belden, A. D. 3.41

Belial 11.212; 17.59

Beliar See Belial

Belloc, H. 1.353

Benaiah 16.133

Bengel, J. 2.122f; 3.80, 174; 4.193; 6.126, 219; 8.59; 10.177; 11.13, 67, 163; 13.57; 14.220, 252, 300

Benjamin, *Testament of* See Index VI

Bennett, A. 4.137; 10.158

Bernanos, G. 5.233

Bernard, saint 16.147

Bernard, J. H. 5.74; 6.120; 10.135

Bernice 7.93, 174

Berokah of Chuza, rabbi 2.14

Beza 9.13; 12.173

Bias 14.55

Bigg, C. 14.143, 151, 176, 224, 230, 247, 300, 334, 348

Bilney, T. 4.91; 11.112; 13.56; 14.128

Binyon, L. 6.148

Birkett, N. 1.100; 3.153

Bishop, E. F. F. 1.121

Bithia 13.156

Black, J. 8.169

Blackie, J. S. 1.41

Blake, W. 2.373

Blastus 7.97

Boadicea, queen 17.5

Boanerges 5.16, 18

Boaz 6.146

Booth, W. 3.362; 4.68, 116; 9.208

Boreham F. W. 1.236; 4.8, 235; 8.124f; 10.89; 12.46

Borrow, G. H. 3.122

Boswell, J. 1.190; 3.152; 9.83, 160; 10.90

Botherich 12.205

Bottomley 15.161

Bradley, A. C. 1.244

Bridges, R. 1.223

Britannicus 17.91

Brooke A. E. 15.43, 47, 65, 77, 83, 97, 103, 115

Brooke, R. 1.115; 4.259f; 8.20

Brooks, C. 8.188

Brown, E. F. 11.103; 12.38, 40, 44, 55, 63, 80, 120, 129, 139, 193, 205, 248, 255

Brown, J. 1.285; 6.20; 7.18; 15.22

Brown, R. 1.227

Brown, R. McAfee 6.102

Brown, T. E. 3.186

Browne, T. 1.275; 14.92

Browning, E. B. 1.400; 3.186; 4.274; 5.142

Browning, R. 1.117, 214; 4.124; 5.155, 191; 6.32, 198f; 7.104; 8.20; 9.200, 202; 13.89, 178; 14.43, 247

Bruce, A. B. 3.5f; 4.195; 6.162; 9.179; 12.126; 13.70

Brugman 1.306

| 11 Phil, Col, Thes | 13 Heb | 15 John, Jude | 16 Rev, v.1 |
| 12 Tim, Tit, Phlm | 14 Jas, Pet | | 17 Rev, v.2 |

Brunner, E.   15.143
Brutus   11.3; 13.125
Bryant, A.   1.251
Buchan   A.   3.113; 10.178
Buchan, J.   11.197
Buchanan   10.89
Bultmann, R.   2.234; 9.14, 22
Bunyan, J.   1.51, 106, 395, 396,
    397; 3.20, 77, 184, 314; 7.12,
    24; 9.173; 12.132, 134;
    13.128, 129, 151; 14.90, 128;
    15.163, 182
Burke, E.   1.279
Burke, R.   1.279
Burkitt, F. C.   2.246; 11.52
Burns, J.   3.123, 277
Burns, R.   1.227, 240; 2.119;
    3.25, 139; 4.66, 185; 8.146,
    164, 194; 9.68, 174; 10.8,
    152; 13.137; 14.52; 16.117
Burroughs, E.   2.52
Burrus   17.92
Burton   8.2
Bushnell, H.   9.132f
Butler, bishop   4.71

Cadoux, C. J.   3.89
Caedmon   5.46; 9.12
Caesar   8.172; 12.78; 16.81
    godhead of   2.134; 3.192;
    9.107, 222
    image of   3.287
Caiaphas, J.   2.326, 373f; 4.3,
    32; 6.104f, 225
    house of   2.373
Cain   13.131–133; 15.17, 84,
    159, 164, 189f
    daughters of   14.323
Cairns, J.   3.156; 4.190; 6.162;

8.164
Caleb   9.88; 13.36; 14.35; 16.25
Caligula, emperor   2.97; 3.310;
    8.31; 14.40, 221; 15.63;
    16.18; 17.89, 90, 93, 95, 139,
    146, 155f, 159
Callimachus   12.243; 14.346
Callistus   1.377; 14.211
Calvin, J.   9.257; 10.61; 12.173;
    13.8; 14.259, 277, 285, 348
Cambyses   1.264
Cameron, R.   1.213; ˈ4.14
Campbell, T.   3.140
Candace, queen   7.68
Capitolinus   13.87
Carabas   6.247
Carey, W.   9.121
Carleton, W.   5.28
Carlyle, T.   1.251, 284; 3.16, 28;
    4.44, 63, 113f; 6.112; 8.97,
    164; 9.44, 78, 235; 11.194;
    12.196
    father of   6.62; 8.161
Carr   1.37
Carrington, P.   16.2
Carswell, C.   1.189
Caspar   1.31; 3.64
Cassander   11.180
Cassandra   4.246
Cassian   5.18
Cassiodorus   15.18
Cassius   11.3
Castor & Pollux   7.189
Catullus   9.155; 11.203; 13.136;
    14.187
Catiline   13.177
Cato   1.302; 2.80; 10.179;
    12.77; 14.218, 220, 222
Cavour   3.218; 13.147

Cebes 1.278

Celsus 1.34, 289; 2.350; 5.73;
9.19, 21, 141; 10.122; 14.204
Against Celsus Sèe Index VI

Cephas See Peter, apostle

Cerinthus 5.12, 18, 21; 15.7f,
108, 144; 17.190

Cervantes 3.226

Cestius 2.328; 3.324; 4.263

Chalmers, J. 3.227; 4.35; 9.261;
13.22

Chamberlain, N. 3.140

Chanina, rabbi 1.390

Chapman, J. 1.244, 247

Charlemagne, emperor 4.111

Charles, R. H. 16.29, 89, 98,
103, 173; 17.40, 120, 123,
149, 172, 180, 232

Charlie, prince 9.92f

Charrington, F. W. 9.222

Chase, bishop 14.286

Chesterton, G. K. 1.14, 348;
3.264, 316; 4.44, 75, 77, 92,
96; 6.18; 8.181; 10.130;
12.171; 13.24; 14.349

Chija ben Abba, rabbi 1.327

Chillingworth, W. 10.90

Chirgwin, A. M. 3.82f; 6.94;
12.146, 199f

Chiyya, rabbi 3.86

Chloe ix.6, 8, 13

Chopin, F. 4.272

Christ See *Jesus*

Christie, W. M. 1.317

Chrysippus 2.313; 14.341

Chrysologus, P. 1.302; 14.211

Chrysostom 2.349; 3.3; 5.211;
6.49; 8.42, 168; 9.19, 20,
119, 212, 213, 218; 10.50,

116, 138, 167, 173; 12.11,
102, 256; 13.60, 152; 14.303,
324; 15.73; 17.113

Churchill, W. 1.132, 374, 380;
3.201; 5.28; 8.199

Chuza 4.96

Cicero 1.14, 139, 153; 2.164;
3.125; 6.250; 7.163; 10.82,
83, 113, 161; 12.78, 104;
13.2; 14.38, 99, 207, 303;
16.74, 138

Clark, A. 9.124

Clark, G. N. 10.85

Clarkson, T. 2.76

Claudia 12.222

Claudia Procula 2.359

Claudias Lysias 7.4, 167; 14.23,
36

Claudius, emperor 1.114, 344;
3.134, 320; 7.136; 8.7, 32,
106, 208f, 213; 12.222;
16.18, 59; 17.89, 90f, 93, 139,
144, 146

Clement of Alexandria, 1.160,
307, 379; 2.207; 5.10, 17,
21; 6.154; 8.28, 32; 9.109;
10.160; 12.249; 13.5, 7, 149;
14.10, 64, 134, 277, 280, 285;
15.19, 28f, 97; 16.67

Clement (N.T.) 11.74

Clement of Rome 9.214; 12.10,
60, 158; 13.161; 14.137, 141

Clementine
Letters of See Index VI
Recognitions of See Index VI

Cleopatra of Egypt 5.98; 7.168;
17.156

Cleopatra of Jerusalem 3.150

Clogg, F. B. 14.286

Clough, A. H. 2.82; 4.122; 12.154

Clovis 9.24

Cnaeus Domitius Ahenobarbus 17.90

Cockburn, Lord 9.188

Cogidubnus 12.222

Coleridge, S. T. 1.251, 280; 8.178; 9.85; 10.62, 123, 157

Colman, R. 1.262

Columella 8.4

Confucius 1.274; 4.79

Conrad 7.63

Constantine 1.25, 120

Copernicus 1.339; 3.101

Coponius 6.233

Cornelius Gallus 17.51

Cornelius (N.T.) 1.301; 2.145; 7.4, 5, 19, 79f, 88, 114; 14.178; 15.90

Cotton 9.244

Courvoisier, Prof. 2.31

Cousin, A. R. 11.193

Cowley 3.174

Cowper, W. 8.166; 16.65

Cranfield, C. E. B. 14.169, 190, 195, 205f, 225, 227, 252

Cranmer, T. 1.255

Crassus 5.109

Crescens 12.218

Crispus 9.5, 16

Croesus 16.113f

Cromwell, O. 1.394; 3.253; 4.130; 7.45, 53; 8.183; 9.34, 88; 10.184; 13.52, 165; 14.340; 15.145; 16.91

Cromwell, T. 3.329

Cronin, A. J. 4.128

Crooks, W. 3.138f

Curzon, Lord 3.223

Cybele 9.117; 10.44; 12.17; 16.74f

Cynics 3.127; 9.37, 65

Cyprian 12.59; 13.5; 16.84

Cyrenius 3.285

Cyril of Alexandria 6.283; 14.323

Cyril of Jerusalem 6.23; 9.168; 14.280

Cyrus 2.33; 6.5; 9.89; 11.92; 12.186; 13.60; 15.36; 16.114f; 17.110, 128f

Dale, R. W. 1.184

Damaris 7.133

Damocles 14.158

Dan, *Testament of* See Index VI

Daniel 1.234; 13.164

Dante 3.156, 328

Daphne 7.89

Darius 3.202

Darwin, C. 4.162; 6.114

David, King 1.9, 13, 47, 101, 225; 2.23; 3.22, 50, 63, 85, 193, 281; 4.40, 70; 5.82; 6.142; 11.10, 54; 13.90, 163f; 14.293; 15.69; 16.25, 133; 17.59, 81

city of 1.24

covenant of 13.90

house of 2.145

key of 2.144; 16.127

kingdom of 17.206

line of 4.26; 7.23, 105; 16.2

servant of God 6.178

Davidson, A. B. 10.118

Davies, T. W. 9.97

Davies, W. H. 7.32; 12.214

Deborah 4.47; 13.163; 16.105; 17.132

Deeping, W. 5.155

Deissmann, G. A. 4.76; 8.xif; 11.218; 17.100

Demas 4.286; 11.171; 12.212–215; 14.103; 15.153; 17.106

Demetrianus 12.59

Demetrius, prophet 15.132, 135, 153

Demetrius, silversmith 7.146; 12.214; 15.153

Demetrius, critic 8.ix

Democritus 12.131

Demonax 14.55

Demosthenes 1.153; 5.195; 10.170; 11.199; 12.106, 240; 13.11, 132; 15.36f

Denney, James 1.285; 2.8, 79f; 4.1; 7.67, 177; 8.87; 12.280; 13.22; 15.204

Diana 2.207; 7.140f; 12.67, 89; 15.124; 16.59

Dibelius 8.1

Dickinson, G. L. 13.111

Didymus 5.90; 6.87; 14.285 called Thomas 7.100

Didymus of Alexandria 14.303; 15.168

Dill, S. 17.154f

Dio Cassius 10.79; 14.38

Dio Chrysostom 12.125, 207

Diocletian 13.57

Diogenes 1.44, 333, 386; 3.127; 9.23, 186; 14.315

Diogenes Laertius 12.75; 15.37

Diognetus, *Epistle to* See Index VI

Dion Cassius See Dio Cassius

Dionysius of Alexandria 16.13;

17.190

Dionysius the Areopagite 7.133; 9.21

Dionysius the Great 5.23

Dionysius of Halicarnassus 4.7

Dionysos 5.104

Dionysus 9.117

Diotima 1.155

Diotrephes 15.131f, 135f, 152f

Dismas 1.34f; 4.286

Dives 4.213f; 6.34, 102; 17.113

Dixon, McN. 8.185

Dodd, C. H. 2.82; 8.25, 92, 111, 112, 178; 14.140; 15.29, 39, 43, 56, 58, 65, 84, 98, 101, 115, 142, 144, 145, 153

Domatilla 8.212, 216

Domitian, emperor 5.17; 8.216; 9.21; 12.60; 15.173; 16.14, 19, 41, 164; 17.8, 89, 93, 101, 139–141, 147
    persecution of 13.6

Don Carlos 9.180

Dorcas 5.90; 6.87

Dore 6.268

Doris 3.149

Doryphorus 17.91

Drake, F. 7.10

Drinkwater, J. 10.131

Driver, G. R. 17.49

Drusilla 7.93f, 168, 171

Duguid, J. 1.135; 5.236; 7.175

Dumachus 4.286

Dundas 12.232

Dunsany, Lord 8.52

Easton 12.117; 14.30

Eby Kermit 13.40, 58, 73

Edersheim, A. 2.48, 114, 127,

161; 6.225

Edward I 7.44

Edward the Confessor 6.95

Edwards, T. C. 9.167

Egnatius 14.218

Eleazar 4.214; 6.105; 8.137;
13.168

Elektra 15.19

Elgar, E. 14.273

Eli 2.42; 12.134; 17.59

Eliakim 2.145; 7.100; 16.128,
133

Eliezer, rabbi 1.56, 192, 194,
274; 2.48f, 116; 10.111

Eliezer ben Hyrcanus, rabbi 1.34

Eliezer ben Jacob, rabbi 1.368

Elijah 1.44f, 49, 64, 282; 2.14,
136f, 160, 287, 369; 3.16, 22,
147, 211, 213, 364; 4.19, 48,
90, 126; 5.244; 6.45; 8.120,
144; 13.164, 166; 14.29,
132; 15.69; 16.6, 25; 17.42,
79, 143

meaning of name 4.17

at Passover 3.338

return of 2.6, 164f; 3.195f;
4.115; 5.78f; 17.70f

at Transfiguration 2.156–63;
4.123

Eliot G. 1.247; 9.150

Eliot, T. S. 6.242

Eliphaz 3.47; 4.173; 6.126;
10.158

Elisha 1.239; 2.159, 287; 3.24,
127; 4.48, 86, 134; 13.164,
166; 15.69; 17.42

Elizabeth 2.96; 4.4, 10f, 17

Ellicott, C. J. 11.13

Elliott, W. H. 1.312

El Shaddai 9.188

Elymas 1.26; 7.19, 100; 12.54

Emerson, R. W. 6.244; 12.34

Enoch 8.104; 13.133–135;
14.238–240; 15.159; 16.122;
17.70

Book of See Index VI

Book of the Secrets of See
Index VI

legends of 13.134

Epaenetus 8.8

Epaphroditus 7.192; 9.230;
11.6f, 48–50, 74; 12.159

Epaphras 11.94, 107, 171;
12.269; 16.25

Ephraim 5.152

Epicharmus 1.278f

Epictetus 1.274, 283, 336, 396;
3.114; 4.65, 278; 8.19, 113,
197; 9.55, 69, 140, 204, 254;
10.13; 11.85, 132; 12.19,
58, 125, 159, 204, 265; 13.62,
139; 14.76, 207, 220, 304,
326; 15.115

Epicurus 1.55; 8.19; 9.22;
12.129; 13.129, 139, 195

Epidaurus 9.110

Epimenides 7.132; 12.243

Epiphanius 13.17

Erasmus 1.385; 11.124; 12.208;
13.57; 14.277; 15.111

Erastus 9.21; 12.222

Esau 4.17; 8.120, 128; 11.58;
16.133

legends of 13.183f

Esdras, *Apocalypse of* See
Index VI

Eudemus 12.236

Eumenes 16.88

Eunice 11.47; 12.68
Euodia 11.71–74; 12.68
Euripides 8.202; 9.140, 155;
   10.25, 48; 12.80, 107f, 236,
   239; 13.111, 132; 14.95,
   298; 17.4
Eusebius 1.81; 2.360; 4.112;
   5.3, 17, 18, 23; 12.11, 61,
   118; 13.5; 14.5, 12, 151,
   204, 285; 15.7, 38, 127, 167;
   16.14; 17.79, 141, 190, 231
Euthymius Zigabenus 6.290
Eutychus 7.149
Evans, C. 6.124
Evans, E. 1.312
Evans, M. 1.247
Eve See *Adam & Eve*
Evelyn 1.37
Ezekiel 14.79
Ezra 1.12, 74; 2.281; 4.40;
   5.150; 7.65
   Apocalypse of See Index VI

Faber 1.341; 4.6; 11.83; 13.162
Fabiola 2.80
Falconer, R. 12.144, 158, 164,
   235
Farmer, H. H. 5.112
Farrar, F. W. 9.2, 4; 14.147
Farson, N. 1.294
Faustus 6.83
Felicitas 14.211
Felix 3.312; 7.94, 166–168, 171;
   12.283
Festus 3.312; 7.4; 172–176,
   178; 11.188; 14.12
Findlay, J. A. 2.319; 3.62; 5.192
Fisher, H. A. L. 10.85
Fisher, Lord 14.82

Flaccus 11.93; 16.139
Flavius Clemens 8.216; 9.21
Flavius Sabinus 8.217
Fleming, A. L. 14.128
Foch, Marshal 4.53; 12.160
Foligras, Andela di 3.123
Forbes, R. 8.72
Fortunatus 9.6, 8, 166
Fosdick, H. E. 1.288; 3.42;
   4.68; 6.129; 7.101; 9.120;
   12.218; 13.130; 16.65
Foster, J. 7.10; 13.43
Fowler, W. 12.61; 14.304
Fox, G. 1.161, 396; 15.145, 161,
   162
Foxe, J. 4.151; 9.214
Francis of Assissi 2.326; 3.24;
   4.95; 6.138; 10.56; 12.254f
Francis of Sales 2.107
Frankau, G. 1.262; 6.87
Frazer, J. G. 5.178
Freeman, K. J. 2.80
Freud, S. 9.86
Friedlander, L. 14.202; 17.154
Frohman, C. 13.138
Froude, J. A. 5.58; 6.112;
   8.26; 9.147; 14.340; 17.86
Fry, E. 3.107

Gabriel 10.93f; 13.18, 156;
   14.323, 325; 16.31, 174;
   17.41, 175
Gaius 15.131f, 135, 147f, 150
Gaius of Augustus 3.229; 15.37
   of Corinth 8.220; 9.16; 15.148
   of Derbe 15.147
   of Macedonia 15.147
   of Rome 1.302; 10.180
Galba, emperor 3.257; 8.130;

16.19; 17.89, 92f, 139
Galen 3.146; 12.176; 13.82, 193; 14.129; 16.89
Galerius 12.59
Galileo 3.101f; 4.68
Gallio 7.3f, 137; 9.5; 16.15
Galloway 6.93
Galsworthy, J. 3.28
Gamaliel 7.49f, 160; 11.59
Gamaliel II, rabbi 6.89
Gandhi 2.254
Garfield, president 1.231
Garibaldi, G. 1.375; 3.201; 6.191
Gee, H. L. 1.399; 2.62f; 6.206; 9.172, 261; 10.129
Gehazi 1.239
George V 6.275; 9.172
Gibbon, E. 3.205; 4.85; 8.173
Gibbs, P. 3.108; 6.242; 10.91, 113
Gideon 4.47; 13.163; 17.180
Gilbert, H. 7.184
Gilbert, W. S. 13.136
Gladstone, W. E. 4.148
Glaucus 12.151
Glover, R. 2.143, 145, 175
Glover, T. R. 1.323, 394, 397; 4.130; 5.73; 6.138; 7.128; 8.15, 185; 11.85; 15.41
Godet, F. L. 5.91; 6.100
Goethe, W. 1.75; 5.48; 8.181
Gog 17.60, 194
Goldsmith 10.90
Goodspeed, E. J. 3.287; 5.7, 26; 10.68; 11.126; 12.269, 274; 14.30, 138; 15.7; 16.16
Goodwin, T. 12.46
Gore, C. 9.145

Gorgias 12.156
Gorion 5.123
Gosse, E. 3.122
Gossip, A. J. 4.8; 6.162; 10.13; 12.160; 13.45, 72
Gough, J. B. 10.54
Graham, Billy 3.13
Gray, T. 1.279
Green, B. 7.72
Gregory the Great 2.235; 3.258
Gregory of Nazianzen 13.82
Gregory of Nyssa 2.234; 3.258; 8.16; 12.127
Grenfell, W. 1.135; 5.105, 191, 236f; 7.175
Grenville, G. 2.76
Grice, S. Le 1.220
Gunkel, H. 17.133
Gunther, J. 10.11

Haarhoff, T. J. 10.123
Hadrian 1.25; 9.54; 13.87
Hagar 8.128; 10.41; 11.58
Hamilton, W. 6.162
Hananiah 2.240; 3.339
Handel 6.195; 9.195; 16.151
Hankey, D. 6.140; 8.15; 14.337
Hannah 4.15; 14.112; 17.59
Hannibal 13.126f
Hanum 16.143
Hanway, J. 1.339; 6.185
Hardy, H. E. 1.208
Hardy, T. 1.215; 3.344; 4.189; 5.219; 8.15; 10.91
Harnack, A. 3.33; 10.69; 13.9, 193
Harris, R. 14.238; 15.130
Harrison, P. N. 12.155
Hastings, J. 9.97

Hawkins **1.**190
Hazael **15.**69
Healy, G. **1.**16
Heawood, G. **1.**353
Hegesippus **14.**10, 12, 14
Heine **1.**204; **8.**43
Heli **4.**41
Heliodorus **12.**149
Helofernes **13.**164
Helvidius **14.**20
Henley **8.**74
Henry V **1.**126; **7.**111; **9.**216
Henry VI **12.**176
Henry VIII **1.**386; **3.**206; **4.**186
Henry, O. **3.**230; **4.**15; **6.**109;
    16.64
Heracles **17.**103
Heraclitus **3.**57; **5.**34f; **15.**124;
    16.60
Herbert, G. **1.**41, 183; **9.**65;
    12.123, 128
Hercules **12.**26
Hermas, *Shepherd of* See Index VI
Hermes **5.**222; **7.**109
Hermogenes **12.**156; **17.**140
Herod Agrippa I **2.**97, 135;
    3.256; **7.**93, 96f; **14.**9
Herod Agrippa II **7.**93
Herod Antipas **1.**39, 71, 331;
    2.1, 93–98, 133, 136; **3.**53,
    146, 150, 160, 187f, 213, 237,
    284; **4.**3, 31, 35f, 115, 186,
    222, 237, 278–280; **6.**237;
    7.93
Herod the Great **1.**12, 28–30,
    36–39, 43; **2.**95, 134; **3.**53,
    149–153, 284; **4.**31, 35f, 237;
    5.116, 237; **7.**93, 167; **12.**78
Herod Philip **2.**94, 97; **3.**150,

191; **4.**3, 31, 35, 173, 237;
    6.237; **7.**93
Herodias **2.**94–96; **3.**149f, 152f;
    4.35f; **7.**93
Herodion **8.**213
Herodotus **1.**365; **4.**7; **6.**119;
    9.154; **11.**92, 180; **12.**17,
    151; **13.**48; **14.**261; **17.**103,
    128
Histories of See Index VI
Hervey, H. **12.**216
Hesiod **1.**278; **5.**178; **10.**82
Heywood, T. **16.**75
Hezekiah **5.**134; **6.**43; **12.**150;
    13.164, 166; **16.**128; **17.**22
Hieronymus See Jerome
Hilarion **2.**81
Hilary of Poitiers **14.**3
Hillel, rabbi **1.**170, 263, 273,
    284, 367, 390; **2.**198, 200;
    3.113, 164, 239, 293; **4.**79;
    6.70; **10.**169
    school of **1.**152; **4.**212
Hind, L. **3.**51
Hippocrates **12.**280; **16.**89
Hippolytus **14.**312; **15.**70;
    16.67; **17.**25, 85
Canons of See Index VI
Hitler, A. **5.**234; **15.**63; **17.**100
Hogan **9.**244
Holland **3.**181
Holmes, O. Wendell **1.**120
Homer **3.**138, 335; **5.**98; **9.**167;
    10.109; **12.**234; **13.**110, 117;
    14.216; **16.**73, 75
Honorius **3.**204
Hood, T. **9.**203
Horace **1.**279; **9.**155; **12.**78,
    245; **17.**156

Horder, Lord 3.140

Hort, F. J. 12.24, 25, 207;
　　14.42, 45, 46, 55

Housman, A. E. 1.180

Huldah 16.105

Huna, rabbi 2.14f

Hunt, H. 1.32; 16.148

Hunt, L. 9.30

Hutton, J. 5.132; 9.25

Huxley, T. 5.92; 9.240

Hymenaeus 12.53, 174f, 178

Iamblichus 12.80

Iberina 1.157

Ibsen 1.120; 13.58

Ignatius 2.175; 6.283; 12.19,
　　106, 275; 14.137, 139; 15.8,
　　142; 16.28, 42, 58, 60; 17.11

Inchfawn, F. 4.295f, 298

Inge, R. 12.214

Irenaeus 5.18, 20, 115; 6.154;
　　8.125; 12.94, 192; 14.129,
　　141, 278, 309; 15.29, 108,
　　137, 166; 16.67, 160; 17.101,
　　189, 231

Irwin, M. 6.242

Isaac 1.62, 210; 4.54; 8.120,
　　128; 10.41; 12.76; 13.151–
　　154; 14.35, 42, 78
　　covenant of 8.125

Isaiah 2.136; 4.157; 8.145;
　　13.13, 166; 16.25
　　Ascension of See Index VI

Iscariot See Judas Iscariot

Ishii, T. 3.60, 80; 6.94

Ishmael (O.T.) 8.120, 127f;
　　10.41

Ishmael, rabbi 1.171

Ishtar 17.80

Isis 2.65
　　Mysteries of 3.91; 5.222;
　　12.51

Isocrates 1.274; 4.79; 12.97,
　　207

Israel See Jacob

Issacher, *Testament of* See
　　Index VI

Jacob (O.T.) 1.23–24, 93, 210;
　　3.62; 4.17, 54; 5.90, 147,
　　152; 6.79; 8.120, 128; 11.39;
　　13.3, 183; 14.35; 16.25,
　　98, 133; 17.180
　　blessing of 13.153f
　　covenant of 8.125
　　called Israel 5.90

Jacob (N.T.) 14.31

Jah 17.169

Jahweh 3.298; 6.210; 13.99;
　　14.101; 15.53

Jair 6.118

Jairus 1.342; 3.8; 4.110–112;
　　5.9, 89; 6.86, 100

Jambres 12.194

James, apostle 1.77; 2.228,
　　230f; 3.54, 253; 4.127, 129;
　　5.16, 23; 8.221; 10.93;
　　14.8f, 162; 17.148

James of Jerusalem 6.164, 178;
　　7.96, 115; 9.144; 10.145;
　　14.9–12, 14–23, 292; 16.134
　　Book of See Index VI
　　'the just' 7.115; 9.144
　　legends of 9.144; 14.11
　　martyrdom of 14.12–14
　　and Paul 10.17; 14.22f, 73f
　　religion of 13.1

James, father of Judas 14.8

James, son of Alphaeus 14.8, 15
James the Younger 2.229;
    14.8, 15
James of Compostella 14.9
James VI 1.385
James, M. E. C. 11.163
James, W. 9.85
Janet 1.306f
Jannes 12.194
Jason (N.T.) 7.128; 8.219f
Jason (Gk) 9.3
Jay, W. 8.55
Jeans, J. 1.207
Jeffrey, G. J. 3.18, 314; 15.182
Jeffrey, Lord 1.262
Jehoida 2.298
Jehovah 3.298; 4.143; 5.60;
    6.210; 9.107; 11.39; 17.179f
Jehu 2.239; 3.266; 4.47; 15.69;
    17.132
Jehudah, rabbi 17.175
Jephthah 13.163
Jeremael 16.31
Jeremiah 2.136f, 240, 337;
    5.215; 14.79
  covenant of 13.92-94
  legends of 13.166; 16.94
Jeremias, J. 2.349
Jeroboam 2.240; 16.3
Jerome 2.361; 4.139; 5.18,
    96, 111; 6.65, 284, 290;
    9.120, 144, 258; 10.132, 171;
    11.173; 12.11; 13.8, 178;
    14.3f, 10, 11, 15-17, 32, 187,
    286; 15.110, 167, 168, 196;
    16.14, 41; 17.190
Jerome, J. 7.18
Jesse, root of 16.170
Jesus

acceptance of 5.190f
  accursed 10.26
advocate 15.14, 35-38
alpha and omega 16.37f;
    17.204, 225f
the Amen 16.140
anger of 2.247, 281, 288; 3.7,
    272-275; 5.14, 105, 108-
    114; 10.156
anointing of 2.329f; 5.5f
apostle 13.30f
appearances of 12.149f, 203;
    15.75f
arrest of 2.350-352; 3.345f;
    4.273f; 6.223f
ascension of 4.299; 5.1, 227;
    6.127, 149, 270; 7.13f;
    10.144f; 12.91; 14.286;
    15.171; 17.78
authority of 1.133-135; 3.35,
    37, 279; 4.51; 6.14, 223;
    13.75
awe of 3.6
baptism of 1.58-60, 83, 358;
    2.3; 3.18-20; 4.37f; 5.1, 80,
    83-85; 6.127; 13.47; 15.70,
    107, 108, 109
birth of 1.20, 23-27, 30; 3.11;
    4.12f, 21-25; 5.1; 6.28, 36;
    17.21, 78
blood of 5.221, 223-226;
    9.103-105; 11.122; 14.141,
    170; 15.15, 30; 16.34; 17.30-
    34, 83f
body of 9.103-105; 13.103,
    119, 197, 15.7
the Branch 1.40
the Bread of Life 5.9, 216-
    220; 9.103-105

the Bridegroom 1.336; 5.143

burial of 2.371f; 3.365f; 4.289f; 6.262–4

carpenter 1.41f, 59; 2.17; 3.6, 76, 138, 193, 254; 4.37, 237; 5.123, 174, 219, 236, 239; 6.20, 107, 160, 222; 11.218

centrality of 1.79; 5.82; 9.130; 14.337; 15.22, 93, 178; 17.180

and children 2.174–181, 211f; 3.7, 224, 241; 4.127, 225–227

Christ, The 2.137f; 3.196; 5.88; 8.86; 10.32, 132; 11.11, 15, 32, 67, 104, 131f, 148f, 152f; 15.13f

commission of 2.378

compassion of 1.297f, 354f; 2.15–18, 99; 3.6f, 182f; 4.86, 117; 5.9; 6.39; 11.18

courage of 2.19f, 242, 350; 3.252, 268, 283, 335, 351; 4.107, 230, 239f; 5.187, 236, 243; 6.108, 119, 126, 223, 244

courtesy of 4.295

and creation 5.40f; 6.18; 11.95, 114, 119f; 13.15, 31; 14.185; 16.140f

cross of 1.32f, 60f, 65, 70, 104, 337; 2.18, 33, 99, 120, 136, 147–149, 156f, 161f, 211, 227f, 230, 326, 343; 3.60, 192, 210– 212, 215f, 220, 241, 251, 282, 327, 340, 343f, 350f; 4.67, 119f, 127, 196, 230f; 282– 289, 297f; 5.135; 6.19f, 101, 171, 204; 7.26; 9.33; 10.25,

26f, 114; 12.9; 13.58f; 14.185f; 15.107

crucifixion of 2.363–370; 3.8, 360–365; 4.153, 288, 297f; 5.2, 5, 13, 134f; 6.234, 245, 292; 7.33f; 9.15; 15.8

day of 9.12; 15.118

death of 3.362f; 4.287f; 5.135, 251; 6.67, 261; 8.93; 9.17, 202, 209; 11.122f, 142; 14.185, 242; 15.109; 16.177f; 17.30–34

deity of 2.135, 206; 3.6; 4.51, 138; 5.14f, 39, 52, 74, 148, 183, 188; 6.68f, 74f, 161, 215, 217f; 7.25; 9.151; 11.34–37, 39, 70, 95, 115; 13.4, 14, 19, 31, 44, 119; 14.154, 294; 16.110, 127, 180; 17.138

deliverer 9.23

and Hades 14.232, 236–243; 16.52

disciples of 2.77f, 120f, 125f, 133, 212, 224, 229, 249, 304, 333, 377; 3.27–29, 38, 74, 83, 155, 218, 252f; 4.267f, 274, 292; 5.5, 16, 85–95; 6.190, 213f; 7.15

the Door 6.58f

emotions of 3.6f

eternal 6.36; 16.49; 17.226

exaltation of 13.15, 84, 86f; 117f; 14.141, 185

example of 4.293; 11.34f; 13.173; 14.214

exodus of 2.160, 162

expiation of 15.14f, 39f; 17.31

faithful 17.178

family of 2.229; 4.102; 5.231
233; 6.83, 257; 7.15, 95;
14.9f, 14–20; 15.171
fasting of 1.234, 325
feeding of five thousand 2.98–
103, 125f; 3.1f, 7; 5.4, 10,
10, 200–208
finality of 2.130; 11.95, 116–
118; 16.23
the Firstborn 11.119, 121;
16.32
the First-fruits 9.149–151
the Forerunner 6.155; 13.63
forgiveness of 2.345; 3.49–
52; 6.203, 231
the Foundation 2.140; 9.32
friendship of 1.369; 2.10;
3.26; 6.177
fullness of 5.71; 11.118f
and the future 2.300
in Galilee 2.126f; 3.41, 70,
73, 237, 262f; 4.45; 5.2, 4,
91, 106, 141
genealogies of 1.8–9, 11–13,
14–15; 3.298; 4.3, 12, 40f;
7.23; 13.74, 161
generosity 14.297
and Gentiles 3.177–179
gentleness of 9.238
in Gethsemane 1.65; 2.148,
191, 256, 343, 348, 350f; 3.8,
343, 347f; 4.271f; 5.1, 89,
126, 221; 9.199; 13.47, 74;
14.272; 17.97
glorification of 6.81, 123, 204
glory of 2.162; 3.211; 5.9,
14, 68–70; 6.81, 148f, 219f;
11.210; 13.14f, 86f; 16.150,
180

'Lord of glory' 1.25; 8.197
goodness of 8.81
gospel of 8.221; 12.149
grace of 7.142; 8.199; 9.144,
169; 10.143; 12.44, 48;
17.232
greatness of 3.190; 5.226;
6.152, 195; 14.296–298
healings of 1.80, 83, 354;
3.39, 119, 131f; 4.177f, 187
the Herald 1.352f, 362
the High Priest 6.254; 13.4,
31, 41–48, 70f, 79, 80–82,
119f; 15.93; 16.45f
and history 4.137f; 8.222;
12.230; 15.93
holiness of 13.83; 16.127
honesty of 1.111, 374, 393f;
2.231, 310; 3.201, 250; 4.131,
259; 6.154
honour of 16.180
our hope 12.19–21
hour of 3.70; 4.37, 45; 5.102,
231; 6.78, 81
humanity of 2.314; 3.6f; 4.41,
50, 138; 5.14, 65, 147f, 223;
6.50, 258, 261f; 8.103;
11.34–37, 95, 98, 115, 118;
12.90, 164; 13.4, 31, 44, 84;
15.9, 14, 23f, 93f, 143, 180
humility of 6.137; 11.6, 38
image of God 11.116–119
incarnation of 1.104; 3.80,
139; 4.23, 40, 274; 5.13, 14,
63–70; 6.148; 8.14, 157, 222;
9.18f, 141, 157; 10.144f;
11.36f; 12.90, 127, 256f;
13.103f, 15.6–9, 14, 23f, 61,
93, 105, 142f; 16.22, 63, 160;

17.58, 62

influence of 2.6; 6.164

and Jerusalem 2.158f, 160, 299; 3.262f; 4.124, 186; 5.2f, 106f; 6.101

of Judah 13.70, 79; 16.169, 172

the Judge 2.316; 3.51; 5.9, 189f; 6.15, 20, 246; 7.14, 132; 9.206f; 12.202; 13.111; 14.22, 141, 195; 15.176; 16.146; 17.194f

justice of 14.294

and the keys 2.144; 16.48

kindness of 2.127, 231

kingship of 1.9, 32f, 40, 115, 371; 2.104, 137, 239, 242f, 361; 3.15, 27, 144, 160, 256f, 265; 4.26, 169, 238–240, 247, 278; 5.43, 50, 80; 6.116, 130, 241f, 243, 246f, 252; 9.107; 10.141; 11.39, 111; 12.136, 203; 13.15, 110, 118; 14.122, 347; 15.93; 16.32, 46, 146; 17.183

knowledge of 11.63–65; 14.178f

'Lamb of God' 4.23, 5.80–82, 153; 14.185; 15.77

the Lamb 16.27, 157, 168–172; 17.30, 83, 96, 98, 102, 107f, 112, 118, 141f, 147, 172f, 208

language of 1.88, 314; 6.271

and the Law 1.9, 126–133, 298; 2.118; 4.72; 10.114f

law of 10.78; 14.21

legends of 4.286

liberator 1.13; 2.341

life of 1.40–43; 2.11; 3.1f, 5f, 139f; 4.1, 134, 185f; 5.75, 106f; 6.279; 7.9, 10; 9.24, 130

life-giver 5.43, 189; 6.60, 158; 15.15, 100

the Light 1.122–125; 5.9, 10, 45; 6.10f, 13, 64; 6.85; 10.164f; 13.56; 16.53

limitlessness of 5.72

loneliness of 3.7, 251; 6.202

lordship of 1.114; 2.123, 234, 312, 342; 4.261; 6.183; 7.14, 26; 8.11, 139; 9.11, 107; 10.141; 11.9, 39, 70–72, 122, 132; 12.91, 136f; 13.118; 14.21, 184f; 15.24, 68; 16.16, 33, 169; 17.89, 183

love of 1.293f; 6.149f; 9.125, 144; 10.9, 132f; 11.18, 56; 16.33

loveliness of 2.211f; 3.80, 191

made sin 2.369; 3.19f, 364

majesty of 6.243; 9.184; 16.172

master 2.239; 4.3; 5.76

mediator 12.29, 62f; 13.15, 89; 17.176

meekness of 16.172

mercy of 15.54

merits of 9.13

messiahship of 2.353; 3.264f, 350; 4.239; 5.154, 161f, 185f, 192; 6.72, 118; 14.24; 15.6, 68, 93, 107, 110; 16.170

miracles of 1.308f; 2.101f; 3.37f; 5.9, 52, 119, 232

mission of 1.72, 80; 4.14

the Morning Star 16.110f; 17.228

names of 1.19; 2.177, 361f; 3.225; 5.63; 6.200; 7.144; 9.9, 15, 16; 11.38f, 160; 15.53

nature of 15.13–15

obedience of 4.30, 120; 5.136, 165f, 188; 6.20, 33, 66, 148, 206, 219f, 224, 273; 11.38; 13.105, 114f

omnipotence of 16.171

omniscience of 5.15

only begotten 5.74

opposition to 1.324f, 358; 4.147

parables of 1.8; 2.53–56, 78f, 88, 320; 3.93; 4.99, 236; 5.2; 6.200

and passover 2.338–340; 5.2, 4; 9.45

patience of 10.139

our peace 8.72; 10.114

'Prince of peace' 3.357f; 6.118

perfection of 13.26

personality of 1.312

pioneer 13.25f

pity of 6.8

power of 2.83, 378; 3.23, 270; 4.87f; 14.297; 16.179, 180

praise of 16.173

and prayer 1.197f; 3.41; 4.4, 261, 288; 6.165, 213–220

preaching of 1.75f, 82, 210; 3.84; 4.211; 7.11

pre-existence of 5.14, 37; 6.36; 12.90; 16.49

presence of 1.233; 8.186; 9.42; 11.11, 164; 12.245; 13.173; 17.216

priesthood of 1.32f; 16.160

promises of 14.297

and prophecy 1.16; 9.176f; 17.37

prophet 2.305, 328; 3.303–322; 4.173, 247; 5.206, 235, 252; 6.45, 51; 16.46

the Propitiation 15.38–40

rabbi 3.138; 4.3, 94, 96; 5.87

the Ransom 2.234f; 14.317; 16.177

redeemer 1.58, 200; 14.184–186; 16.177

resurrection of 2.50, 143f, 156, 206, 218, 228, 256, 343, 375f; 3.212, 283, 368–371; 4.231, 291–293, 297; 5.23, 48, 55, 117, 227; 6.149, 168f, 207, 266–272, 282, 288; 7.4, 24, 27f, 34, 132, 177; 8.14, 139; 9.17, 78, 115, 137, 142–151, 202; 10.92, 146; 11.39, 64, 69, 121f; 12.90, 164; 14.24, 140, 185f, 245, 286, 310; 16.12, 32, 45–51, 81f, 103; 17.224

resurrection and life 5.10; 6.93, 103; 13.118

revealer of God 2.130, 280; 3.25, 51; 4.19, 137; 5.38, 40, 74f, 133; 6.33, 98, 161, 186f; 7.132; 9.146, 197; 11.115, 116–119; 12.33; 13.12, 14, 28, 117, 188; 14.197; 15.54, 88; 16.23, 32

riches of 11.100; 13.51; 16.179

our righteousness **9**.22

robe of **2**.367; **6**.254

the Rock **2**.140

sacrifice of **2**.264; **8**.58; **9**.45,
229; **10**.161; **11**.124; **13**.4,
15, 79, 81, 85, 102–105, 106,
109f, 113–115, 116f, 187,
197; **14**.170, 185, 233;
15.14f, 54, 81, 100, 109f;
16.161, 171f, 177; **14**.234;
17.33f, 84, 96, 227

Saviour **1**.19, 22f, 33, 41f,
200, 334, 341; **3**.58; **4**.2,
39, 71, 237, 283; **5**.43, 51,
170–172; **8**.55, 135; **11**.9;
12.91, 230; **13**.48, 82; **14**.195;
15.15, 88, 94, 100, 110;
16.89, 108; **17**.138

sayings of **1**.148; **2**.118;
3.233f, **5**.228; **6**.14, 98f;
9.103; **12**.177; **16**.94

'orphan sayings' **2**.84, 289,
349; **3**.98; **13**.149; **14**.168

second coming of **1**.7, 381f;
2.304, 308f, 312–317; **3**.208,
303, 306f, 315, 320–322; **4**.167,
220, 258, 261; **6**.155f, 184;
7.14, 24, 36; **8**.177; **9**.17, 58,
61, 70, 160, 169; **10**.172;
11.16, 69, 76, 148, 182f, 197,
201, 202–205, 212; **12**.182,
257; **13**.123; **14**.21, 26, 121–
124, 139, 141, 148, 248, 249f,
284, 287, 310–312, 337–339,
343–347; **15**.46, 71, 75f, 142;
16.4, 26, 36f, 119, 132f, 146;
17.224, 232

self-determination of **5**.15

self-renunciation of **11**.38

serenity of **4**.188, 274

the Servant **5**.1; **13**.82, 110

the Suffering Servant **1**.60,
311; **4**.54; **5**.236; **14**.185,
214

the Shepherd **6**.52–63; **7**.152;
10.148; **13**.201; **14**.215, 270;
17.38f

the Chief Shepherd **14**.269

sin-bearer **12**.282; **14**.244;
15.14

sinlessness of **2**.158; **3**.18;
6.158, 193; **8**.103; **9**.151;
12.90; **13**.41, 48, 71, 83–85;
14.214, 228; **15**.14; **16**.49

Son of David **1**.8, 9, 11, 13,
15, 341, 349, 393; **2**.35, 48,
123, 237, 279; **3**.261f, 265,
297; **4**.252; **5**.7; **7**.23;
8.101; **16**.170, 172; **17**.228

Son of God **1**.35f, 60, 70, 200;
2.15, 135, 137, 140, 143, 147,
158, 161, 169, 257, 264, 266,
280, 353, 367; **3**.6, 20, 71f,
148, 192, 365; **4**.14, 23, 29,
87, 203, 247, 272, 276f;
5.43–45, 51, 82f, 135f, 151,
187, 189, 245; **6**.15, 26, 50,
51, 72, 77, 99, 169, 201, 243;
8.127; **13**.14, 20f, 85; **15**.13,
67, 68, 88, 101, 105, 110;
16.160

Spirit of **3**.236; **9**.193f;
17.229

the Stone **2**.264f; **4**.247;
8.135; **14**.193–195

the Corner Stone **2**.141

submission of **3**.256; **4**.272;
9.151

sufferings of 2.147, 227, 348f,
363f; 3.342; 4.271f, 275f;
5.14; 6.244, 246f; 11.64;
12.168f; 13.26f, 47; 14.258,
286, 311; 15.14; 16.131f
sufficiency of 10.65f; 11.134f;
12.241
supremacy of 5.12, 92, 142,
144; 13.14, 16, 31, 33
our surety 13.61
sword of 16.93f
sympathy of 2.344; 4.87;
5.149; 6.96–99, 203; 13.27f,
42f
and the synagogue 2.53f;
3.29–32
the Teacher 1.311, 353;
2.339; 3.31, 84, 138; 5.152
teaching of 1.4, 8, 83–87;
2.1, 54, 273; 3.32f, 144;
5.2, 20–23; 14.25, 60
and the Temple 2.20, 243–
248; 5.2, 4, 107, 114–117;
6.101; 10.51
temptations of 1.61–70, 83,
224f, 358; 2.36, 148, 171,
252; 3.6, 21–24, 160, 199;
4.41–44; 5.1, 80, 204;
6.161; 13.42; 16.33; 17.82,
143
transfiguration of 2.156–163;
3.209–211; 4.123f; 5.4;
16.51
trial of 2.343, 352–362, 373;
3.354f; 4.275f, 277–281;
5.53; 6.233–249; 12.136
the Truth 5.66f; 13.13;
14.316; 17.178
touchstone of truth 2.42, 129;

15.143
unifier 10.66
uniqueness of 5.165; 6.66;
8.139; 11.95, 115, 134;
12.31, 153; 13.33, 87, 101;
14.233; 15.13, 68, 163, 165,
180; 16.23, 32
victory of 2.220, 228, 312,
369f; 4.288; 6.258; 8.21;
9.183; 11.87, 142f; 13.118;
14.242f; 15.77f, 106; 16.178;
17.3f, 66, 167f, 177–183
the Vine 5.9; 6.172–176; 9.80
voice of 17.229
the Way 5.46; 9.17; 13.82
wisdom of 2.308; 5.242;
9.22; 16.179
the witness 16.32
woes of 2.288-299
work of 2.3; 3.23; 5.52, 104;
6.205f, 209–211; 7.82f; 8.23,
103; 10.101–104, 122–125;
11.143; 14.231–243; 15.35–
40, 112; 16.33–35; 17.17,
31f
worship of 1.30, 297f; 2.123
yoke of 2.17f
Jesus Barabbas 2.361f
Jesus ben Sirach 14.45, 63, 82,
113
Book of See Index VI
Wisdom of See Index VI
Jesus called Joshua 7.100
Jesus called Justus 11.170
Jezebel (O.T.) 1.64, 152; 2.198;
3.175, 239; 4.48; 9.266;
10.47; 16.105
Jezebel of Thyatira 16.66, 102–
110

Joab **16**.133

Joachim **13**.18

Joad, C. M. **4**.175; **11**.151

Joan of Arc **4**.14; **6**.124, 133, 204f; **9**.199; **12**.221

Joanna **4**.96

Joash **2**.298

Job **14**.29, 35, 125; **16**.25

Jochanan, rabbi **1**.368, 387f; **2**.182; **5**.150; **13**.103, 199

Jochebed **13**.155

John, apostle **1**.77; **2**.228, 230f; **3**.54, 253; **4**.127, 129, 265; **5**.15–18; **6**.266f; **7**.1, 32, 38; **8**.221; **14**.162; **16**.134; **17**.148

  Acts of See Index VI

  beloved disciple **3**.329; **5**.19; **6**.145

  legends of **5**.96; **10**.94

  name of **4**.17

  religion of **13**.1

  the un-named disciple **6**.228

John, Augustus **1**.348, 371

John the Baptist **1**.7, 43–60, 71; **2**.1–7, 10, 92–98, 99, 136, 258; **3**.11–20, 30, 146, 150f, 154, 213, 279; **4**.31–36, 89f, 115, 244; **5**.141–146, 245; **6**.25, 163; **9**.261; **14**.72; **15**.23, 109; **17**.143

  baptism of **4**.37; **5**.79f, 84; **6**.79; **7**.139, 141

  birth of **4**.8–11, 14, 16–19

  death of **7**.93

  disciples of **1**.78; **2**.2; **4**.5; **7**.141f

  emergence of **4**.3; **5**.2f

  in John's Gospel **5**.49f, 70f, 141

  prayers of **4**.143

  preaching of **3**.20f; **4**.6; **5**.45; **7**.141f

  sect of **5**.11f, 50

  witness of **5**.75–82, 85, 195f; **15**.112

John of Damascus **14**.4

John the Divine **16**.11–13

John the Elder **5**.23f; **14**.162; **15**.128

Johnson, L. **1**.350

Johnson, S. **1**.190, 242, 268; **2**.218; **3**.39, 247, 361; **4**.134, 156, 191; **5**.206; **9**.83f, 160; **10**.155; **11**.154; **12**.171, 216; **13**.73; **14**.336; **17**.198

Johohanan **4**.17

Jonadab **12**.119

Jonah **2**.49; **4**.151

  and Jesus **2**.20

  sign of **2**.129

Jonathan **16**.46

Jones, S. **4**.15

Jose ben Chalafta, rabbi **13**.29

Jose ben Jehuda, rabbi **2**.193

Joseph of Arimathea **2**.219, 372–374; **3**.263, 366f; **4**.289f; **6**.263

Joseph, husband of Mary **1**.8, 18f, 33f, 39, 41; **3**.65, 139; **4**.12f, 21, 29f, 41; **5**.96; **14**.17–19

Joseph (O.T.) **1**.15f, 39, 93; **4**.40; **5**.147; **7**.56f; **13**.153f; **14**.31; **15**.37; **16**.143; **17**.23

  Life of See Index VI

Josephus **1**.12, 27, 37, 45, 72, 77, 161, 295f, 359; **2**.28f,

37f, 84, 93, 96f, 98, 121, 134f, 179f, 182, 196, 197f, 307f, 328, 329; 3.27, 68, 134, 177, 22ɔ, 300, 308, 311, 324, 333; 4.35, 45, 147, 234, 258f, 263, 281; 5.178, 248; 6.23, 59, 104, 233, 237; 7.58, 97; 9.266; 10.47, 112; 11.155, 157; 12.76, 77; 13.164, 168, 191; 14.11, 37, 40, 277, 291, 322, 326; 16.45; 17.95, 213

Joses 2.229

Joshua 1.19; 2.281; 3.102, 178; 6.178; 8.12; 9.88; 11.10; 12.227; 13.37; 14.35, 79, 293; 16.25; 17.134
  called Jesus 2.362; 7.100
Joshua, High Priest 17.81
Joshua ben Levi, rabbi 3.178
Joshua ben Nehemiah, rabbi 1.176

Josiah 1.141; 2.183; 3.231; 4.47; 9.221; 17.132
Jotham 3.89
Judah 1.234; 8.47; 16.133
  Testament of See Index VI
Judah the Patriarch, rabbi 6.37
Judah the Prince, rabbi 3.85
Judah, rabbi 3.129
Judas Barsabas 14.275; 15.169
Judas of Damascus 15.169
Judas the Gaulonite 3.285
Judas of Galilea 1.395; 4.121; 6.23; 7.50; 15.169f
Judas Iscariot 2.328; 331–338, 350f; 3.8, 23, 173, 221, 328–330, 335, 345f, 348; 4.153, 172, 263, 273f; 5.5, 15, 48, 229; 6.109, 111–113, 142–

148, 151, 222, 292; 7.15–17; 10.3, 146; 14.267, 279; 15.169; 16.133; 17.82
  meaning of 'Iscariot' 7.16
Judas of Jerusalem 7.116; 15.170, 173
Judas Maccabaeus 2.136, 241, 306; 3.267; 5.82; 6.70; 13.160, 170; 17.69
Judith, *Book of* See Index VI
Julian the Apostate 1.120; 2.264f; 4.112f, 195; 7.90; 13.58; 16.81
Jülicher, A. 16.6
Julius Caesar 6.60; 9.3f; 11.137; 13.125; 14.38, 221; 16.17; 17.159
Julius, centurion 7.181
Julius Vindex 17.92
Junias 8.212; 10.145; 14.17
Juno 17.140
Jupiter 1.379; 10.129; 17.40
  crown of 9.184
  J. Stator 14.147
Justin Martyr 1.24; 2.360; 5.244; 6.25, 246; 8.41, 172; 12.59, 76, 100; 13.12; 14.129, 242, 279; 15.150; 16.26; 17.189
Justus 9.5
Juvenal 1.157; 3.12, 236; 5.203; 8.31f, 48, 49, 50; 10.171, 180; 11.199; 12.78, 151, 270; 14.187, 202; 16.166; 17.141, 144, 154f, 161

Kagawa, T. 2.233; 12.56, 102
Kant 1.208; 5.58
Keats 1.262; 4.87, 167; 8.177; 13.137

Keble, J. 12.250
Kennedy, A. R. S. 2.194
Kennedy, S. 6.253; 10.46
Kepler, T. S. 16.1; 17.100, 169
Khayyam, O. 1.212, 259; 8.75
Kingsley, C. 3.217; 6.175;
    12.171
Kingsley, H. 6.265
Kipling, R. 1.221; 3.28, 257,
    357; 4.68; 5.58; 6.128;
    8.43; 9.122, 205, 208, 244,
    265; 10.14; 14.77
Kirkpatrick, A. K. 14.194
Klausner, J. 2.364
Klopstock 3.328
Knox, C. 1.262f; 4.65; 9.68
Knox, J. 1.386; 2.94; 4.161;
    5.27f, 165; 7.41; 9.179f;
    10.61; 11.32; 12.49f, 52, 55;
    17.100
Kollybos 5.110
Korah 2.16; 9.89; 12.177;
    15.159, 164, 191; 17.152
Kuria 15.130, 138

Laban 4.17
Lacordaire 12.129
Lactantius 1.377
Lagrange 3.274
Lamb, C. 1.220; 3.270
Lamb, M. 9.182; 11.163
Lang, A. 1.223
Lang, C. 6.123f
Langton, S. 9.223
Laodice 16.137
Latimer 1.386; 4.186
Laubach, F. 6.40
Laurentius 1.242
Law, W. 14.96

Lawrence, Brother 2.84
Lawrence, J. 14.208
Lawrence, T. E. 5.219; 6.146;
    8.76
Lazarus of Bethany 2.329;
    3.263; 5.5, 9f, 15, 69; 6.80f,
    96, 101, 109–111, 114
  as Beloved Disciple 5.19;
    6.145
Lazarus, rich man 4.213f; 6.34,
    102; 11.54; 17.113
Lecky 1.157; 5.26
Legion 3.118; 4.108
Leighton 4.73; 8.169
Leontinium 1.155
Lessing 1.201; 5.136
Levi (N.T.) See *Matthew, apostle*
Levi (O.T.) 13.70
  Testament of See Index VI
Levi, rabbi 1.195
Levison 2.73, 79
Lewis, C. D. 6.242
Lewis, S. 5.155
Licinius 13.193
Lightfoot, J. B. 9.90, 121, 211;
    10.138; 11.18, 26, 28, 49, 53,
    60, 67, 81, 91, 92, 116, 132,
    155; 12.271; 14.19
Lilley, P. 14.92
Lincoln, A. 1.109; 3.28; 4.130,
    175, 205; 6.204; 9.120, 173,
    263; 14.66; 15.145; 17.165
Lind, J. 3.219
Lindsay, D. 12.49
Linklater, E. 1.383
Linus 12.222
Lipman, W. 11.126
de Lisle, R. 5.28
Lister 1.339; 4.68; 13.51

Liszt 4.272
Livingstone, D. 4.292f; 7.12, 129; 8.203
Livy 8.31; 10.113
Lock, W. 12.55, 129, 236
Locke, W. J. 4.195
Lois 11.47; 12.68
Loisy 3.292
Lollia Paulina 14.221
Lombard, P. 2.235
Longfellow 13.138
Longinus 9.33; 13.172
Lord, W. 1.348
Lot 9.221; 12.79; 14.327; 17.151
Lovelace 1.394
Lowell, J. R. 3.19; 11.106
Lucan 8.4, 204; 13.178
Lucian 3.53; 9.186; 12.125; 14.99; 15.133; 16.73
Lucifer 3.81; 12.73; 15.183; 16.111; 17.59, 133
Lucius 7.98; 8.219
Lucius Antoninus 8.49
Lucius Valerius 14.220
Lucretius 8.31; 9.254
Lucullus 5.178
Luke 1.76; 4.2, 82; 7.6, 121f, 148, 192; 9.229, 231; 12.215f, 233
  author of *Acts* 7.1–3; 12.11
  doctor 4.1f, 52, 86; 7.3, 189; 11.171
  historian 7.6
  and *Letter to Hebrews* 13.7
Lull, R. 9.82
Lunn, A. 11.151, 163
Lunn, H. 11.103
Luther, M. 1.65, 209, 357; 3.61,

99, 102; 5.205; 6.107, 214; 7.42; 8.25; 9.182, 257; 10.22, 157, 178; 11.163; 12.127, 169; 13.5, 8f; 14.3, 5–8, 24, 59, 77f, 169; 15.143; 16.1; 17.100
Lydia 7.123; 11.5, 73f; 16.102, 105
Lysanias 4.3, 31
Lysimachus 16.74
Lyte, H. F. 6.195; 10.132

Maartens, M. 9.86
Macaulay, Lord 1.37; 6.224
Macauley, R. 3.41
Maccabaeus, J. 2.28; 12.149, 156f
Macdonald, chief 4.89
Macdonald, A. B. 4.58
Macdonald, C. M. 1.244, 246f
Macdonald, G. 1.253; 2.212, 250; 3.206, 241f; 6.160
Macdonald, R. G. 1.v
Macdonald Maclean, C. 1.244, 246f
Macgregor, W. M. 3.145; 4.195; 5.22; 6.162; 9.244; 11.193; 12.126; 13.46, 73; 15.41
Mackail, D. 4.168; 14.113
Mackay, J. 1.287
Maclaren, A. 1.44
Maclaren, I. 5.238
MacLean, A. 1.259f; 9.202; 10.75
Magog 17.60, 194
Mahafty, J. P. 1.391
Mahomet 3.229
Maimonides 1.53, 57; 2.22;

6.90, 227
Malchus 2.351
Maltby, F. R. 4.77; 10.124
Malthake 3.150; 4.35
Manaen 7.98
Manasseh 1.58; 3.231; 5.150,
152; 9.221; 13.166
Manasses 13.164
Manoah 10.129; 13.3, 192
Marcion 10.68; 12.3, 139;
15.144; 17.106
Marcus 12.192
Marcus Antonius 12.39
Marcus Aurelius 1.154; 3.11,
25; 4.285; 5.58, 64; 10.170;
13.87, 111, 139
Marduk 11.212; 15.61; 17.58,
77, 133, 198
Mariamne the Boethusian 3.150;
4.35
Mariamne the Hasmonaean
1.29, 36; 3.149; 4.35; 7.93f
Mark, John 3.3f, 72, 347f; 7.97,
101f, 192; 10.39; 11.169f;
12.217f; 14.278
Marlow, N. 1.339
Marlowe, C. 6.83
Martha 1.104; 2.329; 3.263;
4.4, 141f; 6.80, 91, 96f, 109–
111; 15.138
Martial 1.157; 8.4, 204; 10.171;
12.222; 14.187
Martin, H. 2.77, 225
Martin, J. 1.v
Martin, K. 11.200
Martin of Tours 11.326
Martineau 12.204
Marvell, A. 4.171; 8.177
Matthias 16.133

Mary, queen 2.194; 9.180
Mary of Orange 2.320; 11.205
Mary Tudor 12.52
Mary of Bethany 1.104; 2.329;
3.263; 4.4, 141f; 6.80, 91,
96f, 109–111
Mary, wife of Clopas 2.229;
6.255; 14.16
Mary, mother of James & Joses
2.374; 5.96–98; 14.16
Mary, mother of Jesus 1.18–20,
33, 41; 2.79, 96, 373; 3.139;
4.4, 5, 12–16, 21, 29f, 39, 41,
181; 5.19, 101f; 6.28, 82f,
255–257; 11.136; 12.68;
13.11f; 14.17, 19f; 15.138
Mary Magdalene 2.229, 376;
4.4, 96; 5.19, 48; 6.256,
264–267; 12.68; 14.16
Mary, mother of Mark 3.3,
347; 7.95; 12.217
Mary, the other 2.376
Mary (Rome) 8.214
Masterman, E. W. G. 1.295;
3.43
Mathathias 13.170
Matheson, G. 9.124; 10.103
Matthew, apostle 1.4–5, 329–
332, 359; 2.189; 3.53–57,
74, 83; 4.64, 75, 82; 5.3, 23,
94; 11.136; 14.8, 162
Maugham, S. 2.205; 14.223
Maurice, F. D. 6.175
du Maurier 10.97
Maurois, A. 1.380; 10.85, 155
Maximus of Egypt 4.21
Maximus of Tyre 12.51
Maxwell, W. D. 1.195
Mayor, J. B. 14.46, 47, 134,

286; **15.**157
McCaig **4.**197
McCosh, A. **1.**v
McFadyen, J. E. **6.**92, 93;
  9.138; **14.**117
McNeile, A. H. **1.**335; **2.**163,
  200; **10.**64; **14.**21
Meander **1.**173
Meir, rabbi **3.**85
Melanchthon **12.**127
Melba, N. **1.**262
Melbourne, Lord **12.**191
Melchior **1.**31; **3.**65
Melchizadek **5.**157; **13.**63–72,
  80f
Meleager **3.**125
Melito **16.**42
Melville, A. **1.**385; **3.**102; **4.**36;
  9.147; **12.**167f
Men **16.**138
Menander **2.**46
Menippus **3.**125
Menuhin, Y. **8.**160
Meredith, G. **13.**138
Merrick, L. **3.**277
Meshach **1.**117
Mesori **1.**26
Messalina **17.**144
Metallus **12.**77
Metillus **1.**157
Meyer **14.**30
Micah **4.**157
Michael, archangel **13.**18;
  14.324f; **15.**158, 166; **16.**31,
  54, 174; **17.**11, 40, 41, 80f,
  96, 175
Michelangelo **5.**91; **8.**201
Milligan, G. **8.**x; **10.**24
Milton **1.**355; **8.**43, 53; **14.**266,

334
Mimnermus **13.**110
Minerva **17.**140
Minucius **14.**114
Miriam **13.**155; **16.**105
Mithra **5.**222; **17.**33
Mnason **14.**254
Modestinus **1.**156
Moffatt, J. **6.**19, 97, 108; **9.**139,
  143; **10.**64; **11.**73; **13.**117,
  121, 122, 129, 133, 158, 174,
  182, 191, 202; **14.**32, 138,
  142, 150, 191, 238, 276, 286,
  294, 299, 305, 327, 336, 345;
  15.19, 62, 92, 151, 157, 160,
  192, 203f; **16.**104, 118, 142
Moiseiwitsch **9.**244
Mommsen **14.**39; **16.**75
Monobaz **1.**241; **12.**137
Montaigne **1.**264; **3.**26; **9.**110
Montanus **15.**90
Montefiore, C. G. **1.**52f, 172;
  2.6, 223
Montgomery, Lord **11.**163f
Montrose, Earl of **6.**205
Moody, D. L. **1.**125f; **8.**56, 203
Moore, G. F. **1.**52f
Mordaunt, E. **10.**178
Mordecai **11.**58; **17.**228
More, H. **10.**156
More, T. **12.**235
Morley, J. **3.**226
Morris, W. **7.**30; **13.**135
Morrison, G. **12.**204
Morton, Earl of **4.**36; **9.**147;
  12.50, 167
Morton, H. V. **1.**25, 77; **4.**139;
  5.167; **6.**56f, 222, 229, 281
Moses **1.**47, 98, 234, 375; **2.**281;

3.21f, 132, 211, 281; 4.133; 5.52, 134, 215, 237–239, 241; 6.27, 45, 54f; 9.88, 189–192; 10.27; 11.10, 187; 12.70, 134, 177, 194, 227; 13.3, 31, 33, 89, 154–159; 14.35, 181, 262, 292; 16.25, 123; 17.70f, 98, 143, 152, 196, 200

Ascension of See Index VI
Assumption of See Index VI
body of 15.158, 166
and the Law 1.366; 2.160f; 3.293; 5.72; 8.118, 123; 10.6, 29f; 16.24, 161
law of 2.16, 281; 4.250; 5.5; 7.21; 8.81; 10.6; 13.17, 185f
legends of 7.58; 9.125; 13.18, 155, 156, 201f
pre-existence of 17.96
and Samaria 2.359; 5.157
seat of 1.7
servant of God 6.177; 8.12
Song of 17.117–120
at Transfiguration 2.159f, 163; 4.123
uniqueness of 13.28f
veneration of 1.187
Moule, C. F. D. 11.106, 108, 110, 150, 152, 165, 168
Muir, E. 1.220
Muirhead, L. 6.162
Muller, M. 11.155
Muratori 5.21; 14.152
Muratorian Canon See Index VI
Muretus 4.16; 14.47
Murray, A. V. 3.215
Murray, G. 12.20, 80; 16.159
Mussolini 15.63

Myers, F. W. H. 3.132, 191; 8.124; 9.254; 15.121, 122; 16.52

Naaman 1.239; 3.127; 4.5; 5.187; 14.112, 116
Nabal 17.59
Naboth 4.47
Nain, widow of 4.4; 5.9; 6.100; 16.168
Nannacus 7.107
Naphtali, *Testament of* See Index VI
Napoleon 1.39; 2.138; 5.211, 235; 6.5f; 7.109; 9.121; 13.159; 15.28, 63; 17.100, 132
Narcissus 8.9, 213
Nathan 3.50, 85, 89
Nathanael 2.252; 5.91–95; 16.150
Nebuchadnezzar 8.166; 13.129, 164; 14.39; 17.77
Necho 17.132
Nehemiah 1.74, 230; 2.168, 281; 4.40; 5.150; 6.117; 7.65
Nelson, Lord 1.32; 4.265; 7.30; 8.169; 10.48; 12.88
Nelson, J. 11.52
Nemeseis 16.75
Nepos 17.190
Nereus 8.9, 216f
Nero 1.27, 112; 2.135, 328; 3.324; 4.263; 6.183; 7.167; 8.4, 106f, 172f, 204, 213; 9.21, 53f; 10.121f; 11.128; 12.11, 18, 59, 78, 166f, 211; 13.6, 58, 130; 14.10, 138,

146f, 156–159, 209, 221;
15.63; 16.14, 18f, 59; 17.7,
63f, 89, 93, 129, 139, 145,
146f, 155f, 160
life of See Index VI
N. redivivus 15.63; 17 64, 90,
93, 101f, 129, 138, 141f, 184
'saviour of the world' 17.89
Nerva 16.14, 20
Newbigin, L. 3.62; 7.55; 13.144
Newman, B. 11.186
Newman, J. H. 13.3; 14.327
Newton, F. E. 1.121
Newton, I. 4.57
Newton, J. 11.163; 12.46
Nicanor 12.149
Nicholls, B. 1.353
Nicias 17.103
Nicklaus 9.244
Nicodemus 2.219; 5.5, 120–125,
131f, 152, 163, 237, 254;
6.86, 263; 16.32
Gospel of See Index VI
Nicolaos 7.53
Nicolaus 16.66f
Nicoll, W. R. 1.253
Nicolson 1.324
Nicomedes 5.123
Niger (N.T.) 3.361
Niger, sophist 12.124f
Nightingale, F. 9.79; 10.150;
13.121
Nimrod 13.143
Noah 2.315; 12.79; 13.140–142;
14.238, 240, 325f
covenant of 8.125; 16.161
legends of 13.140
North, B. 3.353; 7.176
Northcott, C. 1.269; 2.76, 233

Nympha 11.171

Octavia 8.107; 17.91
Octavius See Augustus
Oerstterley, W. O. E. 3.92
Onesimus 11.164, 169; 12.269f,
271, 274; 14.213
Onesiphorus 12.155, 222
Onias 2.136f; 12.149
Onosander 12.75
Origen 1.34, 217, 289, 320;
2.96, 149, 207, 234, 361;
3.232, 258; 6.153; 8.176;
9.33f, 120; 10.54, 98; 11.124;
13.5, 7–9, 192, 193; 14.4, 9,
134, 280, 285; 15.167; 16.54,
70; 17.106, 190
Ormuzd 2.364; 3.23; 5.47;
9.196; 17.59, 130
Orpheus 3.336
Osiris 2.65; 3.91; 5.222
Otho 9.54; 16.19; 17.89, 91,
93, 139
Ovid 8.98; 12.35, 78; 14.55
Oxenham, J. 1.278; 3.19;
4.104; 6.249

Paedaretos 3.223
Paley 1.207
Pallas 7.167, 171
Palmer 5.100; 9.244
Palmerston, Lord 9.188
Panthera 6.28
Papias 1.4f; 2.345; 3.4; 5.23;
6.291; 14.161, 278, 309;
15.127, 137; 17.189
Paris 17.140
Parry 12.25, 241
Pascal, B. 14.92

Passfield, Lord   See Webb,
  Sidney
Pater, Walter   **2.**55
Paterson, J.   **5.**27; **17.**81
Patmore, C.   **1.**326
Paul   **1.**15, 79; 161, 301, 363;
  2.128, 256; **3.**77, 89, 202,
  248f, 312, 315; **4.**2, 77, 95,
  120, 285; **5.**16, 94; **6.**164,
  190, 193, 287; **7.**1, 3, 6, 19,
  97, 101, 117f; **8.**94, 98; **10.**17,
  18–20, 39; **11.**57–61; **12.**41–
  43, 45–48; **13.**130, 201;
  14.146, 347f; **17.**93
  Acts of   See Index VI
  ambassador   **9.**209–212
  Apocalypse of   See Index VI
  apostleship   **8.**12; **9.**78f;
    10.3f, 74; **11.**9, 27, 103;
    12.17f, 63f, 142f, 148, 227f;
    14.17
  apostle to Gentiles   **7.**100,
    151; **8.**45f, 148; **9.**14; **14.**22
  appearance of   **9.**242f, 257;
    12.279f
  in Arabia   **10.**14
  in Athens   **9.**23; **10.**6
  authority   **9.**267; **12.**228
  baggage of   **7.**154
  bonds of   **11.**174f
  businessman   **9.**231
  chronology of   **7.**73; **12.**9–12
  in Cilicia   **10.**15
  conversion of   **7.**5, 70–72;
    10.12f
  in Corinth   **8.**19; **9.**4–8, 14,
    23f, 31, 41; **11.**45; **17.**93
  courage   **7.**73f, 110, 129, 147,
    152–154; **10.**14f; **12.**50

  courtesy of   **11.**48–50, 169
  in Crete   **12.**9
  'crisis legislation'   **9.**70
  in Damascus   **7.**73; **10.**14
  death of   **12.**208f
  at Ephesus   **9.**4, 5, 13, 31, 154,
    166f, 172; **11.**45, 93; **16.**60;
    17.93
  epilepsy of   **9.**258
  eyesight of   **9.**258
  in Galatia   **10.**38f
  greatness of   **8.**17; **9.**40, 181
  and healing   **7.**189
  humility of   **9.**38–40, 145, 188f,
    217; **11.**216
  humour of   **12.**283
  imprisonments of   **8.**206; **10.**61,
    121, 182f; **11.**20, 21f, 27, 47,
    168, 174; **12.**10f, 145, 155,
    165–167
  independence   **9.**80f, 248;
    10.4; **14.**266
  industrious   **7.**143
  influence of   **2.**6
  and Jerusalem   **10.**4, 14f;
    17.93
  and Jesus   **4.**13; **9.**42, 193f;
    11.27, 34–40, 46; **12.**244
  and Jewish feasts   **7.**150
  and Jews   **3.**148, 168f; **7.**191
  journeys of   **7.**97, 119, 138;
    9.254f
  letters of   **8.**ix–xiii, 45;
    10.68f, 172; **11.**47, 52, 104,
    172, 174; **12.**8f, 275; **14.**288,
    348
  prison-letters   **7.**192; **10.**61;
    12.165
  love of   **9.**169, 178f, 218;

10.39
in Macedonia 11.179
marriage of 9.60f; 10.73;
 11.75
ministry of 9.82–84
mother of 3.361
at Neopolis 11.5
obedience of 11.9
opposition to 9.176, 242, 251,
 259; 10.3f; 11.182, 188;
 14.26
parchments of 12.219
pastor 9.255; 10.44f; 11.194–
 196; 14.192
persecutor 7.64; 11.11, 60;
 12.45; 17.85
Pharisee 7.70; 8.13; 11.59f
at Philippi 8.19; 10.7, 8, 248;
 11.3, 5, 13, 86, 188; 17.93
prayers of 10.28; 11.128,
 196f
preaching of 7.103–105; 9.23f,
 195; 10.24f; 14.28
rabbi 7.98, 135, 160, 180;
 8.118; 9.60, 79, 131, 243;
 10.27, 29, 41; 11.218
in Rome 7.5; 8.2f; 12.10
and Sanhedrin 10.172
servant of God 6.178
sickness of 7.102f, 121
slave of Christ 8.11f, 202;
 9.40; 10.9f, 124; 11.9;
 12.227
in Spain 8.3f, 204; 12.10–12,
 283
strategy of 8.4
style of 10.64; 14.142
sufferings of 9.253, 257–260;
 10.38f, 56f, 124; 11.30, 126,

128; 12.197
in Syria 10.15
tact of 8.201
of Tarsus 7.62, 70f; 9.252;
 10.15; 11.58f
tent-maker 7.136, 175; 11.167
at Thessalonica 8.19; 11.47,
 86, 181f
thorn of 9.257; 10.38
trial of 7.161f, 169–173;
 11.20; 12.220
in Troas 9.183, 224; 11.5
visions of 9.256f
vocabulary of 10.64; 12.8f
vows of 7.138
Paul of Nisibis 14.4
Paula 8.216
Pausanias 5.104; 6.153
Peake, A. S. 1.v; 13.158
Pekah 1.75
Pelagius 12.237
Penn, W. 3.226
Pericles 1.155, 231; 10.108f;
 12.87; 16.97
Perpetua, saint 14.211; 17.118
Perrot, A. 2.31
Perseus 12.26
Persius 6.42; 12.20; 14.335;
 15.121
Peter 1.8, 15f, 65, 77; 2.156–
 163, 169, 171, 175, 193, 220,
 226, 343–347; 3.54, 80, 214,
 248, 250, 346, 351–353, 369;
 4.4, 57, 119, 121, 126f, 153,
 265, 269–271, 285, 292, 296;
 5.19, 23, 88ff, 163; 6.87,
 151f, 224f, 266f, 282f, 285–
 288; 7.1, 4, 19, 32, 38–42,
 44f, 76f, 80–88, 95, 100, 114;

8.100, 221; **9.**14f, 36, 143f;
    10.17, 18–20, 102; **14.**145,
    162, 292, 347f; **16.**134;
    17.108
Acts of See Index VI
character of **2.**106f
Chief Apostle **14.**262
confession of **2.**137–139;
    3.180, 192f; **5.**230; **14.**195
courage of **2.**351; **14.**154f;
    17.97
denial of Jesus **3.**351–353;
    6.227–231; **14.**90, 268;
    15.119
faith of **2.**140f
and Gnosticism **11.**136
Gospel of See Index VI
house of **3.**39
and James **4.**16; **14.**10
and John **4.**16
in John's Gospel **6.**101, 141
and the keys **2.**139–146
legends of **3.**145; **10.**93; **13.**58
and Mark **3.**72
and Paul **10.**17, 18–20;
    14.347f
preaching of **2.**345; **3.**4f, 7–8,
    157; **7.**5, 24–29, 33f
rebuked **1.**65, 225; **2.**51, 148–
    150; **3.**174, 199; **5.**4
religion of **13.**1
wife of **14.**277
wife's mother **1.**307f; **3.**36–38
Peter Lombard **3.**258
Peter Pan **1.**149f; **9.**160; **13.**51,
    138
Petronius **17.**157
Phaniel **13.**18
Pharaoh **8.**120, 131; **12.**194

Philemon **1.**173; **11.**164, 169;
    12.270, 273, 274, 278, 283
Philemon the Greek **14.**46
Philetus **12.**174, 178
Philip, apostle **1.**39; **5.**5, 15, 16,
    23, 52, 91, 94, 202, 204f;
    6.120, 159, 163; **7.**62;
    14.162; **17.**107
Philip, evangelist **7.**4, 19, 62,
    64f, 69, 88; **12.**68; **15.**89;
    16.105
Philip II **9.**120
Philip of Macedon **2.**84; **7.**122f;
    11.3, 180
Philip of Neri **13.**173
Philip, Tetrarch **2.**95, 133, 135;
    3.53, 150
Phillips, J. B. **16.**118
Philo **1.**134; **2.**358, 364; **3.**196;
    4.79; **5.**36, 64, 83, 183;
    6.237, 247; **8.**96; **10.**99;
    11.117, 159; **12.**39, 80, 107,
    131; **13.**2, 12, 52, 80, 91, 134;
    14.55, 60, 84, 98, 126, 323;
    15.37, 190; **16.**70
Philodemus **3.**125; **12.**236
Philostratus **9.**19; **12.**124, 125
Phineas **11.**60
Phocylides **12.**131
Phoebe **8.**7, 207; **9.**186
Phygelus **12.**156
Pilate **1.**8; **2.**353, 357–363, 377;
    3.354; **4.**3, 31, 153, 172f,
    277–281; **6.**231–249; **13.**130
Acts of See Index VI
bodyguard **2.**363
character of **6.**237–240
shade of **2.**362
wife of **2.**359

Pindar 8.46
Pitt, W. 2.76; 12.98
Pius 1.377
Pizarro 1.374f; 6.191
Plato 1.27, 136, 173, 279; 2.203,
313; 3.17, 113, 174; 4.36,
124; 5.8, 73, 140; 6.38, 168;
7.63; 8.167; 9.35, 51, 53, 79,
140, 186; 10.52, 83, 90, 113,
153, 183; 12.80, 81, 98, 107,
109, 207; 13.1, 2, 39, 88, 191;
14.99, 114, 186, 203, 217,
288, 316, 337, 341; 15.41,
42, 123, 149; 16.151; 17.199,
211
  Definitions of See Index VI
Plautius 9.21
Plautus 1.385
Pliny 1.378, 398; 5.212; 6.42,
189; 8.36, 49; 9.21, 107;
10.179; 11.159; 12.67, 78,
99, 270; 13.193; 14.128,
155f, 161, 221; 16.97, 137;
17.155, 158f, 160, 213,
214
  Letters of See Index VI
Plotinus 9.204
Plummer 1.73, 311, 359, 374;
2.14, 46, 288; 15.107, 118,
121
Plutarch 1.119; 3.202; 5.64,
8.45; 9.18, 19, 40, 71; 10.51,
83, 99, 156; 12.62, 124, 182,
185, 237; 13.43, 46, 207;
14.295, 302; 16.21; 17.103
Pluto 14.346
Pole 9.120
Polybius 1.301; 4.84; 12.237,
242, 258

Polycarp 1.115; 5.20; 9.107,
171; 11.7, 15; 12.19, 169;
14.137, 141f, 162; 15.9, 144;
16.76
Polycrates 6.228
Pompey 2.28; 3.68, 125; 5.123;
12.78; 14.38
Pomponia 12.223
Pomponia Graecina 9.21
Pomponius Mela 8.4
Pope 3.129
Popilius Laena 13.30, 167
Poppaea Sabina 6.183; 12.78,
14.149; 17.91
Potter, G. 2.24
Pouyanne 2.31
Praxiteles 7.141
Premanand 2.99, 101, 111, 211,
291; 11.103
Prescott 1.375
Primasius 17.142
Prisca See Aquila and Prisca
Priscilla See Aquila and Prisca
Priscillian 15.110
Prometheus 1.200
Propertius 8.31; 12.78
Prudentius 17.33
Psammetichus 14.39
Ptolemy 1.155; 16.88; 17.179
Ptolemy Lagos 2.29
Publius 7.188f
Publius Sempronius Sophus
14.219
Pudens & Claudia 12.222
Pusey 1.294; 4.106
Pythagoras 2.47; 8.112; 9.26;
10.99, 156; 12.80; 13.52,
62, 196; 16.21
Pytho 7.124

Quartus 8.220; 11.103
Quintilius 1.279
Quintillian 1.97; 8.4, 204; 9.35; 13.195; 14.220
Quintus Fabius Cunctator 3.202f
Quintus Lucretius Vespillo 12.78
Quirinius 4.20; 7.50
Quiroga, V. 12.201

Rab, rabbi 2.14
Rabbula 14.4
Rachab See Rahab
Rachel 1.24, 38; 11.58
Rafael See Raphael
Raguel 16.31; 17.41
Rahab 1.17; 13.161, 191; 14.29; 15.62
  legends of 14.78f; 17.58, 77
Rainy 11.201
Ramsey, W. 9.98; 16.41, 68, 87, 113, 125, 137
Raphael 13.8; 14.323, 325; 16.31, 174; 17.41, 175
Rawlinson, A. J. 3.80, 286
Rebecca 8.128; 12.76
Redwood, H. 3.54
Rehoboam 1.24; 2.240; 12.134; 13.92; 16.3
Reith, Lord 6.87; 8.74
Remiel 17.41
Renan, E. 6.101f; 14.138; 17.83
Resh, rabbi 3.276
Reuben 1.233; 16.133; 17.25
  Testament of See Index VI
Rhine, J. B. 1.306
Rhoda 16.54
Richard of Chichester 1.v
Richards, L. 1.231
Rieu 6.97

Robert of Burgundy 2.180
Robertson, E. H. 14.234
Robertson, F. W. 10.156
Robertson, J. A. 4.283; 6.175
Robinson, A. T. 2.288
Roby, W. 8.56
Rockefeller, J. D. 4.268
Rogers, E. 14.185
Roland 4.111; 6.190; 16.80
Roma 1.113; 6.182; 16.17, 75
Ropes 14.33, 45, 64, 80
Rossetti, C. 11.215; 13.41; 16.173
Rough, J. 11.32; 12.49
Rowe, N. 13.137
Rufinas 12.205; 17.231
Rufus 2.366; 3.249, 361; 4.283; 8.7, 214–216
Ruinhart 17.106
Ruskin, J. 4.195
Russell, G. 13.1
Ruth 1.17, 24; 6.146
Rutherford, M. 1.202, 244, 246f; 264; 4.58; 11.209
Rutherford 9.170; 11.193
Ryle 15.185

Sadd, A. 6.224
Saiguael 16.31
Salisbury, F. 5.239
Sallust 10.80; 13.177
Sallustius Lucullus 17.140
Salome, of Herodias 2.95f; 3.150, 152f, 7.93
Salome 2.229; 3.353; 5.16, 96; 6.256; 14.16
Sambathe 16.101, 105
Sammael 6.31
Sammlai, rabbi 3.293

Samson 10.129; 13.163; 14.115f
Samuel 1.234; 2.276, 296; 4.17;
5.82; 6.126; 12.134; 15.69
Samuel, Viscount 1.340
Sanballat 5.150
Sanday, W. 1.65; 8.1
Saphira See Ananias & S.
Sarah 8.128; 10.41; 14.222
Sariel 17.41
Satan 1.65; 2.36f, 40, 51, 148–
150, 317; 3.22f, 78f, 174, 330;
4.150, 263, 270, 273f; 6.31,
126; 8.34, 219; 9.181f, 195f,
246; 10.182; 11.193; 12.91,
93; 14.50; 17.47, 59, 80–84,
86, 88, 130, 168, 184, 190,
191f
   and death 16.141
   delivery to 9.44; 12.53f;
   15.118
   depths of 16.108f
   power of 11.112, 212
   prosecuting angel 13.18
   seat of 16.88–90
   synagogue of 16.80
Saturninus 12.94
Saul, king 2.276; 4.17, 47;
11.54, 58; 15.69; 16.46, 133
Saul of Tarsus See Paul
Schopenhauer 3.25; 5.231
Schürer 2.303; 3.194
Schweitzer, A. 9.83
Scipio 12.18
Scott, E. F. 5.160; 10.66, 67,
68; 12.217; 13.5; 14.283
Scott, R. 4.126; 11.72
Scott, W. 4.19; 8.74; 9.219;
13.83
Scythinus 3.57

Seago, E. 5.112
Seeley, J. 6.3; 14.229; 15.204
Selwyn, E. G. 14.143, 178, 190,
257
Semjaza 14.322
Seneca 1.27, 32, 139, 157, 283,
344; 3.12, 25; 4.26, 181;
5.55, 58; 6.23; 7.137; 8.4,
19, 31f, 39, 98, 204; 9.54,
140, 204, 235, 254; 10.81,
171, 176; 11.199; 12.19,
34, 51, 78, 130, 131, 159,
231, 245; 13.139, 157; 14.60,
64, 82, 113, 207, 221, 335:
15.100, 121; 16.117, 159;
17.91f, 145, 161
   Epistles of See Index VI
Serapis 1.111; 3.181; 9.72
Sergius Paulus 7.3, 100; 9.21
Seth (Greek) 2.65; 3.91
Seth (O.T.) 14.323
Sennacherib 6.43; 17.22
Severus, A. 14.129
Shackleton 1.375
Shadrach 1.117; 8.166; 9.119;
13.129, 164
Shaftesbury, Lord 1.94, 166;
10.155
Shakespeare, W. 1.117, 244;
2.225, 297; 3.19, 206, 329;
5.224; 6.51; 8.33; 10.64, 82;
12.128, 189; 13.117, 135, 136,
137; 14.92, 266, 329; 17.28
Shammai, rabbi 1.273; 2.198,
200; 3.164; 6.70; 10.168
   school of 1.152, 158; 3.239;
   4.212
Shaw, G. B. 3.28; 4.11; 5.58;
6.129; 7.75; 8.40

Shearjashub 8.145
Shebna 16.133
Shelley 4.87; 6.128
Shemaiah 12.134
Shemachsai 3.34
Sheppard, D. 1.218; 9.187;
13.124
Shibta 3.165
Shimei 17.59
Short, A. R. 2.80, 112; 3.33,
36, 119f
Shylock 5.110
Sidney, P. 3.85
Silas 7.117, 125, 136; 9.5, 74;
11.181; 12.22; 14.17, 143,
274; 15.169
Silesius 13.128
Silvanus 10.145; 14.143f, 145,
274–276
Sim, A. F. 9.121
Simeon ben Jocai, rabbi 4.224
Simeon 4.26
Simeon, called Niger 3.361;
7.98f
Simeon (O.T.) *Testaments of*
See Index VI
tribe of 14.31
Simeon (Peter) 2.145, 4.26, 228
Simeon, rabbi 1.257; 14.55
Simeon ben Yohai, rabbi 1.55
Simon the Canaenaen 1.359;
3.74; 4.3
Simon of Cyrene 1.168; 2.366;
3.360f; 4.282f; 7.98f; 8.215f
Simon ben Eleazar, rabbi 1.139f
Simon ben Gamaliel, rabbi
2.246; 3.274
Simon the Leper 2.329; 3.325
Simon Maccabaeus 1.74, 233f;

2.239; 3.266; 6.117
Simon Magus 1.26, 69; 15.89
Simon Peter See Peter
Simon the Pharisee 2.329; 4.4,
5, 94; 11.157
Simon the Righteous, rabbi 3.293
Simon ben Shetah 12.77
Simon the Sorcerer 7.66f
Simon the Tanner 7.80; 14.254
Simon the Zealot 1.359; 3.83;
4.3, 75
Simpson, E. K. 12.106, 122, 130,
158
Simpson, J. Y. 1.41f, 119, 224,
338; 3.127; 4.68, 136
Sirach See Jesus ben S.
Slessor, M. 8.184
Small, A. H. 8.71
Smart, W. J. 12.56
Smith, Adam 10.86
Smith, Alexander 3.13
Smith, D. 10.177
Smith, G. A. 1.63; 2.247; 4.47,
201; 5.28; 6.53; 9.118;
14.216; 15.184–186; 17.38
Smith, R. 17.103
Smith, W. H. 1.276
Smith, W. T. 3.134
Snowdon, R. 8.76; 10.113, 115
Socrates 1.78, 154, 155, 278,
396; 2.313; 5.140; 6.23,
168, 187; 8.112; 9.53, 79,
132; 10.170; 11.45, 85;
12.61, 186, 205, 239; 13.130,
142; 14.114, 120f, 304, 341;
15.41, 42, 85, 122f
Solomon, King 1.17, 45, 225;
2.37, 50; 3.22, 210; 4.147,
151; 5.82; 11.187; 13.19;

14.42; 15.87; 16.3; 17.81,
206
and Jesus 2.20
Odes of See Index VI
Psalms of See Index VI
temple of 2.161
Solomon, pianist 9.244
Solon 1.154; 10.162; 12.38,
106; 16.114
ben Soma 9.256
Sopater 8.220
Sophocles 1.173; 8.202; 9.136,
158; 10.25, 110; 14.172,
298
Sosipater 8.220
Sosthenes 11.103
Spence 5.142f
Spenser 12.209; 17.114
Sporus 17.91
Spurgeon, C. H. 5.100, 163;
12.204
Spurius Carvilius Ruga 1.156;
8.32; 10.171
Stalin, J. 4.114
Stalker 9.7
Stanley 7.12
Stanton 6.204; 9.120
Starbuck, E. D. 6.40f
Statius Quadratus 9.107
Statilla Messalina 12.78
Stephanas 9.15f, 166
Stephanatus 9.6, 8
Stephanus 3.299; 9.223; 15.111
Stephen 4.285; 6.86, 233; 7.4,
5, 19, 53f; 14.259
defence of 7.54–61
and Paul 7.74f
prayer of 7.62, 72; 8.168
Stevenson, R. L. 1.100, 121,

222f; 3.153, 245; 4.66, 106,
167; 5.55; 8.22, 64, 91, 177;
9.196, 203, 235f; 10.182;
13.120, 150; 14.92; 15.55;
16.82
Stewart, H. F. 14.92
Stewart, J. 9.24
Stilicho 3.204
Stoddart, J. 1.276
Stowe, H. B. 9.188
Strabo 11.91; 14.40; 16.58, 74,
87, 126; 17.45, 166
Strachan, R. H. 6.87
Stradivari, A. 7.45
Strahan 16.41
Streeter, B. H. 14.151, 163
Struma Nonius 14.221
Struthers, J. P. 1.285; 3.327;
7.31; 13.151
Studd, C. T. 3.58; 12.56
Sulla 12.78
Suetonius 1.27; 3.181, 229, 313;
6.182; 8.31; 10.171; 14.157;
17.139f, 154, 156
Suidas 14.107
Sullivan, A. 10.123
Sulpicius Gallus 14.218
Sulpicius Severus 14.149
Sunday, B. 3.12
Sutherland, H. 12.213
Swedenborg, E. 1.305
Swete, H. B. 3.80; 16.33, 38,
50, 51, 121, 151, 154, 156,
159, 169, 172; 17.17, 26, 41,
77, 79, 83, 93f, 110, 117, 120,
130, 131, 132, 133, 151, 171,
172, 176, 177, 180, 190, 192,
197, 209, 219, 221, 224, 225,
227, 229

---

11 Phil, Col, Thes
12 Tim, Tit, Phlm
13 Heb
14 Jas, Pet
15 John, Jude
16 Rev, v.1
17 Rev, v.2

Swinburne 1.120, 213; 4.195;
 8.72; 13.135
Symeon (Peter) 14.291f
Syntyche 11.71–74; 12.68

Tabitha 5.90; 6.87; 7.77
Tacitus 1.27; 2.218, 364; 3.313,
 320; 6.41f, 182, 250; 7.168;
 8.31, 49, 50; 12.20, 36, 78,
 167, 190; 13.111, 178; 14.147,
 149, 202; 15.124; 16.138;
 17.83, 145, 146, 154, 160
 Histories of See Index VI
Tagore 10.8
Tamar 1.17
Tarphon 1.367
Tatian 12.59; 14.152; 17.106
Tatlock, R. 11.33
Tauler 1.260f
Taylor, Fr. 10.113
Taylor, J. 3.122, 174; 8.36;
 12.80; 13.27
Taylor, V. 10.45; 15.143
Telemachus 2.77; 3.203–205
Temple W. 2.117; 3.89
Tennyson, A. 1.227; 2.321;
 3.200, 226; 4.226, 276; 13.1,
 20, 27; 14.132
Terah 13.143
Tertius 8.xii, 45, 220; 11.174
Tertullian 1.111, 267; 2.349,
 360; 3.13, 317; 8.27, 172;
 9.63, 222, 258; 12.1, 59, 64,
 170; 13.5, 8, 149, 192;
 14.20, 129, 279, 280; 15.70,
 169; 16.26, 70, 92; 17.12, 70,
 141, 189
 and Scripture 14.3, 151
Tertullus 7.168f

Thackeray 9.219
Thaddeus 1.82
Thalasius 2.80
Thecla, *Acts of Paul* See
 Index VI
Theocritus 11.203
Theodore of Mopseuestia
 2.349; 12.116f, 204
Theodoret 1.266; 2.349; 8.34f;
 11.124
Theodorus 3.125
Theodosius 12.159, 205
Theodota 1.155
Theognis 10.110
Theophilus (N.T.) 4.1, 3; 7.2, 9;
 12.11
Theophilus of Antioch 12.59
Theophorus 2.175
Theophrastus 8.37, 38; 12.186;
 13.191; 14.105, 265; 15.58,
 197
Theophylact 8.37; 12.186;
 13.182; 14.105
Theresa, saint 8.71
Thermouthis 13.156
Theudas 1.69; 7.50; 9.18
Thomas, apostle 5.5, 23, 90;
 6.87f, 101, 156f, 270, 275–
 279; 14.161, 162, 179, 294
 Acts of See Index VI
 called Didymus 7.100
Thomas à Kempis 15.87
Thompson, F. 6.160; 8.153;
 9.199
Thomson, W. M. 1.77, 316, 322,
 344; 2.21, 72f, 76, 84, 134,
 253; 6.57, 61, 281
Thorwaldson 2.249; 9.92
Thurio 12.127

Thucydides 9.3, 155; 14.82, 108, 143

Tiamat 11.212; 15.61; 17.58, 133, 198

Tiberius 2.359; 3.125, 286; 4.3, 31; 6.239; 8.31; 10.171; 11.21, 137; 16.18, 75, 115, 126, 135; 17.89, 93, 139, 146, 160

Tiberius Claudius Cogidubnus 12.222

Timothy 3.4, 71; 7.120, 136; 8.219; 9.5, 6, 8, 41, 165; 11.47f, 74, 103f, 181, 195; 12.21–23, 49, 50, 51f, 96, 98, 133f, 138, 164f, 197; 15.171

Tiridates 1.27

Titus (Emperor) 2.302, 306; 9.183; 16.19; 17.89, 93, 101, 139, 146

Titus (N.T.) 9.7, 8, 183, 224–226; 10.16; 12.71, 218f, 232

Tobias 1.273

Tobit, *Book of* See Index VI

Tolstoi 4.40; 9.188

Toplady 6.262

Torpacion 14.129

Toscanini 1.135; 3.17; 4.51; 10.126

Tournier, P. 1.327; 2.31; 3.35, 37f, 47; 6.5; 13.60

Trajan 1.391; 6.189; 9.21, 107; 11.159; 12.99; 13.193; 14.128, 155f, 159

Trench, R. C. 8.42; 9.170; 10.51, 136; 11.157; 12.37, 61, 80, 83, 236, 239, 240; 14.330; 16.60, 63, 133, 140, 141, 144, 145, 148

Tristram, C. 1.345; 2.157, 251; 5.153, 212f

Trophimus 7.157; 10.112; 12.222

Tryphaena and Tryphosa 8.214

Trypho, *Dialogue with* See Index VI

Tsze-Kung 1.274

Tullia 12.78

Tulloch, Mrs 1.105

Turgeniev 9.262

Turner, C. H. 7.4

Twitchell, J. 9.132f

Tychicus 7.192; 10.61f, 185; 11.169; 12.219, 265

Tyndale, W. 1.255; 3.180; 4.152; 6.189; 8.167; 12.220

Tyrimnus 16.101

Tyrranus 7.142f

Tyrrell 5.51

Ulysses 3.336; 8.186; 9.52

Unamuno 4.182; 10.124; 17.118

Urban VIII 3.101f

Uriah 1.17; 3.85

Uriel 13.18; 14.325; 16.31; 17.41

Valentine 12.127

Valentinus 12.8

Valerius Maximus 17.156

Varro 1.302; 10.179; 14.211

Varus 1.395

Vaughan, C. J. 8.55, 96; 13.14

Vedius, P. 10.180; 12.270

Verrall, A. W. 1.153

Verrius Flaccus 9.249

Verus 1.154; 10.170

Vespasian 2.170; 3.181; 6.41f;
 8.216; 11.137; 14.14; 16.19,
 126, 135; 17.89, 93, 101,
 139, 146
Vettius Epagathos 15.38
Victor of Capua 11.173
Victoria, Queen 1.105
Victorinus 16.14, 161
Vidyasagar 2.100
Vincent of Lerins 12.139
Vincent, M. R. 11.11, 77
Vinicius 3.145
Virgil 1.27, 279; 4.87; 8.30;
 9.129; 14.76; 16.11, 16
Vitellius 2.359; 11.21; 16.19;
 17.89, 93, 139, 157
Voltaire 3.227

Wagner 9.191
Waldmeier, M. 1.314
Walker, A. 6.270
Walpole, H. 2.218; 3.341
Walton, I. 14.138
Warren, M. 9.240
Washington, B. 7.188; 8.170
Watkinson 4.132
Watson, W. 4.91, 132; 6.80;
 13.15
Watt, J. 4.57
Watts 8.196
Way, A. S. 9.155; 12.107
Weatherhead, L. 10.7, 126;
 13.194
Webb, S. 4.177; 6.5
Welch, A. C. 4.149; 10.166
Wellington, Duke of 11.186
Wells, H. G. 1.100, 315; 2.78;
 3.77, 108; 4.63, 177, 269;
 6.22; 7.41; 8.72, 110, 200;

10.91; 15.31
Wendt 1.314
Wesley, C. 4.130; 13.119;
 14.234; 16.71; 17.84
Wesley, J. 3.61, 84, 110; 4.56,
 73, 130, 164, 195; 7.110, 111;
 9.46, 214, 259; 10.133, 156;
 11.51f; 12.171, 181; 14.109,
 131; 15.161, 162, 182; 16.80
Wesley, Samuel 4.130
Wesley, Susannah 2.163
West, B. 10.178
Westcott, B. F. 3.5; 5.71; 6.111,
 273; 13.104, 182, 183;
 14.151, 176; 15.35, 44, 47,
 56, 64, 82, 116, 122, 123
Wetstein, J. J. 1.188
Weymouth 15.92
Whale, J. S. 12.127
Wharton, Lord 1.394
Whitefield, G. 3.84; 6.5; 8.163;
 12.260
Whitley, Bishop 2.101
Whittier 1.215; 2.25; 3.252;
 8.157; 15.26
Whyte, A. 1.361; 8.196; 9.115;
 10.13; 15.22
Wilberforce, W. 1.166; 2.76;
 5.165; 9.243; 10.155; 14.134
Wilde, O. 1.309; 10.84f, 100
William, Conqueror 2.181
Williams, K. 3.226; 15.92
Williamson, K. 4.216
Wilson, Bishop 12.205
Winn, G. 1.183
Wishart, G. 7.62; 12.55
Withers, J. H. 1.16
Wolsey 3.206, 329
Wood, H. G. 6.114

1 Matt, v.1	3 Mark	5 John, v.1	7 Acts	9 Cor
2 Matt, v.2	4 Luke	6 John, v.2	8 Röm	10 Gal, Eph

Wordsworth 1.208, 262; 5.22, 155; 9.191, 202; 10.98; 15.3

Wren, C. 3.89; 10.121

Wyclif 1.255; 3.53; 4.151; 6.167; 7.10

Wyon, O. 2.107

Xenophanes 5.73

Xenophon 1.78, 155; 8.38, 112; 10.170; 12.61, 87, 186, 239; 13.176; 14.114, 304; 15.36, 41, 122; 16.69f

Xerxes 5.178; 11.92, 180

Yeats, W. B. 1.305, 309, 326, 347, 348, 350; 2.16

Young, E. 3.249; 6.64

Zachaeus 2.189, 219; 3.53; 4.5, 234f

Zacharias (N.T.) 2.298; 4.9–11, 17–19; 5.76; 16.160

Zacharias (O.T.) 4.159

Zadok 16.133

Zadok, rabbi 1.284, 367

Zarephath, widow of 4.5

Zebedee 2.229; 5.15; 6.229

Zechariah 13.166

Zedekiah 16.171

Zenas 12.266; 17.176

Zeno 3.279; 14.55

Zera, rabbi 3.86

Zeus 1.201, 271; 3.267; 10.129; 13.25, 167; 14.321; 16.29f, 89, 91; 17.226
  of Olympias 2.241, 306; 3.310; 6.70; 17.60
  and Paul & Barnabas 7.109
  temple of 16.74f
  tomb of 12.243

Zeus Xenios 12.81f; 13.191; 15.149

Zeuxis 16.138

Zophar 14.295

Zwingli 16.1

11 Phil, Col, Thes
12 Tim, Tit, Phlm
13 Heb
14 Jas, Pet
15 John, Jude
16 Rev, v.1
17 Rev, v.2

INDEX OF FOREIGN WORDS,
TERMS AND PHRASES

A 17.159
Abaddon 17.51
Abba 2.349f; 3.8, 344; 10.35
Acharistos 12.187
Acharista mathemata 13.48
Achreioo 8.55
Adiaphora 8.189
Adelphos 14.16f
Adiakritos 14.97
Adikia 8.34
Adokimastos 12.173
Adokimos 12.246
Adolos 14.192
Adonai 17.180
Adoxos 10.135
Ad salutem 12.231
Ab umbris et imaginibus ad
  veritatem 13.3
Adunaton 13.57
Aeons 12.6; 15.164
Aergos 2.46
Agallian 17.172
Agalliasthai 1.116
Agapan 1.173; 4.78; 16.144
Agape 1.113, 173–175, 224, 376;
  6.184; 9.95, 99f, 216; 10.18,
  49f, 139f; 12.98, 134f; 14.148,
  203; 15.139
Agape, he 15.192; 16.80
Agapetos 15.148
Agathos 1.125; 3.326; 6.62;
  7.31; 8.42; 14.202
Agathosune 10.51, 164
Agenealogetos 13.74

Agennes 10.135
Aggareuein 1.168
Aggareus 1.168
Aggelos 7.47f; 13.17; 16.54
Agon 12.210
Agorazein 16.177
Aionios 2.182, 216; 5.44, 129;
  6.207; 12.228; 15.113
Aischrokerdes 12.237; 14.265
Aischrokerdeia 14.265
Aischrologia 11.153
Akakos 13.83
Akatastasiai 9.265
Akatharsia 9.265; 10.47; 11.188
Akeraios 8.218; 11.43
Akeratos 1.106
Akolasia 14.303
Akoulouthein 6.12
Akrasia 14.303
Akrates 12.189
Akratisma 8.178; 9.53; 16.147
Akropolis kakon 12.186
Alazon 8.38; 12.185f; 15.58
Alazoneia 8.38; 12.186; 14.114;
  15.58
Ale 12.185
Aleph 5.213; 16.38; 17.226
Aletheia 5.9; 10.164
Alethes 5.9, 54; 16.127
Alethinos 5.9, 54; 6.173;
  16.127; 17.178
Allotriepiskopos 14.259
Allotrios 14.259f
Alpha 16.37

Amachos 12.84, 259
Amarantos 14.174
Amemptos 11.43, 60
Amen 9.177; 16.37, 140
Ameth 5.213
Ametor 13.74f
Amiantos 13.84; 14.173
Amixia 8.50
Amnos 16.171
Amomos 10.78; 11.44; 15.207;
  17.108, 161
Amphiblestron 1.77; 2.88f;
  3.27
Anagke 9.213
Anakainosis 8.158
Analuein 11.28
Analusis 12.209
Anamartetos 6.4
Anapempein 12.274, 281
Anastrephesthai 12.88
Anastrophe 14.201
Anathema 8.124
Andrapododes 10.135
Androphonoi 12.38
Andropodistai 12.39
Aneleemon 8.39
Anemeros 12.190
Anepileptos 12.75
Anhupotaktoi 12.37
'Ani 1.91
Anoche 8.42
Anomia 1.221; 3.357
Anomoi 12.37
Anosios 12.37, 188
Anothen 5.125
Antallagma 2.154
Anthropos 6.244
Anti 15.61
Antilutron 16.177

Antistrategos 15.61
Antitheseis 12.139
Antitupos 14.244
Anupokritos 14.97
Aorgesia 1.96
Apagoge 1.144
Aparabatos 13.82
Aparche 17.108
Apatheia 6.98; 9.18; 13.42;
  14.75f
Apator 13.74f
Apatouria 10.34
Apaugasma 13.14
Apechein 1.186
Apecho 1.186
Apeitheia 8.38
Aphanismos 13.92
Aphilagathos 12.190
Aphorozein 8.12
Aphrosune 3.175
Aphthartos 14.173
Apo 11.26; 16.21
Apokalupsis 3.305; 14.122;
  16.2, 21
Apokaradokia 8.110f; 11.26
Apokatallassein 10.117
Apokruphos 11.130, 148
Apokruptein 11.148
Apollyon 17.51f
Apologia 11.17
Apolutrosis 8.59; 10.81
Apostellein 5.165; 10.74; 12.17;
  15.176
Aposthesthai 14.189
Apostolos 4.74; 7.177; 10.74f;
  11.49f, 103; 12.17, 148; 13.30;
  15.176
Aproskopos 11.19
Aptaistos 15.206

Arbel **17.50**
Arbiter bibendi **5.99**
Arbitri **13.89**
Arche **11.121**; **16.141**; **17.204f**
Archegos **13.25f**
Archetheoria **8.202**
Architriklinos **5.99**
Archomenoi **13.52**
Archon **5.123**
Areskeia **12.62**
Areskos **12.236**
Arete **11.81**; **14.301f**
Argurion **2.332**
Ariston **16.147**
Arles **9.177**
Arnion **16.171**
Arnoumai **17.101**
Arnoume **17.101**
Arrabon **9.177, 205**; **10.87**
Arsenokoitai **12.38**
Artemisia **17.44**
Asebeis **12.37**
Asebes **12.37**
Aselgeia **3.174f**; **8.179**; **9.265f**;
  10.47, 153; **14.319**; **15.180**
Aselgese **15.180**
Asher **4.56**
Ashere **1.88**
-Asmos **8.91**
Asotia **12.234**
Asotos **12.235**
Aspondos **12.188**
Assarion **1.389**; **4.171**
Asthenein **1.365**
Asthenes **1.365**
Astorgos **8.39**; **12.188**
Astrateia **8.49**
Asunetos **8.38**
Asunthetos **8.38f**

Ataktein **11.217**
Ataktos **11.217**
Ataraxia **8.199**
Atheotes **8.49**
Athetesis **13.79**
Athlein nominos **12.161**
Atimia **9.217**
Augustus **17.138**
Autarkeia **9.235**; **11.84**; **12.128**
Autarkes **11.84**
Authadeia **12.62, 236**
Authades **12.236**; **14.329f**
Autodiakonos **1.90**
Autos **14.329**
Ayont **9.203**; **13.150**
Azazel **13.100**

Baptizein **3.255**; **4.169**; **5.84**
Barbaroi **7.187**; **13.148**
Basileia **16.40**
Basilikos **5.174**
Bastazein **6.112**; **8.197**
Bath **5.98**
Bath qol **3.20**; **6.127**
Bdelugma **12.246**
Bdeluktos **12.246**
Be **16.34**
Bebaiosis **11.17**
Bebaptismenos **3.255**
Bebelos **12.37f**; **13.182**
Bela **16.66**
Bema **9.206**
Beneficiarius **9.185**
Biblia **12.219**
Biblos **1.12**
Blasphemia **1.324**; **3.175**;
  11.153; **12.187**
Brekekekex coax coax **17.130**
Brosis **1.239**

Burnous 1.99

Capax dei 12.55
Carob 3.16
Cavaletta 17.50
Centuries 7.79
Chaburah 5.120
Chairein 14.23, 36; 17.172
Chairete 2.376
Chalepos 12.182
Chalkolibanos 16.49
Challah 9.80
Chamaizelos 10.135
Chara 10.50
Character 13.14
Charagma 17.99
Charaz 4.81, 160; 8.55; 14.30
Charis 9.163; 10.9, 75f; 11.12
Charisma 8.91, 160; 9.12
Charismata 8.160; 9.108
Charosheth 2.340; 3.333, 338
Chazzan 3.31; 4.48
Cheirographon 11.141; 12.283
Cherem 6.47; 7.166
Chesedh 1.103; 12.24f
Chilios 17.186
Chiton 1.167; 3.141f
Chliaros 16.141
Chloros 17.9
Choinix 17.7
Choregein 14.299
Choregia 8.202; 10.25
Choregos 14.298
Chortazesthai 5.203
Chremata 3.246
Chrematizein 13.188
Chrestologos 8.218
Chrestos 2.17; 8.42; 10.51, 159f

Chrestotes 8.42; 9.216; 10.51; 11.157; 12.261
Christemporos 15.135
Christos 3.297; 10.107; 15.70; 17.60
Cilicium 7.136
Cognomen 8.212
Conversari 11.29
Cor 16.10
Corban See Korban
Cubit 3.308

Damnatio memoriae 10.69f
Dayyaneh gezeloth 4.222
Dayyaneh gezeroth 4.222
Deesis 12.57
Deilos 17.206
Deipnein 16.147
Deipnon 9.103; 16.147f
Delator 3.313; 17.83
Delatores 12.190
Deleazein 14.332
Denarius 1.389; 2.194, 222, 329; 3.159, 285, 326; 4.171, 247; 5.202; 17.7
Derush 10.41; 13.67
Desmios 11.21
Deus pater 10.129
Diabolos 1.227; 3.22; 10.157; 12.74, 189; 17.82
Diadema 11.70, 193; 16.83; 17.3, 179
Diakonia 8.161; 9.163; 10.149
Diakonos 9.163
Dialogismos 3.173; 11.43; 12.65
Diaspora See Subject Index
Diatheke 13.90, 107
Didache 7.22; 9.25f

Didaktikos 12.82
Didaskalos 1.311; 5.87
Didrachma 2.168; 4.172
Diekrithete 14.65
Dikaios 8.23; 9.79f; 12.239; 13.142
Dikaiosune 8.23, 34; 10.164; 11.62; 12.134
Dikaioun 8.22, 57
Dilogos 12.85
Diolkos 9.1
Diorussein 1.239
Dipsuchos 14.46
Dispensator 14.255
Dives 4.213
Divus 17.89, 138
Dokein 5.13, 65; 11.26; 15.7, 180
Dokimazein 11.18
Dokime 8.74
Dokimion 14.43
Dokimos 12.173; 14.48
Dolos 3.174; 8.35f; 14.190
Doloun 8.36
Domina 15.138
Dominus 17.89, 138
Dorcas 7.77
Douleuein 1.248
Doulikos 10.135
Douloprepes 10.135
Doulos 1.248; 6.177f; 8.11f; 11.9; 12.227; 14.35f, 210, 292, 293; 15.175; 16.24f
Doxai 14.323
Drachma 2.168, 222; 4.172, 202
Dunamis 5.119; 7.180
Dusnoetos 14.349
DWD 1.9

Ebedh 16.25
Ebion 1.91
Ecclesia haeres crucis est 12.169
Echein 14.318
Echthroi 8.152
Egguos 13.81
Egkomboma 14.270
Egkombousthai 14.270
Egkoptein 11.193
Egkrateia 10.52; 14.302f
Egkrates 12.239
Eikon 11.116–118; 13.112f
Eikonion 11.118
Eile 11.19
Eilein 11.19
Eilikrineia 9.174, 185
Eilikrenes 11.19; 14.337
Eilikrines dianoia 14.337
Eimi 16.30
Eirein 11.12
Eirene 10.9, 50, 76; 11.12; 14.95, 97
Eirenikos 14.95
Ek 15.92
Ekbasis 9.90
Ekklesia 2.142; 12.88f; 14.21, 26
Eklektos 14.167
Ektenes 14.252
Ekzetesis 12.5
Electrum 16.49
Eleemon 1.103
Eleemosune 9.164
Elegchein 6.192; 12.239; 16.144
Elegchos 16.145
Elekte 15.19, 129f, 138
Elekte kuria 15.129f, 138
Eleos 12.24; 14.96
Eleutheria 12.9

Elohim   6.77; 13.24
Eloi, eloi, lama sabachthani   3.8
Emathen aph hon epathen   13.48
Emblepein   5.90
Embrimasthai   6.97
Emphutos   14.57
En   9.104
Enarchesthai   10.25; 11.17
Endeiknumai   12.219
Energein   11.41
En kairo eschato   14.176
Ennoia   13.40
Enteuxis   12.57f
Enthumesis   13.40
Entugchanein   12.58
Eophema   11.80
Epaggelia   8.68
Epagonizesthai   15.179
Epainos   8.47
Epekteinomenos   11.66
Eperotema   14.244
Ephebos   10.34
Ephphatha   3.8
Epichoregein   14.298f
Epieikeia   9.238; 11.75f; 12.83
Epieikes   12.83, 259; 14.95, 124
Epignosis   14.294f
Epikaleisthai   14.67
Epiorkoi   12.39
Epiousios   1.216f
Epiphaneia   12.149f, 203; 14.122
Epiphanes   16.87
Epipothein   14.192
Episkopein   12.71
Episkopos   12.70f, 81; 14.139,
   216; 14.259
Epistomizein   12.242
Epitage   12.17
Epitelein   11.16

Epiteleisthai   10.25
Epi ten gen   2.126
Epi ten thalassan   2.105
Epi thumia   8.28f, 176; 10.100
Epitropos   4.97
Epoptes   14.310
Eran   1.173; 4.78
Eranos   9.99, 162
Ergon   2.46
Eris   8.35, 179; 9.263
Eritheia   9.264; 10.48; 11.23;
   14.91
Erithos   10.48
Eros   1.173; 10.49, 139
Errimenoi   1.356
Eschato   14.176
Eskulmenoi   1.355
Eta   9.15
Euaggelion   .3.24
Euanthas   17.101
Eucharistia   12.58
Euergetes   4.267
Eulogetos   14.90
Eulogia   9.164
Eupeithes   14.96
Euphemia   11.16
Eusebia   12.61, 134; 14.297,
   303f
Eusebes   14.304
Euseistos   11.91
Exagorazein   16.34, 177
Exaleiphein   11.142
Exedoke   5.20
Exia   14.318
Exodos   2.160; 14.308
Exousia   1.134; 3.37

Familia   13.17
Fortis   6.167; 7.10; 9.171

Frail 3.184
Fugitivus 10.180; 12.122, 270

Galil 1.72; 4.45
Gallicinium 2.347; 3.352; 6.230
Gan 4.56
Gazam 17.50
Geneseos 1.12
Genomenos 16.30, 81
Genus Boswellia 17.162
Geraskon 13.92
Geron 12.280
Gerousia 12.70
Gignesthai 11.37
Gignomai 16.30
Ginoskein 11.63
Gnesios 12.22f
Gnosis 9.109, 130; 12.139;
   14.294, 302; 15.10
Goggusmos 5.237; 11.43
Goggustes 15.197
Graphein 6.3
Gumnasiarcha 8.202
Gumnos 13.40
Gunai 5.98
Gunaika 16.104
Gune 16.104

Ha'am 16.66
Hadon 14.329
Hadrotes 9.163f
Haggadah 3.338
Hagiasmos 8.91; 13.181f
Hagios 15.4, 176; 16.93, 127;
   17.152
Hagiazo 9.10
Hagiazein 6.77, 216
Hagiazesthai 1.205
Hagios 1.205; 6.77, 216; 7.78;

8.94; 9.10; 10.77, 108; 11.10;
   13.181; 14.188, 199
Hagnos 11.80; 14.95
Hagnotes 9.215
Hairein 12.265
Haireisthai 14.316
Hairesis 10.48; 14.316
Hairetikos 12.265
Halal 17.169
Hallel 2.342; 3.338; 5.249;
   6.116; 17.169
Hallelujah 17.168f
Halusis 11.21f
Hamartia 1.220; 6.17; 10.95f;
   14.233; 15.33
Hamartolos 3.56f; 12.37;
   14.107
Hanukkah 6.69
Haplos 1.245
Haplotes 1.245; 8.161f
Haplous 1.245; 8.162
Hargol 17.50
Harpagmos 11.36
Harparchein 11.35
Harpax 9.53
Hasil 17.50
Hathos 8.118
Hedraioma 12.89
Helkuein 5.220
Heupferd 17.50
Herrenvolk 1.304; 2.224
Hestiasis 8.202
Heteira 1.154f
Heteros 8.118
Hieron 2.244, 336; 3.272f
Hilaskesthai 15.39
Hilasmos 15.38–40
Hilasterion 8.58
Himation 3.142

Holokleros   14.44
Homilia   7.23
Honestus   14.202
Hora   5.231
Horan   15.23
Hosanna   2.239; 3.267f; 6.116;
   17.169
Hosios   12.37, 239; 13.83
Hubris   8.37; 9.266; 12.45;
   17.154
Hubristes   8.37; 12.45
Hugiainein   12.40
Huios   1.29, 109; 12.9
Huiothesia   12.9
Hupage satana   2.150
Huparchein   11.35
Huper   9.152f
Huperephanos   8.37; 12.186;
   14.105
Huperetes   1.145; 9.36
Huper hamartion   14.233
Hupo   8.54
Hupodeigskia   13.88
Hupogrammos   14.214
Hupo hamartion   8.54f
Hupokrinesthai   14.190
Hupokrisis   14.190
Hupokrites   1.188; 2.288;
   3.168; 14.190
Hupomenein   9.124
Hupomone   8.73f, 196; 9.170,
   212f; 11.83, 109f, 210; 12.135,
   197; 13.173; 14.43, 125,
   303; 16.40, 62; 17.97
Huposchesis   8.68
Hupotithesthai   12.96
Hupotuposis   12.48
Hupselokardia   1.97
Hupsoma   8.118

Hupsoun   5.134
Hus   1.29
Hyperephania   3.175

'Iakobos   14.31
-Iani   7.90
Ibis ad crucem   6.250
Idiotes   9.247
IHWH   6.210f; 13.99; 17.179f
Illi servire est regnare   11.10
-Im   13.17
Imsh' Allah   14.114
-Inos   9.29
Intermundia   13.43
Iodh   1.127
IOGD   14.257
Iota   9.15
Io triumphe!   9.184
Isos   14.291
Isotimos   14.291
Ius gladii   6.233; 16.90

Jaba   2.349
Jeshuah   3.213
Jot   1.85, 127

Kaboth   8.125
Kadasha   1.267f
Kadosh   1.267; 11.10
Kainos   8.158; 9.189; 10.116;
   13.92; 16.98, 176
Kairos   5.231; 8.165
Kakia   8.35; 11.153; 13.83;
   14.189f
Kakoetheia   8.36
Kakos   3.174; 8.35, 38
Kakos krites   8.35
Kalein   1.333; 15.175
Kalos   1.125; 3.326; 6.62; 7.31;

---

1 Matt, v.1   3 Mark   5 John, v.1   7 Acts   9 Cor
2 Matt, v.2   4 Luke   6 John, v.2   8 Rom   10 Gal, Eph

12.52; 14.202
Kalupsis 16.21
Kaluptesthai 1.317
Kamelos 2.217; 4.229
Kamilos 2.217; 4.229
Kara 11.26
Kartarizein 14.273
Kartartismon 10.149
Kartartizein 10.149
Kata 6.3; 8.159
Katagraphein 6.3
Katalalein 14.111
Katalalia 9.264; 14.111, 190
Katalalos 8.36
Katalambein 5.49
Katanoein 13.29
Katapausis 13.35
Kataphilein 2.335; 3.345
Katastrophe 12.172
Katatemnein 11.55
Katergazesthai 11.41
Katharizein 15.30
Katharos 1.105f; 10.47; 12.33f
Kathekonta 8.33
Katheudein 1.345
Katiasthai 14.116
Katoikein 10.132; 16.91
Kauson 14.47
Kenoun 11.36
Kephas 2.139
Kerugma 7.22; 9.25; 14.140
Kerussein 1.75, 362
Kerux 1.75, 362; 12.148; 14.326
Khan 4.21
Kethubah 12.77
Kiddush 2.202; 3.337
Kinnor 4.56
Kiomasthai 1.345

Kleptes 3.173
Kleronomia 14.173
Kleros 14.267f
Klopai 3.173
Koimeterion 1.345
Koinonia 9.163
Koinonia pisteos 12.278
Koinos 3.164
Koite 8.178
Kolakeia 11.189
Kolaphizesthai 9.40
Kollubistai 5.110
Kollubos 5.110
Kollurion 16.138
Kolumban 5.178
Kolumbethron 5.178
Kombos 14.270
Komos 8.178; 10.49
Kophinos 2.126; 3.158, 184; 5.203
Kopian 8.214; 11.44f; 16.62
Kopos 9.215; 16.62
Korban 2.115f, 214f; 3.8, 169–171; 6.239
Korinthiazesthai 9.2
Kosher 2.112
Kosmios 12.80f
Kosmos 6.18; 14.86f, 103; 15.56, 105
Krabbatos 5.180
Krasis 14.58
Kraspedon 1.346; 2.286
Kratein 12.189; 16.61
Krauge 13.47
Kretizein 12.243
Krinein 11.19
Krites 8.35
Krustallon 16.156
Kubeia 10.151

Kuberneseis 9.116
Kunaria 2.122
Kuppah 7.51; 12.85
Kuria 15.130, 138
Kurios 1.248; 3.298; 8.11, 139,
    165; 9.107; 10.141; 11.39;
    15.130; 17.89, 138, 179
Kurios kai theos 16.164
Kuriotes 14.323
Kusi ballomena 11.62

Lalein 13.188
Lambanein 14.62
Laos 9.10; 16.66
Lapis lazuli 17.213
Lateinos 17.101
Latreia 6.190; 8.156
Latreuein 8.156
Latreuein kallei 8.156f
Legatus 9.209f
Legion 3.118; 4.108; 7.79
Leipesthai 14.44
Leitourgia 8.202; 9.164
Leitourgos 8.202f; 11.49f
Lepton 3.302; 4.171, 255
Lestes 3.173; 4.248
Lex talionis 1.163
Libellus 1.114
Liberalia 10.34
Lictors 9.184, 253
Lilin 3.35
Lilith 1.320; 3.35
Limne 1.76
Log 4.155
Logia 8.52; 9.163; 14.256
Logikos 14.190
Logizesthai 9.122
Logos 5.7f, 35f, 56; 8.113;
    11.117; 14.191, 230

Logos akoes 15.24
Logs 5.249
Loidoresthai 9.40
Lolium temulentum 2.72
Loudaioi 5.76
Louein 16.34
Luein 16.34
Lulabs 6.116
Lumen Asiae 16.58
Lutron 16.177
Lutroun 10.81
Lutrousthai 16.177

Ma'ah 4.241; 5.109
Machai 14.98
Magna est veritas et praevalebit
    2.377
Major domo 9.36
Makarios 1.89
Makrothumein 9.119
Makrothumia 8.42; 9.216;
    10.50, 138; 11.110, 158; 12.196
Mal'akim 13.17
Malakos 9.52
Mamon 1.249
Mancipatio 8.106
Mandata dei 12.127
Manthanontes 13.52
Maran atha 9.169; 14.124
Marin 6.247
Martha 15.138
Martus 7.13; 16.92
Massah 13.33
Mataiologoi 12.241
Mataios 12.241
Mathein 13.48
Mathetes 6.20
Mazzikin 3.34
Mechitsah 1.296

Megabyzi **15**.124
Megalopsuchia **9**.40
Melissae **12**.67
Mellon aion **13**.57
Memphesthai **11**.60; **16**.197
Mempsimoiros **15**.197f
Memra **5**.30
Menein **11**.28
Mens sana in corpore sano
 12.119
Meribah **13**.33
Merimna **1**.255
Merimnan **1**.255
Merismos **16**.32
Mesites **13**.89
Mesos **13**.89
Messiah **10**.107; **15**.69; **17**.60
Metamorphousthai **8**.157
Metanoia **3**.26; **13**.53, 184
Methe **8**.178
Methistemi **11**.111
Methos **9**.53
Methuskein **17**.159
Metraloai **12**.38
Metriopatheia **13**.47
Metriopathein **13**.46
Mezuzah **3**.295
Miainein **14**.173
Millenium **17**.186
Mimesis **10**.160
Min **5**.213
Minah **4**.172
Misanthropia **8**.50
Miseria **6**.4
Misericordia **6**.4
Mnemonic **1**.13
Moicheiai **3**.173
Moira **15**.197
Monai **6**.153

Monogenes **5**.74
Moriturus **8**.85
Moros **1**.140
Morphe **8**.157f; **11**.35–37
Mulos onikos **2**.179
Mumcheh **5**.110
Muopazon **14**.306
Murex **17**.160
Muscipula **2**.235
Musterion **2**.64; **3**.92; **9**.26;
 16.153; **17**.143

Nai **16**.37
Naos **2**.243, 305, 336; **3**.273
Neos **8**.158; **9**.189; **10**.116;
 13.92; **16**.98, 176
Neotes **12**.98
Nephalios **12**.79f, 247
Nephein **12**.207; **14**.252
Nephilum **14**.322
Ne plus ultra **15**.90
Neron **17**.102
Nezer **1**.40
Nikan **16**.66
Nimbus **16**.84
Nomen **8**.212
Nomenclatores **17**.163
Nomikos **12**.266
Nominos **12**.161
Nothros **13**.49
Nouthetein **9**.41
Nun aion **13**.57

Odinai **16**.7
Odium theologicum **2**.34;
 12.162; **14**.92
Ofanim **13**.17
Oiketai **14**.210
Oikiakoi **1**.383

Oikonomia 10.84
Oikonomos 9.36; 10.84
Oikos 12.88; 13.31
Ololuzein 14.115
Omega 16.37
Onos 2.179
Opheilema 1.221
Opisthograph 16.166
Opsonia 8.91
Orge 1.139; 10.159; 11.153;
 12.236
Orgilos 12.236
Orgilotes 1.96
Orgizesthai 1.138
Orphanos 6.168
Orthotomein 12.173
Ouai 2.12, 288
-Oun 8.57

Paggim 2.252
Paidagogos 9.41; 10.31
Paidia 15.51
Paliggenesia 12.262
Palkos 11.151
Paneguris 13.186
Panta 11.123
Pantokrator 16.38f; 17.173f
Para 11.28
Parabasis 1.220f; 13.22
Parabolani 11.50
Paraboleuesthai 11.50
Parachrema 2.251
Paragellein 1.362
Parakalein 11.129; 15.36
Paraklesis 7.22; 11.83; 13.9
Parakletos 4.162; 6.166f;
 15.14, 36–38
Parakoe 13.22
Parakolouthein 12.195

Paralambanein 11.81
Parallage 14.54
Paramenein 11.28; 13.82
Paraptoma 1.221; 10.53, 96
Pararrein 13.21
Parastesai 12.173
Paratheke 12.4, 138f, 150–153
Paratithesthai 12.50; 14.261
Pareisduein 15.179
Parepidemos 13.148, 200
Paroikein 13.148
Paroikos 10.118; 13.148;
 14.167, 200
Paroimia 6.200
Paroinos 12.79f, 237
Parousia 2.312; 14.122
Parresia 15.114
Parthenos 15.19
Paschein 1.103
Pastor 6.54; 10.148
Panthei mathos 13.48
Pathein 13.48
Patientia 14.303
Patraloai 12.38
Patria potestas 1.156; 8.38,
 106; 10.79f, 175; 11.161;
 13.176; 14.218
Paupatheia 12.135
Pax romana 3.287; 6.182;
 8.174; 10.67; 12.231; 14.95;
 16.16, 137
Peah 5.203
Peirasmos 14.42
Peirazein 1.62, 224; 14.42
Pempein 5.165
Penes 1.90
Penia 16.78
Penthein 9.44
Pera 1.367; 3.143

Pergamene charta 16.88
Peri hamartias 14.233
Periousios 12.257
Peripatein 2.105; 11.29f
Perisseia 14.57
Peritemnein 11.55
Peshat 10.41; 13.67
Petalos 6.228
Petra 2.139
Phainole 12.219
Philadelphia 14.304
Philadelphos 16.125
Philagathos 12.238
Philanthropia 12.261
Philautos 12.184
Philein 1.173; 2.335; 3.345;
   4.78; 7.2; 16.144
Philia 1.173; 10.49f, 139
Philostorgos 8.164
Philoxenos 12.81, 238
Phobeisthai 13.38
Phoinos 17.160
Phonos 3.173; 8.35
Phos 17.209
Phosphora 9.165
Phoster 17.209
Phosteres 11.44
Photismos 13.56
Photizesthai 13.56
Phratmai 10.34
Phronesis 10.82f; 14.251
Phrourein 11.78; 14.174
Phthonos 8.35; 10.48; 14.90
Phusioseis 9.264f
Phusis 8.45
Pietas 12.61; 14.304
Pikria 10.159
Pinein 6.109
Pisteuein 5.44

Pistikos 6.109
Pistis 10.51; 12.134; 14.301;
   17.97
Pistos 6.109; 12.158, 179
Pithanologia 11.131
Planos 9.217
Plektes 12.83, 237
Pleon 14.318
Pleonektes 9.53
Pleonexia 3.173f; 8.34f; 10.153;
   11.151f; 14.318, 332
Pleroma 5.71; 11.118f
Pneuma 1.22, 49; 5.131f; 8.101–
   103; 9.28; 13.39; 14.93; 15.11,
   165f, 201f; 17.129
Pneumatikos, oi 9.28f; 15.11,
   165f, 201f
Poderes 16.45f
Poiein 1.361
Poikilos 10.36; 14.177
Poimen 14.215
Polemoi 14.98
Polis 4.47
Politeuesthai 11.30
Polu- 13.11
Polumeros 13.11, 13
Polupoikilos 10.127
Polutropos 13.11, 13
Poneria 3.174; 8.34
Poneros 1.245; 3.174; 8.34
Pontifex 1.32; 6.254; 12.1;
   13.31, 66; 14.196; 17.193
Porneia 3.173; 9.265
Pornoi 12.38
Poros 10.152
Porosis 8.146; 10.152
Poroun 8.146
Porte 2.143
Praenomen 8.212

---

11 Phil, Col, Thes   **13** Heb   **15** John, Jude   **16** Rev, v.1
12 Tim, Tit, Phlm   **14** Jas, Pet   **17** Rev, v.2

Praetor 8.106; 10.80
Praitorion 11.20
Praktor 1.145
Praotes 1.96; 10.51f, 137;
    11.158
Prasiai 3.158
Praus 1.96; 10.52, 137f; 12.259
Prautes 9.238; 14.58
PRDS 10.41
Presbeutes 9.209f; 12.280
Presbuteros 12.70f; 15.127
Presbutes 12.280
Proagon 15.143
Prodotes 12.190
Prodromos 6.155; 13.63
Prographein 10.24f
Proi 5.88; 6.265f
Proistasthai 12.264
Prokope 11.20; 14.299
Prokoptein 11.20; 12.174
Prokoptontes 13.52
Propetes 12.191
Prosagein 14.235
Prosagoge 8.73; 14.235
Prosagogeus 10.117; 14.235
Prosechein 13.21
Proselutos 2.290
Proseuche 12.57
Proskunein 1.297
Prosopolempsia 14.62
Prosopon 14.62
Prosopon lambanein 14.62
Prosphiles 11.80
Prostasia 13.18
Pros thanaton 15.120
Proton 5.88
Prototokos 11.119; 16.32
Pseustai 12.39
Psithurismoi 9.264

Psithuristes 8.36
Psuche 9.28; 13.39; 14.93;
    15.11, 166, 201
Psuchikos, oi 9.28; 14.93;
    15.11f, 165f, 201f
Psuchros 16.141
Ptocheia 16.78
Ptochos 1.90
Ptoein 6.271
Ptossein 1.90
Publicanus 3.53
Pule 17.210
Pulon 17.210

Qolbon 2.245
Quadrans 4.171
Quahal 2.142
Quaternion 6.250; 7.95
Quelle 1.4
Qui cessat esse melior cessat esse
    bonus 13.52
Quo vadis? 13.58

Rabban 7.49
Rabbi 1.311; 6.269
Rabbounai 6.269
Raca 1.139
Raphis 7.2
Ratio marmorum 17.161
Recto 16.165
Rede 17.162
Religio licita 14.146, 156
Religiones (licitae et illicitae)
    14.156
Remaz 10.41; 13.67
Renatus in aeternum 5.127;
    17.33
Roizedon 14.344

| 1 Matt, v.1 | 3 Mark | 5 John, v.1 | 7 Acts | 9 Cor |
| 2 Matt, v.2 | 4 Luke | 6 John, v.2 | 8 Rom | 10 Gal, Eph |

Ruach 1.22, 49; 5.83, 131; 8.102

Ruparia 14.57

Rupos 14.57

Sacramentum 12.160; 14.245

Sagan 7.37

Sagene 1.78; 2.89; 3.27

Salaam 1.108

Salem 13.69

Sar 4.56

Sarkikos 9.29f

Sarkinoi 9.29f

Sarx, sarka 5.65; 8.101–103, 158; 9.29f, 239f

Satana 2.149f

Satraps 17.141, 147

Schema 8.157f; 11.35–37

Schismata 9.14

Scintilla 12.175; 15.79; 16.159

Scribo 15.50

Scrip 6.55

Seah 10.32

Sebaste 16.43

Sebastos 17.89, 138

Seiros 14.321

Seismos 1.317

Seleniazesthai 2.166

Semeion 5.9, 119

Semnos 11.79; 12.61, 236, 247

Semnotes 12.61f

Senate 12.70

Senechomai 11.27

Senex 12.70

Sepein 14.115

Serif 1.127; 4.211

Sesterces 9.249

Setobrotos 14.116

Shalom 1.108; 6.171; 10.9, 50, 76

Shechinah 2.161f; 5.69; 8.125; 14.259; 17.35f, 94, 202f

Shedim 1.320; 3.35; 9.92

Shekel 2.168; 4.172, 241; 5.109

Shekinah See Shechinah

Shema 1.192, 196; 2.278; 3.295; 17.119

Shomeron 6.31

Shomeroni 6.31

Shemoneh 'esreh 1.192f; 14.89f

Shoshben 5.143

Shub 1.52

Sicarii 2.332

Siloam 6.43

Sindon 3.141f

Siros 14.321

Skandalethron 1.148; 3.342

Skandalizein 2.170; 3.342

Skandalon 1.148; 2.170; 3.342; 4.215

Skene 17.35, 94, 202

Skenoun 17.35

Skia 13.112

Skleros 5.226

Skolops 9.257

Skotia 5.47

Skotos 5.47

Skubala 11.62

Sod 10.41; 13.67

Solam 17.50

Soluitur ambulando 12.171

Soma 14.93; 15.11, 201

Soma sema 12.175

Somatikos 11.95

Sophia 5.31; 9.109; 10.82f, 90; 11.108, 130; 14.295, 302

Sophron 12.80f, 239, 247, 251

Sophronein 14.251

Sophronismos 12.144f

11 Phil, Col, Thes
12 Tim, Tit, Phlm
13 Heb
14 Jas, Pet
15 John, Jude
16 Rev, v.1
17 Rev, v.2

Sophrosune   12.80; 14.251, 302
Soter   12.18; 16.89; 17.138
Soteria   8.19; 9.24f; 14.176
Sou   16.104
Sozein   14.175, 251
Spatalan   14.119
Spectatus   16.96
Speira   2.363; 6.222
Spendesthai   12.209
Spernere mundum, spernere te
    ipsum, spernere te sperni
    13.173
Sphragis   12.176
Sphurides   2.127
Sphuris   2.126; 3.184
Spilas   15.193
Spilos   15.193
Splagchnistheis   1.354
Splagchna   1.354; 9.218f;
    11.17f
Sponde   12.188
Stade   17.212
Stater   2.171
Stauros   12.9
Stauroun   12.9
Stekete   11.71
Stenochuria   9.213
Stephanos   11.70, 193; 14.48;
    16.83, 154; 17.3
Stereoma   11.131
Stergein   1.173
Sterixein   14.273
Sthenoun   14.273
Stigmata   10.56
Stilbein   3.211
Stipulatio   14.244
Stoa   3.279
Stoicheia   10.35; 11.95f, 136f;
    13.50

Storge   1.173; 8.39, 164;
    10.50, 139; 12.188
Strategos   15.61
Stulos   12.89
Sulagogein   11.136
Sumbolon   15.149
Sumposium   10.166
Sunagoge   14.21, 26; 16.80
Sunedrion   1.140
Suneidesis   12.34
Sunesis   11.130
Suntheke   13.91
Sunzugos   11.74
Sur   2.140
Susschematizesthai   8.157
Sustatikai epistolai   8.207
Syn   1.103

Tabitha   7.77
Taborion   3.210
Talaiporein   14.108
Talent   2.194; 4.172
Talith   4.113
Talithi cumi   3.8, 136
Tamhui.   7.51; 12.85
Tapeinophrosune   10.135;
    11.158
Tapeinos   10.135
Tartaroun   14.321
Tau   5.213; 16.38; 17.226
Taurobolium   5.127; 17.33
Taxis   11.131
Te Deum   17.168
Teitan   17.101
Teknia   15.51
Tekton   3.138
Teleioi   13.52
Teleiomenoi   13.52
Teleios   1.777; 9.26; 11.65–67;

13.26, 48, 52; 14.14, 61
Teleiotes 13.52
Teleioun 13.26, 48
Telos 1.177; 17.205
Tephillin 2.286
Tephra phrygia 16.139
Teras 5.119
Terma 12.11
Terumah 4.155; 9.80
Teshubah 1.52
Tesserae 16.96
Tetelestai 2.369; 6.258
Tetrachelismenos 13.40
Tetragrammaton 6.210; 17.180
Tetrarch 2.95; 4.31
Tetuphomenos 12.191
Thalassa 1.76; 5.208; 16.41
Thanatos 17.9
Theasthai 5.64; 15.23
Theion, s 1.119; 17.138
Themelioun 14.274
Theologos 16.13
Theos 5.39; 7.2; 12.50, 138
Theostugeis 8.36f
Thlipsis 8.73; 9.170, 213;
    16.40, 78
Threskia 14.61
Thuia articulata 17.160
Thumos 1.138; 9.264; 10.159;
    11.153; 12.236
Timan 12.138
Time 12.50; 14.291
Tittle 1.85, 127
Toga 10.34
Tolman 14.329
Tolmetes 14.329
Torah 3.31f
Trierarchia 8.202

Trimita 16.138
Triremes 9.3, 36
Trochos geneseos 14.87
Trope 14.54
Truphein 14.119
Tsaraath 3.44
Tupos 14.244
Tzedakah 1.187
Tzelatzel 17.51

Urbs candida 16.122

Vehemens 14.252
Verso 16.165f
Vilicus 14.255
Vilis 11.69
Vindicatio 8.106

Xenos 10.118; 13.148; 15.149

Yada 11.63
Yashmak 9.97
Yetzer hara 8.98; 14.50
Yetzer hatob 8.98; 14.50

Zadik 1.57
Zanah 2.73
Zelos 8.179; 9.263f; 10.47;
    14.91, 104
Zelotes 1.359; 14.229
Zen 5.43
Zestos 16.141
Ziz 6.228f
Zizanium 2.73
Zizith 1.346; 2.286
Zoe 5.43
Zugon 8.55
Zunim 2.73

11 Phil, Col, Thes   13 Heb   15 John, Jude   16 Rev, v.1
12 Tim, Tit, Phlm   14 Jas, Pet   17 Rev, v.2

INDEX OF ANCIENT WRITINGS

Acts of John **15**.7

Acts of Paul and Thecla **9**.242; **17**.106

Acts of Peter and Paul **2**.360

Acts of Pilate **6**.35

Acts of Thomas **6**.277

Ad Uxorem **14**.280

Against Apion **2**.29

Against Celsus See Contra Celsum

Antiquities of the Jews **1**.359; **2**.29, 37, 93, 96f, 179f, 196; **4**.147, 281; **5**.248; **6**.23, 233; **10**.112; **12**.76, 77; **13**.168; **14**.12, 322, 326; **16**.45; **17**.95

Antitheseis, The **12**.139f

Apocalypse of Baruch **1**.373; **3**.194, 290, 313; **5**.187; **8**.63, 109; **13**.145; **14**.246

Apocalypse of Paul **16**.175

Apology, The **8**.172

Apostolic Canons **12**.76, 83, 93, 98, 237

Apostolic Constitutions **1**.266; **6**.291; **12**.106, 109, 111; **13**.192; **14**.162, 280; **16**.67, 139

Ascension of Isaiah **17**.180

Ascension of Moses **3**.198, 319; **15**.167; **17**.12, 14, 199

Baba Kamma **1**.164

Books of Baruch **1**.303; **2**.182; **3**.318, 319; **5**.197; **6**.197; **9**.138; **12**.183; **14**.322; **16**.7, 8, 9, 10, 11, 174; **17**.5, 6, 14, 19, 46, 110, 187, 188, 196, 198, 200

Book of Enoch **1**.373, 374; **2**.182; **3**.197, 290; **5**.186, 187; **6**.122; **9**.50; **13**.111; **14**.51, 117, 239, 246, 322, 325, 340; **15**.80, 168, 183, 196; **16**.6, 7, 8, 9, 31, 158, 167, 171, 174, 175; **17**.5, 13, 14, 15, 16, 19, 47, 48, 80, 81, 113, 148, 187, 196, 198, 218, 220, 231

Book of Esther **3**.183

Book of James **14**.18

Book of Jubilees **1**.373; **2**.22, 182; **3**.313; **16**.7

Book of Judith **13**.164

Book of the Secrets of Enoch **6**.153

Book of Wisdom **6**.38; **9**.50

Canons of Hippolytus **14**.129

Catechetical Lectures, The **14**.280

Clementine Letters **14**.130; **15**.38

Clementine Recognitions **5**.76; **14**.10

Codex Corbeiensis **14**.3, 9

Codex Fuldensis **11**.173

Codex Toletanus **5**.21

Commentaria in Epistolam B. Pauli ad Romanos **14**.280

Concerning Anti-Christ **17**.25
Concerning illustrious Men **16**.41
Confessions, The **15**.6
Contra Celsum **1**.34, 289

De Amicitia **14**.279
De Oratione **14**.279
De Praescriptione **1**.267
Dialogue with Trypho **1**.24;
 6.25; **8**.41; **12**.76
Didache **1**.266, 282f; **4**.134;
 6.106; **7**.91f; **10**.147;
 11.189; **12**.65; **13**.53; **14**.315;
 15.90, 133f; **16**.12f, 42

Ecclesiastical History **1**.81; **5**.3,
 10, 17, 18; **12**.11; **14**.151,
 204; **15**.7, 38; **17**.79, 190
Ecclesiasticus **1**.54, 187, 234;
 2.154; **5**.29, 32f, 59, 150;
 6.178, 208; **8**.63; **9**.138,
 165; **13**.149; **14**.45, 46, 50,
 55, 63, 70, 75, 83, 85, 88,
 94, 110, 113, 119, 322;
 16.69, 141, 145; **17**.218
Epistle to Diognetus **14**.168, 308
Epistles of Seneca **1**.27
Esdras **1**.373; **2**.136, 162;
 3.313; **5**.29; **8**.80; **13**.19;
 14.82; **16**.169; **17**.13, 14, 15,
 113, 188, 198, 199
Ezra **1**.303; **3**.195, 196, 317,
 318, 319; **13**.145; **14**.57;
 16.6, 9; **17**.5, 196

Gospel, according to the Hebrews
 1.59; **2**.30, 215; **4**.228;
 7.96; **9**.144; **14**.11
Gospel of Nicodemus **6**.35

Gospel of Peter **6**.246; **15**.8;
 16.166

Histories of Herodotus **1**.25,
 365
Histories of Tacitus **1**.27

Koran, The **6**.31; **16**.156

Legatio Christianis **14**.280
Letter of Aristeas **1**.273;
 13.148; **17**.231
Letter of Barnabas **9**.15; **14**.137,
 301; **15**.38
Letters of Pliny **1**.378
Life of Adam and Eve **14**.50,
 53
Life of Joseph **15**.37
Life of Nero **1**.27

Maccabees **1**.387; **2**.28, 136,
 137, 239, 241; **3**.172, 210,
 266, 310; **5**.59; **6**.70; **9**.216;
 10.50; **12**.149, 150, 157;
 13.160, 168, 169, 170;
 14.246, 302; **17**.26, 79, 103,
 179, 216
Memorabilia **14**.304
Mishnah, The **1**.129, 303, 367;
 3.129, 164, 166, 195, 274,
 313, 349; **5**.121, 195, 202;
 6.2, 260; **9**.254
Monarchian Prefaces **5**.96
Muratorian Canon **5**.21; **12**.1,
 11; **13**.5; **14**.3, 152, 285;
 15.167; **16**.29

Nicomachean Ethics **14**.300

Odes of Solomon 13.180
On Prescription against Heretics
  16.26

Paedagogus 14.280
Papyrus Oxyrhynchus 17.103
Peshitto, The 14.4, 152
Platonic Definitions 12.186;
  14.58
Protevangelium 13.18
Psalms of Solomon 1.304;
  3.197f, 265, 319; 6.54; 16.8,
  11; 17.177, 218

Sayings of the Fathers 12.67;
  14.55, 81, 91
Septuagint 1.93, 273; 2.68f;
  3.93; 8.198; 12.70; 13.19,
  114; 14.21; 15.183; 16.31, 70
Shepherd of Hermas 12.81;
  14.301
Sibylline Oracles 3.195f, 198,
  318, 319; 8.109; 14.40;
  16.7, 8, 10; 17.15, 90, 110,
  194, 199, 201, 218
Sirach 3.71, 129; 8.80, 99
Song of the Three Children
  16.182
Statutes of the Apostles 14.64
Stromateis 1.307; 14.277

Talmud, The 1.34, 268, 344,
  346, 268; 2.283; 3.37, 129,
  232, 274; 5.110, 121, 213;
  6.90, 226, 233; 9.136;
  17.155, 161

Babylonian 1.130; 5.121;
  14.37, 277
Jerusalem 1.130; 5.121
Targums 5.29f
  of Jerusalem 15.190
  of Jonathan 5.30
Teaching of the Twelve Apostles
  See Didache
Testament of Asher 3.320;
  17.218
Testament of Benjamin 5.187
Testament of Dan 3.296;
  12.62; 16.174; 17.175
Testament of Isaacher 3.296;
  8.161; 12.182f
Testament of Judah 1.234
Testament of Levi 17.175, 218
Testament of Naphtali 14.204;
  17.218
Testament of Reuben 1.233
Testament of Simeon 1.234;
  13.180
Testament of the Twelve Patriarchs
  3.296
Tobit 1.187, 273; 2.38f;3.129;
  12.76; 14.75, 119; 16.9, 31,
  174; 17.41, 175, 201, 217

Wars of the Jews 1.27; 2.38,
  307, 328; 4.258f; 6.104,
  233; 10.112; 14.37; 17.213
Wisdom 1.387; 5.33, 34; 6.38;
  8.41; 9.204; 11.117; 13.134;
  14.94, 117, 120, 322; 15.85,
  94, 189; 17.71, 148, 181

---

11 Phil, Col, Thes   13 Heb   15 John, Jude   16 Rev, v.1
12 Tim, Tit, Phlm   14 Jas, Pet   17 Rev, v.2